D0752737

STRATEGIC DECEPTION
IN THE
SECOND WORLD
WAR

The author of this, as of other official histories
of the Second World War, has been given free access
to official documents. He alone is responsible
for the statements made and the views expressed.

3380754b

D
810
.S7
H6733
1995

STRATEGIC DECEPTION
IN THE
SECOND WORLD
WAR

MICHAEL HOWARD

W. W. NORTON & COMPANY
NEW YORK • LONDON

Originally published under the title *Strategic Deception*, Volume 5 of
British Intelligence in the Second World War.

First published as a Norton paperback 1995 by arrangement with HMSO

© Crown copyright 1990
First published 1990, ISBN 0 11 630954 7

British Library Cataloguing in Publication Data
A CIP catalogue record for this book
is available from the British Library

ISBN 0-393-31293-3

Printed in the United States of America
Manufacturing by the Courier Companies, Inc.

W. W. Norton & Company, Inc., 500 Fifth Avenue, New York, N.Y. 10110
W. W. Norton & Company Ltd., 10 Coptic Street, London WC1A 1PU

1 2 3 4 5 6 7 8 9 0

CONTENTS

PART IV
THE FAR EAST

APPENDICES

PREFACE

THE TEXT of this work was completed in 1980. Since then a certain amount of the confidential material on which it was based has been released to the Public Record Office. Where this is so, full references have been given. Some source material, however, mainly the confidential files of the security and intelligence services, remains withheld from public access and is likely to remain so. As with other volumes in this series, this text must therefore be accepted as the only evidence of the contents of these files that can be made publicly available. This is a situation with which no professional historian can be entirely happy; but most would agree that it is better for such material to be made available in this form rather than withheld from publication altogether. In particular, with few exceptions, the names of officers in the security and intelligence services, including those serving a temporary wartime attachment, are not made public; and *a fortiori*, except when they themselves have chosen to reveal them, the names of their 'double agents'.

During the decade that has passed since this work was completed the whole question of strategic deception has become a matter of major public and scholarly interest and has engendered a large number of publications of varying quality. Some of these have had access to source material in foreign archives which was not used by the author of this work and have made a valuable further contribution to our knowledge of the subject. To take these into account, however, would have involved substantial re-writing of the existing text and resulted in yet further delay in publication. Suffice to say that although this is an 'official' publication, it should not be regarded as the last word on the subject: nor should its judgements (for which the author bears sole responsibility) be necessarily regarded as definitive.

Oxford 1989   Michael Howard

INTRODUCTION

'SURPRISE' WROTE von Clausewitz, 'lies at the root of all military activity without exception'. There have in fact been exceptions; cases when the attacking force has been so confident of its superiority in numbers or firepower that it has, like the British armies in the Battle of the Somme, disdained surprise. But those exceptions have been rare and seldom successful. The defence can spring unpleasant surprises even on the strongest of assailants and may with skill persuade him to misdirect his strength. The weaker a force, indeed, the greater the importance to it of surprise, whether it is taking the offensive or standing on the defensive. It is indeed the only way by which inferiority in strength can be compensated.

All surprise rests upon concealment, and 'security' is one of the classical 'principles of war'. But few intelligent commanders have been satisfied simply with *concealing* their intentions or their strength. The commander who wishes to impose his will on the enemy – which is, after all, the object of all military operations – will seek also to *deceive* him; to implant in the adversary's mind an erroneous image which will not only help to conceal his true capabilities and intentions but will lead that adversary to act in such a way as to make his own task easier. If he is weak he will seek to give an appearance of strength that will deter his adversary from attacking. If an attack is clearly inevitable he may try to manipulate it by giving a false impression of weakness at a particular point well prepared to defend itself, and of strength at one which is not. If he is taking the offensive he will try to weaken the enemy at the point chosen for the attack by feints at other parts of the front. He will, in short, try to get inside the mind of the enemy commander, assess that commander's appreciation of the position on both sides, and then provide for the enemy, through all available channels, the information that will lead him to make the dispositions which will best conform to his own plan. It is not enough to persuade the enemy to *think* something: it is necessary to persuade him to *do* something. The object of deception no less than of military operations is to affect the *actions* of the adversary.

Deception thus demands not only good security, but also good intelligence. These are the two pillars on which all deceptive activity must be based. One can affect a person's actions only if one understands their motivations or, as Field Marshal Montgomery used to put it, 'what makes them tick'. The contribution of good information to this understanding is self-evident, but no less important is that of good psychology – a commodity not always available in equal abundance. At the lowest tactical levels, especially in confrontation with an adversary of similar culture whose military doctrines are easily available for study, one may be able to anticipate enemy reactions with a fair degree of certainty. But at the more senior levels of command, considerations of personality, of logistics and of politics become increasingly dominant, and can only be assessed on the basis of a mass of current information evaluated by experts. Junior commanders may reasonably expect a limited range of stock responses from their opponents on the battlefield. More senior commanders in a theatre of war have to take into account the personality and the logistical position of their immediate opposite numbers. But for those directing the war, to make a sufficiently accurate assessment of enemy capabilities and intentions to impose on him a deception plausible enough to affect his actions is normally so difficult that it has seldom even been attempted.

'Strategic Deception', the deception of the enemy High Command as distinct from his forces in the field, was possible for the British during the Second World War only because they enjoyed two extraordinary, possibly unique, advantages; advantages so extraordinary indeed that one would be rash to assume that we or indeed anyone else could ever possess them in comparable measure again. The first was the insight provided into enemy capabilities and intentions through the intelligence channels described in the first three volumes of this series, and particularly the decrypting of the principal cyphers used by the German Government and High Command for their confidential communications. The second was the high level of security within the United Kingdom itself, an achievement described in the fourth volume. It was this that made possible the virtually total control of communications which in its turn led to the apprehension and control of all active enemy agents in Britain.

These two advantages were complementary and mutually dependent. 'Signals Intelligence', (SIGINT) the result of reading the enemy's cyphers,* made two things possible: first, an ever more detailed grasp of the enemy situation and of the factors that went to the moulding of his strategic intentions; and second, a knowledge of his intelligence operations, not least his arrangements for the despatch of agents to the United Kingdom, which facilitated the counter measures necessary to make British security virtually absolute. 'The Double-Cross System', whereby agents trusted by the enemy were used to feed carefully orchestrated misinformation into his intelligence system, provided a channel of communications to the other side far more continuous and reliable than could be furnished by the normal tactical means of visual or sonic deception, or even the sophisticated measures of radio deception which were an essential component of the whole picture. Outside the United Kingdom double agents played a less central part in the mechanisms

---

* See footnote to p 27.

available for projecting misinformation to the enemy, although the importance of *Cheese* in Cairo, *Gilbert* in Algiers and perhaps *Silver* in Delhi should not be underrated. But by 1943 the Germans, with the German Air Force forced on to the defensive and unable to carry out more than fleeting aerial reconnaissances, were, except for the trickle of information they could get from neutral embassies and scrutiny of a security minded press, becoming almost wholly dependent on the double agents for news of what was going on inside the United Kingdom. Finally, intercepted and decrypted radio traffic revealed the degree to which the enemy were accepting that information and acting upon it; as well as the areas which their disinterest or incredulity made it unwise to exploit any further.

Intelligence and security were the two pillars on which deception rested, but deception itself was a military and operational matter. As it was for the military (including naval and air) commanders at any level to plan and conduct operations, so it was for them to determine and accept responsibility for the deceptive measures that accompanied them. The relationship between the largely civilian security and intelligence services on the one hand, and the military staffs concerned with deception, on the other, might have been delicate, if not acrimonious, and on occasion they were. That they in fact developed so harmoniously and efficiently was due very largely to two men. Rear Admiral J H Godfrey, Director of Naval Intelligence at the beginning of the war, was quick to see the value not only of deception as such, but of the channels provided for it by the double agents. It was he who took the lead among his colleagues in the Services in creating the mutually supportive relationship between the double agents and their controllers, on the one hand, and the armed forces on the other, but for which the successful implementation of the 'Double-Cross System' would never have been possible. And General Sir Archibald Wavell, C in C Middle East, who conducted the earliest independent and sustained British military campaigns of the war, not only appreciated the vital contribution which deception could make to the operations of a small and mobile force, but set the pattern of appointing to his staff, with direct personal access to himself, an officer responsible both for devising deceptive plans and for developing, maintaining and exploiting the channels through which they were to be projected.

General Wavell's relationship with Lieut Col Dudley Clarke, the officer who created and ran 'A' Force, the deception organisation first for the Middle East and ultimately for the entire Mediterranean theatre, was to set the pattern for all other theatres. The Chief Deception Officer (though naturally he was never called that) was directly responsible to the military operational commander, but made use of the channels provided for him by the intelligence and security authorities subject to the constraints which those authorities thought necessary to safeguard those channels. He also used such direct visual or aural means as were available for more direct deception, and co-ordinated the 'tactical' deception measures of subordinate units with the 'strategic' channels directed immediately at the enemy High Command. Wavell was to duplicate in the Far East the arrangements he had established in the Middle East when, on becoming G O C in India, he appointed Lieut Col Peter Fleming to head his deception staff in Delhi; a staff which expanded into 'D' Division in Lord Louis Mountbatten's South East Asia Command. It was on the advice of both Wavell and Clarke that the Chiefs of Staff at the end of 1941 established the London Controlling Section as part of their own staff structure, and the process was to be repeated when in due course major operational commands were created in the United Kingdom. In General Eisenhower's Supreme Headquarters Allied Expeditionary Force (S H A E F) Colonel H N Wild was to occupy the position that Dudley Clarke held in Cairo; though inevitably his activities were more closely co-ordinated with those of all other deception authorities under the general aegis of Colonel J H Bevan's London Controlling Section.

How far all this apparatus achieved its objectives in deceiving the enemy as to British and Allied capabilities and intentions will, it is to be hoped, be shown by this volume. Much of the early years consisted of trial and error, and even after the mechanism was functioning smoothly stories that were gratefully accepted by the enemy's intelligence organisations were still being discounted by his shrewder operational staffs. After its initial successes against the Italians in 1940–1941, 'A' Force could show little for its efforts until its skilful contribution to the battle of El Alamein in October 1942; while the surprise secured by the *Torch* landings in French North Africa owed more to effective communications security and good luck than to the activities of the London Controlling Section, whose attempts to improvise, at absurdly short notice, a threat against North Western Europe in the summer of 1943, were to be almost wholly nugatory.

None the less it was to be during this period of almost continual disappointments that the foundations were being laid on which all subsequent successes were to rest, with the creation, in the mind of the enemy High Command, of a totally false picture of the strength of the Allied forces in the West. A small acorn planted by Dudley Clarke in December 1940 in the shape of a few bogus units in the Western Desert was to grow into the massive oak tree whose branches included the non-existent British Twelfth Army in Egypt (and the barely-existent Ninth and Tenth Armies in Syria and Iraq) and the 1st United States Army Group (F U S A G) in the United Kingdom. Belief in the existence of the first was a major factor in pinning down a considerable proportion of the enemy's strength in the Balkan peninsula and the Aegean in 1943–1944; while the contribution to the success of Operation *Overlord* made by the notional threat posed by F U S A G to the Pas de Calais is now a matter of public knowledge.

The scope of this volume does not and cannot cover all the innumerable deceptions practised on the enemy at the tactical level. These are properly part of the respective campaign histories. Only when these seem to have had particular strategic importance, as did those associated with General Montgomery's attack at El Alamein in October 1942, with General Alexander's attack in Italy, Operation *Diadem*, in May 1944, and with General Slim's crossing of the Irrawaddy in February 1945, have they been included here. Nor does it cover the technical and tactical deceptions practised by the Royal Air Force, which attained the highest possible degree of ingenuity and success. The deception policy of the Royal Navy however was not only 'strategic' in the sense used throughout in this volume, but it made as much use of the double-cross system as any other customer. A special appendix is therefore included, covering naval deception.

PART I

The Foundations, 1939–1942

CHAPTER 1

The United Kingdom,
September 1939–August 1942

(i) The Twenty Committee

BRITISH DECEPTION operations in the Second World War began almost by accident. The intelligence and security services found that they had the means of misleading the enemy, and the urgent need to make use of them, long before their military colleagues had thought seriously about deception at all.

Intelligence and counter-intelligence operations always tend, like any other, to develop a momentum of their own. A major task both of intelligence and of security authorities is to hamper the intelligence-gathering of unfriendly powers. This is done not only by restricting their intelligence-gathering activities, but by inducing them to draw incorrect conclusions from such information as they do acquire. Even if there is no initial intention positively to deceive, even if security is initially visualised only in the most passive and defensive of forms, situations are bound to arise in which, although it is not possible to prevent the enemy from acquiring *some* information, it is possible to ensure that the intelligence he does so acquire is misleading or false.

It may, for example, be impossible to prevent the enemy from carrying out aerial reconnaissance and thus acquiring at least some visual information. In such cases the information can be falsified by camouflage, concealment, and deceptive display. Even more urgent is the requirement to provide misleading information when an enemy agent defects and makes himself available as a channel through which deceptive intelligence can be passed to his employers. If such a 'double agent' is to remain trusted by his original masters, he must either keep going a flow of information of some kind, or provide a credible reason why he cannot – a reason which itself will be deceptive. Should a double agent fall into their hands, the security services thus find themselves virtually compelled to provide him with deceptive information to pass over to the enemy.

Such a requirement was presented to the British authorities before the war even began, in the person of an agent known to the British as *Snow* and to the Germans as *Johnny*. *Snow* was a Welsh-born engineer, travelling on a Canadian passport, who had settled in England

3

in 1933. Whether he was recruited first by the British Secret Intelligence Service (SIS)* or by their opposite numbers in Germany, the Abwehr,† is uncertain. His work with a firm fulfilling contracts for the Admiralty, and his frequent visits to Germany, gave him plenty of opportunity to satisfy both his employers. He does not appear to have informed the Germans about his relations with the British Secret Service, but in September 1938, when war between Britain and Germany seemed imminent, he told the British security authorities that the Germans had nominated him as their principal agent in Britain. His reliability seemed to be confirmed when during the course of 1939 the Abwehr provided him with a radio transmitter, which he turned over to the British authorities. Still, when war broke out in September 1939 the British took no risks. *Snow* was arrested and detained in Wandsworth gaol. There he was reunited with his radio set, and his transmissions to Germany began under the guidance of MI5.

By now *Snow* was not alone. MI5 provided him with a colleague, a retired policeman known as *GW*, whom *Snow* notionally recruited to work for the Abwehr for the same motive that he allegedly did himself – fanatical Welsh nationalism. The Abwehr itself put *Snow* in contact with another of their agents, who when confronted by MI5 allowed himself to be enrolled as a double agent under the name of *Charlie*. A further notional recruit was provided by MI5, one *Biscuit*, who was sent to see the Abwehr authorities in Lisbon, passed their inspection, and was provided with a radio channel of his own. *GW* was also provided with an independent channel through German sympathisers in the Spanish embassy, who passed out the information he provided in the diplomatic bag. By the summer of 1940 MI5 was thus running half a dozen agents who appeared to command the complete confidence of the German Intelligence Service. They did not as yet appreciate that these constituted the sum total of German agents then operating in the United Kingdom.

The misinformation passed by these double or 'special' agents was at first provided very much *ad hoc*. Some preliminary discussion took place between the Service ministries and MI5 on the eve of the war about setting up machinery for co-operating in providing convincing answers to the questionnaires which the Abwehr sent to *Snow* and his colleagues, but nothing initially was done. The Director of Naval Intelligence, Rear Admiral J H Godfrey, and the Director of Air Intelligence, Air Commodore A R Boyle, provided sufficient informal advice and co-operation to prevent the channels from running dry, but MI5 itself was not yet properly equipped to maintain them. Responsibility for

---

* On the outbreak of war SIS became formally part of the Military Intelligence Directorate with the title MI6. The Security Service was entitled MI5. These titles will be used throughout this book.
† See p 45 below.

the running of these double agents lay with B branch of MI5 which dealt with all threats to national security. The enormous tasks which confronted the security authorities at the outbreak of war, and even more those which suddenly emerged during the invasion crisis of 1940, kept MI5 in a state of continuous and unhappy flux. It was not until March 1941, when Sir David Petrie became Director General of the Security Service, that MI5 began to command, and deserve, the respect of the armed forces and of Whitehall which enabled it to function so efficiently for the rest of the war. And only in the summer of 1941 was B Branch, later B Division, under Captain Guy Liddell, able to concentrate its attention entirely on counter-espionage; double agents being the responsibility of its subordinate Branch B1A.

During the 'phoney war' of September 1939–May 1940 B Division had, as we have seen, recruited and successfully run a small number of double agents, mainly through its control of *Snow*, but its scope was restricted by the low level of activity of the Abwehr itself in the British Isles at this period of the war. With the fall of France the situation was transformed. Suddenly required to provide, at practically no notice, a flood of information about Britain in anticipation of the projected invasion, the Abwehr recruited, hurriedly trained and despatched to the British Isles as many agents as it could lay hands on. Some were landed by boat, some dropped by parachute, some posed as refugees, others tried to remain hidden. Most of them were furnished by the Abwehr with identity documents based on information provided by *Snow* which made possible their virtually instant recognition. Some had let themselves be recruited only in order to escape to England, where they at once surrendered to the security authorities. Those who did not do so proved utterly incompetent, and fell sooner or later – in most cases sooner – into British hands. All had assumed that the Wehrmacht would arrive to rescue them within a matter of weeks and were neither morally nor physically equipped for prolonged operations in a hostile environment. A few hard cases had to be executed. There were few difficulties in recruiting double agents from the remainder.

The technical problem of running double agents – the provision of case-officers, of safe houses, of reliable communications, of a credible identity – has been so well described by Sir John Masterman in his book *The Double Cross System** that little more need be added here. It was a task which called for a unique combination of intellectual ingenuity and psychological skill, and understanding of the psychology not only of the agent but of the German spy master who was running him. From 1941 onwards the responsibility for the double agents came to rest mainly with three officials of MI5. Lieut Col T A Robertson, formerly a regular soldier; Captain J C (later Sir John) Masterman, in

---

* J C Masterman *The Double Cross System in the War of 1939–45* (Yale University Press 1972).

peace time a Student of Christ Church, Oxford; and a London solicitor, Mr J A Marriott.[1]

This 'triumvirate' in BiA, assisted by a team of case-officers, looked after the double agents, operating them as credible channels of communication. What MI5 could not do however was determine what messages should be passed over these channels, and throughout 1940 the operatives of BiA found themselves in the situation of having to press the armed forces insistently, and initially rather unsuccessfully, for information which could be transmitted by these 'Special Means'.*

There was a further complication. Since in the summer of 1940 the United Kingdom was, or at any moment was likely to become, a theatre of war, the military authorities considered that the handling of double agents should be their responsibility. G H Q Home Forces, having staked their claim, did not press the matter, having more important matters to worry about. But undeniably it was the responsibility of the military to decide, in the light of the military situation, what, if any, deception policy should be. Should the defences of the United Kingdom be depicted as formidably strong? Should they be depicted, in certain areas at least, as invitingly weak? The question was discussed at a meeting between the Directorate of Military Intelligence and MI5 on 10 September and referred to the Chiefs of Staff Committee; who decided, probably wisely, to attempt no selective deception. Information passed through the double agents was therefore designed simply to emphasise the strength of British defences of every kind.

But clearly the problem extended beyond the competence of the military, even if that term was taken to include naval and air matters as well. As the intentions of the Germans changed from amphibious attack to air bombardment, the information they required from their agents became wider in scope. Whereas during the summer of 1940 *Snow* and his colleagues had been instructed to report on troop dispositions, coastal defences, the location of airfields and the rates of aircraft production, by October the emphasis had switched to the food situation in the United Kingdom, the location of food and other supply depots, the impact of material shortages on public morale, the effect of air bombardment on different classes of the population – anything, in fact, which would enable the Third Reich to conduct siege warfare against the United Kingdom and appreciate its effects. It was easy to see that by manipulating the answers to these questions the whole of German bombing policy might be affected. But in what way *should* it be affected? Should the German Air Force, for example, be encouraged to concentrate its efforts on bombing London, where measures for the protection of the civilian population were relatively advanced and vital targets were widely dispersed, rather than to switch its attacks to the Midlands

---

* See Appendix 5, para 16c for definition.

and the North? What should the Germans be told about the state of stocks of raw materials? These and other questions were raised in a letter which the Chairman of the Home Defence Executive, Sir Findlater Stewart, wrote to G H Q Home Forces on 31 October 1940, 'A decision at the highest level' wrote Stewart 'ought to be obtained before any "slant", real or false, about eg the effect of air raids on civilian morale or of submarine warfare on our raw material situation is given to the enemy'.

It was not simply a matter, however, of obtaining a decision 'at the highest level' on this point alone. Once the decision was obtained there would have to be continuous guidance and control of the information passed through the double agents to meet the changing needs of the war. Since the information might involve any and every aspect of national life as well as material affecting all three Services, such guidance would have to come from a body with very broad competence indeed. On the other hand the very existence of the double agents had, for obvious reasons, to be kept as one of the most closely guarded secrets of the war. Even the Joint Intelligence Sub-Committee of the Chiefs of Staff Committee was felt to be too large and too public a forum for the discussion of so sensitive a subject. So in January 1941 there came into being, without specific authorisation from any political or military authority, a body known as the W Board; consisting initially of the three Directors of Service Intelligence (Rear Admiral J H Godfrey R N, Major General F H N Davidson and Air Commodore A R Boyle), Captain Guy Liddell representing MI5, and the Director of MI6. Lieut Cdr the Hon Ewen Montagu, R N V R, from Admiral Godfrey's staff, acted as Secretary. It was only on the insistence of Liddell, over the objections of the Director of Military Intelligence, that even Sir Findlater Stewart was invited to join. The W Board reported to no one and was responsible to no one. It needed, for its efficient functioning, not only total secrecy, but the greatest possible measure of flexibility and informality in the conduct of its affairs. It would, as Air Commodore Boyle pointed out at the first meeting 'be necessary to pass items of true information to the enemy ... and if such matters had to be referred to others such as the Chiefs of Staff ... either permission would be refused or there would be such delay as to have dire results; also the Twenty Committee and the W Board would have to do some 'odd things' of the kind that it was the job of Directors of Intelligence to authorise on their own responsibility'. This freedom, in the view of the Secretary of the Board, 'was the greatest single factor in enabling double agent work to achieve its successes'.

At the first meeting which he attended, on 11 February 1941, Sir Findlater Stewart confronted the W Board with the issue of public policy with which he was principally concerned: how to obtain approval 'at the highest level' for a deception policy which might lead to certain targets being attacked by the German Air Force in order to spare others (though he pointed out that if it *did* leak out that a town had been bombed as a result of W Board activities they would be damned for it, whether they had secured permission or not). It was hardly a matter even for discussion within the Cabinet. Stewart's own suggestion was that the Lord President of the Council, Sir John Anderson, should be briefed to make a direct and confidential approach to the Prime Minister. Although a member of the Cabinet, he pointed out, Anderson 'was not a politician'. As a former Permanent Under Secretary at the Home Office and a one time Governor of Bengal, Anderson was inured to the need for executive decisions on delicate matters affecting the national interest. So Anderson was approached and duly consulted the Prime Minister. Nothing was minuted, but Stewart was apparently told that 'obviously there was a job to do and he should get on with it'. If ever there were to be a row, he was warned, he would not be able to claim official authorisation for his actions, but he could rely on the unofficial approval of Anderson and of the Prime Minister. That was enough for Stewart, a man very much in the mould of Anderson himself; who thereafter represented civilian authority on the W Board until the end of the war.

The W Board had neither terms of reference nor limitations on its responsibilities. In practice its task was to give guidance on the deceptive material passed to enemy intelligence via double agents. The executive responsibility for selecting and approving such material rested with another body which came into existence at the same time, and was known simply as the Twenty Committee – 'Twenty' from the Roman figures which appropriately constitute a double cross. The first meeting of the W Board, on 8 January 1941, was indeed described in the minutes merely as 'a Meeting to discuss the Twenty Committee'. That body had held its first meeting six days earlier.

Like the W Board, the Twenty Committee had no terms of reference, but in view of the legends which have grown up about it it should be made clear what it did *not* do. It did not 'run' the double agents. That, as we have seen, was the work of MI5's section B1A, and in certain cases overseas MI6. Broadly speaking its task was to elicit, collate, and obtain approval for the 'traffic' which was passed by the double agents, and to act as a point of contact between B1A, the Intelligence Branches of the Service Departments, the Home Defence Executive and the Secret Intelligence Service. All these bodies were represented on the Twenty Committee.

The Chairman was, according to Sir John Masterman 'appointed by the Director-General of the Security Service and responsible to him, but at the same time the Committee was a sub-committee of the W Board and the chairman of the Committee was presumably responsible to them'.[2] But when the Committee was set up, the post of Director General of the Security Service, to which Sir David Petrie was to be appointed in March 1941, had not yet been created. The activities of MI5 were being supervised on behalf of the Prime Minister by Lord Swinton, formerly Secretary of State for Air. Although the situation was no doubt retroactively regularised, a great deal of initiative was obviously exercised at all levels. 'In practice this rather anomalous position proved no handicap', Masterman was to write later. 'Broadly speaking bad men make good institutions bad, and good men make bad institutions good'.[3] The men who ran the Twenty Committee were good.

At the first meeting of the Twenty Committee on 2 January 1941 the Chairman presented a memorandum which defined the problem as it appeared to MI5. MI5 had built up a 'fairly extensive' network of double agents, but unless the Services were prepared to provide traffic for them – traffic which would have to contain a significant proportion of true information – it would be very difficult to keep them in being. But if they could be kept in being and operated successfully, they would provide a very useful instrument indeed. Through them MI5 would not only gain information about enemy intelligence services, but could limit and control the information which those services could obtain from the United Kingdom – as well as diverting enemy secret service funds into British coffers. The radio traffic of these agents would help British cryptanalysts to break enemy cyphers. The questionnaires provided by their German controllers would show what information was already available to German intelligence and for what operations the enemy was preparing. Finally, the double agents could be used to mislead the enemy about British intentions. But if they were to be used for such positive deception it would have to be in accordance with a long range plan. 'We cannot' stated the memorandum, in a phrase which deception experts were to use repeatedly during the next four years, 'put over a new deception suddenly'. But if a few really important agents could be identified, and have their credibility built up through being entrusted with accurate information, then they could 'be held in readiness and at the disposal of the Service Departments for a large-scale deception which could at the critical moment be of paramount operational importance'.

In the light of what eventually did happen, when a few really important agents *were* so built up to become the key elements in a large-scale deception which at the critical moment of the Normandy landings *was* of paramount importance, this was a truly remarkable prophecy. But it is significant how low a priority at this stage was placed on deception as a justification for the running of double agents. For both MI5 and MI6 their principal value lay in the information they provided about enemy intelligence services and enemy intentions. For the Services their value if any lay in confusing the enemy. In the dark days of 1940–1941 the armed forces were in no position to plan the kind of major operations in which a large-scale deception would be of paramount importance, and it was impossible to say when they ever would be able to do so.

Still, as Masterman was to write later, 'This glittering possibility was always the bait used when other authorities had to be persuaded to help us. It served to maintain belief in the system and was a more attractive selling-point than the day-to-day counter-espionage activities which we could secure'.[4] And unknown to the members of the Twenty Committee, in the Middle East, the only theatre where the British were capable of taking the initiative, the first measures of serious operational deception were at that very moment being put into effect, with the ultimate success which was eventually to make the British armed forces the most enthusiastic of customers for the services which the double agents were able to offer.*

This memorandum was considered by the W Board at its first meeting on 8 January 1941; together with an immediate enquiry as to what information should be passed back to the Germans about the effect of air raids. On this the W Board ruled that accounts of the extent of air raid damage should be reasonably true; that the state of national morale should be truthfully reported; that the enemy should be encouraged to disperse his attacks as widely as possible; and that no information should be given about any differing reactions to bombing as between richer and poorer areas of towns – a subject about which the Germans were showing particular curiosity. Thereafter a routine was established. The Twenty Committee met weekly, to discuss both matters of general policy and detailed questions about traffic with the case-officers of individual double agents. The W Board increasingly left matters in the hands of the Twenty Committee, meeting to settle only especially important and delicate questions. Whereas it met seven times in 1941, in 1942 it met only four times, in 1943 twice and in 1944 and 1945 once.

For the first half of 1941 attention continued to focus on air policy. In order to avoid having to make a judgement of Solomon between on the one hand persuading the Germans to diversify their targets and on the other encouraging them to concentrate on London, the Chief of Air Staff suggested that RAF airfields should be indicated to them as attractive targets: that these should be reported as containing a high concentration of aircraft and to be inadequately defended by AA guns. This was approved, and double agents were briefed accordingly: one file full of misleading information being smuggled out by GW through his contacts in the Spanish embassy. By July, however, no identifiable effect had been observed on the pattern of German bombing, and the policy was discontinued. The Germans continued to be embarrassingly curious about the effect of their bombing of British cities, so in July 1941 one double agent was instructed to visit Coventry and report what he saw. BIA arranged for him a notional visit during which police protective activities prevented him from gathering more

---

* See Chapter 2 below.

than the sketchiest of impressions; but even the information which MI5 thought it safe for him to transmit seemed to the Home Defence Executive to be dangerously specific; almost indeed inviting a further German attack. The solution, as the Chairman of the Twenty Committee pointed out to the W Board on 30 July 1941 was for the Home Defence Executive itself to provide the information it wished to have transmitted to the enemy. 'The Germans' he wrote, 'whatever we do or say, will choose some targets to bomb. The choice is not between bombing or no bombing, but between the bombing of this or that objective. Surely therefore it is better to attempt to direct them to places which we consider at least less vulnerable than others, rather than to take no action and let things take their course?' In fact the report of this double agent as finally approved consisted mainly of reported rumours. He was carefully unspecific about the damage he actually saw; and he discouraged further raids by stating that all surviving factories of any importance were being widely dispersed.*

In spite of the appeal by the chairman of the Twenty Committee the Home Defence Executive (HDE) found it difficult to provide anything very positive for his channels to use as traffic. But it was not only about the HDE that BiA felt it had cause to complain. The Service Departments provided general directives, of uneven quality, as to the type of information that might be passed, and in the light of these directives BiA submitted traffic for their approval. All too much of it, to their way of thinking, was not approved. The War Office in particular seemed to them to be more concerned with emphasising the areas on which information could not be passed than those on which it could,† and when Air Commodore Boyle ceased to be Director of Air Intelligence the interest of the Royal Air Force also declined. Only the Royal Navy, where the imaginativeness of the Director of Naval Intelligence, Rear Admiral Godfrey, was compounded by the enthusiasm of the naval representative on the Twenty Committee, Lieut Cdr Montagu, continued to show an active interest in the running of double agents.

The important thing, however, was to obtain enough information of any kind to provide credible traffic, and this BiA was able to do. A few additional tit-bits were provided: a bogus sabotage operation, for example, was mounted in a food store, to satisfy a particular German demand on one of their agents. But throughout 1941 the double agents continued to serve the purposes of MI5 by building up their credibility,

---

* See F H Hinsley and C A G Simkins, *British Intelligence in the Second World War. Volume 4: Security and Counter-Intelligence* (1990), Appendix 8.

† Masterman wrote of this negative attitude with sympathetic understanding: 'The War Office and the Home Forces representatives pointed out that we were still on the defensive and that the great gains of deception could only be garnered when we passed to the offensive. In a defensive phase the chief merit was concealment, in an offensive phase the misinformation we could pass to the enemy'.[5]

persuading the Abwehr that their sources of information in the United Kingdom were so adequate that it was not necessary for them to open any new ones, and by their continued traffic providing the British with an increasing quantity of information about German operational intentions and the structure of the Abwehr itself. From the point of view of MI5 the double agents were earning their keep simply by remaining in being.

For the operatives in BIA however this was only the beginning. It was not enough to have fashioned such an instrument: at some point it must be used for a positive operational purpose. Hitherto misinformation had been passed with the primary object of keeping the agents in being – *defensively*. Had not the time come when the channels should be used *offensively*: to deceive the enemy into making major operational mistakes? This was the view which was being developed with increasing conviction by Lieut Col Robertson and his associates by the early summer of 1942. As Marriott expressed it in a memorandum of 30 June, the double agents must be getting the reputation of 'men who seldom or never say anything untrue but who equally, as must be apparent to the Germans, never say anything which is new'. Would it not be better, he asked, to 'aim at supplying the Germans with so much inaccurate information that the intelligence reports furnished by the Abwehr to the German High Command based on that information would themselves be misleading and wrong?' With this view Lieut Cdr Montagu heartily agreed. 'Our agent goes on a tour' he wrote on 10 July, 'and produces a dull sort of bowdlerised Baedeker – he sees nothing exciting, he sees so few troops of so few units that one would think there were no troops in England; he sees few aerodromes although every recce by the Germans must have shown the country stiff with aerodromes; no factory was making any armaments anywhere, and although he saw some ships he was seldom lucky enough to see a convoy or capital ship under repair'. They were in fact entirely neglecting 'the opportunity of filling the German intelligence files with a mass of inaccurate information ... I feel' he concluded 'that to fill the German files with what we want, and to help deceive them on operations of all sizes, is of such value as to be really worth a real effort'.

The army representative disagreed: they could hardly, he argued on 27 July, put over a planned deception unless they knew what the operational plans were going to be. Moreover he felt that BIA had lost its sense of proportion: Marriott's memorandum, he considered 'emphasises the fact that we must serve the agents rather than that they should serve us ... we must keep a realist outlook, and not become fascinated by the project as though it were a game'. They must not exaggerate the potentialities of the double agents: 'the German General Staff will not move a single division on an agent's report alone, it must be supported by other evidence, e.g. aerial reconnaissance, W/T, R/T, Embassy reports, etc'. Finally, he was highly sceptical of the claims put forward by MI5, that it now controlled 80 per cent of enemy espionage in the United Kingdom. If there were still uncontrolled agents at work, the contrast between the true information they supplied and the false information furnished by the double agents would over a time become apparent, and the double agents would be completely discredited.

Some of this military scepticism was well founded. Although the confident assertion 'the German General Staff will not move a single division on an agent's report alone' was proved untrue in June 1944, the War Office was entirely correct in assuming that German military intelligence placed little confidence in the information provided by the agents of the Abwehr unless they could check it from their own sources. It was also correct in stating that agents' reports had to be seen as only one element in a whole complex of information, all of which had to be consistent if it was to be believed; but the organisation for creating and managing this complex was soon to be created. Where they were at fault was in questioning the extent to which MI5 now controlled the German espionage network in the United Kingdom. This was something that could now be stated with a fair degree of conviction, thanks to 'Signals Intelligence'.

(ii) Signals Intelligence* (Sigint)

The state of emergency imposed in Britain when invasion appeared imminent in June 1940, a condition which remained essentially unaltered for the next four years, gave the security authorities quite exceptional advantages. Apart from any other restrictions, it set very narrow constraints on the capacity of the Abwehr to communicate with its agents in the United Kingdom. With some it could still keep in touch through correspondence via neutral countries, especially Spain and Portugal: The agents wrote apparently innocent letters to cover-addresses in Lisbon and Madrid, the real messages being written between the lines in secret ink. But although very full information could be conveyed by this channel, transmission was slow and by the time it reached Berlin might well be out of date. A limited amount of material could occasionally be passed in the diplomatic bags of neutral embassies such as, as we have seen, that of Spain. The most satisfactory channel was radio transmission, but for this three problems had to be solved. First,

---

* The term Ultra, which has become current as a name for intelligence obtained by interception and decryption of enemy radio communications, was not in general use during the war except as a caveat attached to documents classified as MOST (later TOP) SECRET. 'Special Intelligence' was the term used to describe naval material in this category. Army and Air decrypts were termed 'Most Secret Sources' (MSS), and Abwehr material 'ISOS' or 'ISK'. Signals Intelligence (Sigint) was the phrase in most general use, and seems to be that most suitable for use in this volume, as in the earlier ones.

the agents had to be provided with transmitting and receiving sets, and after June 1940 this was easier said than done. Secondly their transmissions had to evade detection by the security authorities; and finally they had to communicate in a secure cypher.

On the outbreak of war the branch of military intelligence responsible for radio services, MI8, had set up a special unit, the Radio Security Service (RSS) to watch for illicit transmissions from the British Isles. One such quickly came to their attention – the set which was being operated by their colleagues of BıA on behalf of *Snow*; and the traffic between *Snow* and his control in Hamburg provided British cryptanalysts working at the Government Code and Cypher School (GC and CS) at Bletchley Park with valuable information about the Abwehr's communication techniques. So did the communications of another wireless agent, *Tate*, who was parachuted into England with his set in September 1940 and who rapidly became, under the supervision of BıA, one of the Abwehr's chief sources of information about air raid damage. But the most valuable source of cryptographic information came from traffic intercepted and monitored by RSS from the beginning of 1940, which proved to be that of an Abwehr control located in a vessel in the North Sea communicating with agents in the Low Countries. Meanwhile a special section was set up at Bletchley Park to study all communications between Abwehr stations which did not have available the Enigma coding machines on which most high-level German official communications were carried. In December 1940 this section was able to break the hand cypher which carried the bulk of the Abwehr traffic, which became known after the head of the Section as ISOS (Intelligence Service Oliver Strachey).

The breaking of the Enigma cyphers themselves has been fully described in the first volume in this series, and this is not the place to rehearse the story again. The reconstruction of the machine itself at the beginning of the war was an allied effort to which the Polish and the French security services made a major contribution, and thanks to their preliminary work a beginning was made with the reading of the Enigma traffic at Bletchley in January 1940. Little could be done so long as the Wehrmacht remained substantially within its own frontiers and transmitted the bulk of its traffic by land-lines. But when in April 1940 the Germans invaded Norway the volume of their radio traffic increased enormously, and Bletchley was able to read much of their traffic – mainly that of the German Air Force – within a few days. The attack on France and the Low Countries the following month made available a further mass of material. But Bletchley was not yet organised for rapid interpretation and transmission of information to operational commands overseas, and neither were those commands equipped to absorb it. The information from this 'Signals Intelligence' (as it quickly came to be called) was transmitted to General Gort's headquarters as if coming from a well-placed agent, and was not in consequence accorded a very high degree of authority by the users; if indeed it arrived in time to be acted on at all. Sigint therefore provided little or no help to the British forces during the Dunkirk campaign.*

Most of the Enigma keys which were broken at this stage of the war belonged to the German Air Force; partly because of the sheer quantity of air force traffic generated during the Battle of Britain and the subsequent 'Blitz', partly because of the low level of security observed by German Air Force signal sections. This gave useful information not only about the German Air Force itself but about the army units to which German Air Force liaison units were attached. German naval Enigma had also been reconstructed cryptanalytically by early 1941, and during the course of that year a series of successful captures of German vessels provided enough information for much of the German Enigma traffic to become currently readable, at a critical stage in the Battle of the Atlantic. A change of keys the following February did much to restore the security of the communications of U-boats in the North Atlantic, which were then read only with great difficulty until Bletchley achieved a decisive breakthrough in December 1942 which led to victory in the Battle of the Atlantic in the summer of 1943.

But more important for our purposes was the success achieved at Bletchley in December 1941 in cracking the Enigma cypher used by the Abwehr, the traffic so exposed becoming known, after the crypt-analyst principally responsible, Dillwyn Knox, as Intelligence Service Knox (ISK). By 1942 all the cyphers of the Abwehr, both hand and machine, had been broken, and most of their traffic was being currently read.† It was for this reason that in the spring of 1942 MI5 could assert, with a high degree of certainty, that they controlled 80 per cent of the German espionage network in the United Kingdom.

The Army and the Royal Air Force staff attached to GC and CS advised on the distribution of intelligence not only to the Service ministries but, through Special Communications and Liaison Units supplied by the RAF and controlled by MI6, to their operational commands overseas, which ensured that the misunderstandings and delays of the Dunkirk campaign were not repeated. ISOS material and its distribution were the responsibility of the Secret Intelligence Service, MI6, whose Director (later Director General) was also responsible to the Prime Minister for the security of all Sigint material.

This was logical enough. MI6 carried the prime responsibility for

---

* For an account of the difficulties involved in supplying Sigint to the field see Hinsley Vol I pp 144–145.

† The other principal channel of Abwehr communications was in a cypher known as *Fish*, carried over a teleprinter service which automatically enciphered on transmission and deciphered on reception. Each machine used was named after different fish. *Tunny* was broken early in 1942, and its traffic was named *Istun*. For general purposes and cover however the term ISOS continued in use for all intercepted Abwehr traffic. The traffic of the rival service of the SS, the Sicherheitsdienst, was termed ISOSICLE.

the collection of information about the enemy from covert sources. It was, in addition, responsible for the security of its own operations and had its own counter-espionage service, Section V, whose activities inevitably overlapped with those of B Branch of MI5. Broadly speaking, MI5 was responsible for counter-espionage within the United Kingdom and the Empire, including Palestine and Egypt, whereas MI6 was responsible for the collection of all counter-espionage intelligence in foreign countries. It was to Section V that the head of MI6 delegated responsibility for the security of ISOS, and its officials considered it their duty to make available to MI5 only such intercepted Abwehr and other traffic as seemed strictly relevant to the exercise of their responsibilities within the Empire and the United Kingdom.

This duty they carried out in a fashion which for a time appeared to MI5 to be arbitrary and unco-operative. In order to understand and counter the operations of the Abwehr against the United Kingdom, MI5 considered, it needed to build up a complete picture of the operation of German intelligence services all over the world, as well as of the structure and personnel of the Abwehr and its relations with other branches of the German government. Such a picture was indeed being constructed by the Radio Security Service, which had developed an Analysis Bureau specifically for this purpose. But when the decision was taken, early in 1941, to give MI6 control of MSS material, RSS was transferred from its parent body, MI8, to Section V of MI6, and its members were forbidden to communicate directly their conclusions to any branch of MI5. This led to major difficulties in the operation of some of the most valuable of BiA's double agents.

In December 1940 there had arrived in London from Lisbon a twenty-eight year old Yugoslav businessman, Dusan Popov. Popov had been recruited as an agent the previous summer in Belgrade, by an Abwehr official with whom he had been at the University of Freiburg, one Jebsen, and was sent to England as an Abwehr agent. Popov was a young man of remarkable coolness, courage and sense of humour whose character emerges very clearly, in spite of a certain amount of fantasising, from his own book *Spy, Counter-Spy* (London 1974). He reported his recruitment by the Abwehr to the British embassy in Belgrade, and as a result MI6 did all it could to make his journey to London comfortable. On arrival he was contacted by BiA and recruited as a double agent under the code name *Tricycle*.

Tricycle had brought with him a questionnaire from the Abwehr, together with a supply of secret ink for communicating the answers, and it was very largely to provide convincing replies to this particular questionnaire that BiA had called the Twenty Committee into being. He was required to obtain samples of ration cards and identity cards, together with details of the organisation in Britain for dealing with fifth column activities and parachute landings. He was to discover the location of food depots and to report on the state of morale of the working classes. From the Army he was to discover details of coastal defences, anti-aircraft defences, the location of headquarters and the order of battle of all military units. From the RAF he was to discover details of aircraft construction, the location and rate of output of specific factories and the state of supply of raw materials. From the Navy he was to find out what vessels were being built or repaired and where; what ships had been sunk or damaged by mines of torpedoes; what war material was coming in from the United States and where it was being unloaded. In addition he was to make contact with the entourage of the Commander-in-Chief of the Home Fleet, Admiral Sir John Tovey, and with a number of eminent members of the House of Lords who were believed to be in favour of a compromise peace.

For this ambitious programme the Twenty Committee was able to provide answers only of a very vague and general kind. Lieut Cdr Montagu gallantly sacrificed his reputation by posing as a Jewish officer anxious to ingratiate himself with the Germans in order to get good treatment in the event of invasion, and so prepared to pass over information of high quality. A bogus chart of the minefields covering the East Coast was prepared which *Tricycle* took back with him to Lisbon. The Abwehr was impressed, the German Naval Command less so. The Abwehr in general professed themselves disappointed with the generality of the answers which *Tricycle* provided to its questions, but showed no disposition to mistrust him. Nor did it query the authenticity of two sub-agents whom he notionally recruited. One, a former Army officer allegedly cashiered for bad debts and now a registered dealer in arms, known to MI5 as *Balloon*, provided economic and industrial intelligence. The other, a lady known as *Gelatine*, was well-connected, indiscreet, and provided a great deal of confidential political gossip.

Tricycle returned to Lisbon to report in January, and again in March; and in June 1941, on his return to London he was able to give a full account of the Abwehr organisation in Portugal. Then in August his German employers sent him to the United States, and things began to go wrong. The British security authorities in Washington secured the co-operation of the FBI in 'running' him, but that organisation did not appreciate the need for preserving the cover of a double agent in the interests of long-term deception. In its eyes the purpose of a double agent was to entrap other agents, who should then be prosecuted with maximum publicity. Moreover *Tricycle's* extravagant lifestyle, which had merely aroused amused and admiring comment among the tolerant officials of MI5 in wartime London, caused deep offence to J Edgar Hoover's puritanical lieutenants. Deeply mistrusting him, they refused to provide any 'chicken feed' – harmless but accurate information to maintain his credibility. The Abwehr, partly because of administrative difficulties and partly because he was getting no information for it, ceased to provide any money, and its senior officials began to wonder whether he was not merely inefficient, but actually under Allied control. The existence of these doubts was revealed by ISOS decrypts but since *Tricycle* was no longer operating within the British Empire MI6 did not inform MI5 about them. Nor did it provide MI5 with the intercepts of *Tricycle's* own traffic with his Abwehr controls.

By the summer of 1942, therefore, BIA was growing anxious about *Tricycle*. So long as he remained in the United States nothing could go very badly wrong, but in August the FBI refused to handle him any longer. He had to return to London. To maintain his credibility with his German employers he insisted on doing so via Lisbon, somewhat to the alarm of his British case-officers who feared that his chances of surviving German interrogation were remote. MI6 was therefore persuaded to release its intercepts of his traffic and BIA sent an official to Washington to extricate *Tricycle* and brief him for his encounter with the Abwehr. This passed off entirely successfully. On his return to Lisbon in October *Tricycle* took the offensive, berating his employers for failing to provide him with enough funds to do a decent job in the United States. It was clear that whatever doubts about his integrity may have been current in Berlin, *Tricycle's* Abwehr controls in Lisbon still regarded him as a star performer. They proved apologetic and understanding, asked him to return to London, providing him with a new questionnaire and £25,000 in cash. This, needless to say, went to swell the coffers of BIA.

Both the Abwehr and BIA were at one in regarding *Tricycle* as an erratic but reliable agent who had produced little as yet but who was rich in promise for the future. The British expectations were to be amply fulfilled, and we shall return to *Tricycle* later in this story. But while *Tricycle* was in America another agent had arrived from Lisbon, who was almost single-handed to provide a justification for the existence of the Twenty Committee: Juan Pujol Garcia, better known as *Garbo*.

When at the beginning of 1942 Bletchley began reading the Abwehr Enigma traffic between the station in Madrid and their headquarters in Berlin, it was soon realised that reports were being passed, allegedly from a German agent in the United Kingdom, which were rich in ludicrously inaccurate detail. Convoys sailed made up of non-existent ships. British Army regiments were referred to by non-existent numbers. A remarkable situation was reported at Liverpool where there were apparently 'drunken orgies and slack morals at amusement centres'; while in Glasgow dock-workers were prepared to 'do anything for a litre of wine'. It was clear that this agent was not operating from the British Isles and it seemed barely credible that he had even visited them; but his identity remained a mystery until he himself revealed it to a representative of MI6 in Lisbon early in March. He was in fact a 29 year-old Spaniard of good family who, having been profoundly disillusioned with all totalitarian regimes as a result of the Spanish Civil War, was deeply devoted to the cause of British victory. In January 1941 he had offered his services as an agent to the British in Madrid without success. He then turned to the Germans, who were only slightly more forthcoming; but after lengthy negotiations and elaborate deception he succeeded in persuading the Abwehr officials in Madrid that he was about to visit London on behalf of the Spanish security services to investigate a currency racket. The Abwehr thereupon recruited him as an agent and provided secret ink, questionnaires, and an accommodation address in Madrid to which to address his reports. *Garbo* went no further than Lisbon. There he settled down with a map of the United Kingdom, a Blue Guide to England, a Portuguese study of the British Fleet and an Anglo-French vocabulary of military terms. With these slender resources he concocted, between July 1941 and April 1942, when he finally reached the United Kingdom, nearly forty long reports based on his own imaginary observations or those of equally imaginary sub-agents whom he had notionally recruited.

These were the reports referred to above. MI6 initially told MI5 nothing about them. But towards the end of February 1942 MI5 learned of *Garbo's* existence from the Lisbon representative of Section V on one of his periodic visits to London, and on 3 March asked for a full report on this mysterious figure. Two days later the MI6 representative officially informed the Twenty Committee of his existence, and a week later, on 12 March, he was able to give further details. Thanks to the good offices of the US Naval Attaché in Lisbon, MI6 was now in contact with *Garbo*, and he was operating under its control.

This produced a situation that BiA found thoroughly unsatisfactory. It had no official access to the ISOS decrypts revealing *Garbo* traffic, yet it had somehow to harmonise the reports of its own controlled agents in Britain with those fed through this MI6 channel in Lisbon. News of this anomalous situation leaked out at a high level and Sir John Anderson asked Sir Findlater Stewart to convoke a committee to investigate the possibility of a closer co-ordination between MI5, MI6 and the Special Operations Executive 'as it affects the work of the Twenty Committee'. This caused general consternation. To bring in SOE was to extend the number of those who knew about the double agents far beyond anything BiA considered necessary or desirable, and a rather embarrassed meeting of the W Board was held on 28 March 1942 to restore the situation. The head of SOE agreed to forget all he had heard and Sir Findlater Stewart was reassured that liaison would be improved. The immediate problem was eased by bringing *Garbo* to England, which he reached on 24 April 1942. He then came under the jurisdiction of BiA.*

Even now, however, MI6 did not feel justified in making available to the Twenty Committee the decrypts of intercepted Abwehr traffic relating to *Garbo*, and a highly anomalous situation resulted. The Service representatives did not even know of the existence of these decrypts,

---

* For the further history of *Garbo* see Appendix 2.

and they regarded *Garbo* with understandable suspicion. Could anyone possibly be taken in by such obvious inventions? Was *Garbo's* own story not utterly incredible? By June 1942 the position of B1A had become impossible. It knew from ISOS intercepts that *Garbo's* story was true and that his reports were being relayed as accurate by his Abwehr controls. But unless the Services could be convinced of this, they would not provide through the Twenty Committee the material to enable *Garbo* to concoct more credible reports. On 5 June 1942, the chairman wrote to the head of MI6, persuasively explaining the problem. On 11 June he received at last an affirmative and satisfactory reply: copies of all decrypts relevant to double agents would henceforward be made available to the Twenty Committee at each of its weekly meetings.

We have already seen how, by the early summer of 1942, the need for the smooth functioning of a team of double agents whose complete reliability could be tested by intercepts had led to a growing impatience on the part of B1A with the constraints imposed upon it. Now it had won its battle with MI6 over access to all relevant Abwehr material. Next it had to persuade the Services to make more positive use of the instrument that lay to their hand. Quite how powerful that instrument might be was described in a memorandum which Robertson presented to the W Board on 15 July 1942.

'It is reasonably certain' this memorandum opened 'that the only network of agents possessed by the Germans in this country is that which is now under the control of the Security Service'. For this claim three supporting arguments were cited. A watch on mail sent to known Abwehr cover addresses had revealed no uncontrolled agents. There was no evidence of payment being made to any uncontrolled agents through the usual channels in Lisbon and Madrid: indeed one controlled agent in England had £18,000 available for disbursements and had received no instructions to make any. Finally, the Radio Security Service had discovered no uncontrolled agents operating. There was no guarantee that the Germans would not pick up incidental information from miscellaneous sources, but

'it is inconceivable that there should exist in England any organisation or network of agents so carefully concealed, so different in its nature from anything of which we have knowledge, and so wholly divorced from the network which we control that it is able to operate without colliding at any point with the controls we have described above ... It follows from this that if we, being in control of the network, choose to say one thing, and a single agent who is not controlled to say another, it is we who stand a better chance of being believed'.

There was no question of this being a skilful Abwehr plant. Thanks to ISOS decrypts

'we have been able to watch the Germans making arrangements for the [agents'] despatch, discussing arrangements arising from payments sent to them or letters received from them, and passing on from one Stelle* to another their reports and comments on them. In two or three cases we have been able to observe the action (which has been rapid and extensive) taken by the Germans upon the basis of these agents' reports'.

It therefore followed, concluded the memorandum 'that the combined General Staff in this country have, in MI5 double agents, a powerful means of exercising influence over the OKW German High Command'. It could feed the Germans the information it wanted them to have, and on which their decisions would have to be based. 'Once this point is appreciated by our own General Staff it will be realised that they have in their hands a powerful weapon, and one upon the exercise of which it is worth while to spend considerable time'. At present the only time which the Services were so spending was the two hours a week which their representatives spent on the Twenty Committee – normally in a purely passive role – vetting the traffic suggested by MI5. Something more positive was needed if the German files were to be filled, as Lieut Col Robertson put it, with the information that the British would like to see there. He suggested indeed that there should be a permanent Inter-Services Section which could 'devote its whole time to the framing of double agents' traffic, enquiries resulting from such traffic, and similar problems'.

To these suggestions the Services now responded affirmatively. This was not because the MI5 paper was in itself persuasive. During the last weeks in July the whole aspect of the war had changed. With the decisions taken, during the visit of the American Joint Chiefs of Staff to London at the end of July, to launch an allied invasion of French North Africa, the Chiefs of Staff Committee at last had a positive operational plan; and as had been frequently pointed out during the past two years, it was a great deal easier to have a deception policy when one knew what one *was* going to do than when one did not. The Director of Naval Intelligence gave Lieut Cdr Montagu responsibility for naval deceptive activities. The Army appointed a full-time staff officer from GHQ Home Forces, and the RAF promised that its own representative on the Twenty Committee would devote more time to the matter. But more important than any of these changes was the appearance at the Twenty Committee, on 27 August 1942, of Colonel J H Bevan from the War Cabinet Offices; head of the London Controlling Section of the Chiefs of Staff Committee.

(iii) The London Controlling Section

We have seen how the W Board and the Twenty Committee came into being primarily to supervise the supply of information and misinfor-

---

* Stelle = station. See p 46 below.

mation on which the successful running of double agents depended. They were in no way responsible for 'deception policy' as such: they had neither advisory nor executive authority and only a handful of people in Whitehall even knew of their existence. If any body was responsible for deception as a whole in the early years of the war it was the Joint Inter-Service Security Board. This had been set up in February 1940 under the auspices of the Joint Intelligence Sub-Committee of the Chiefs of Staff Committee, when the British and French were planning their abortive intervention in Finland. It was later given responsibility 'for the co-ordination of all means of preventing leakage of information to the enemy, and for the preparation and executive action in connection with measures designed to deceive the enemy as to our plans and intentions'. On it sat representatives not only of the three Services but of MI5 and MI6, who assisted when necessary in putting over false information through their own channels. But its deceptive activities, such as they were, were confined to the protection of convoys or the movement of troops overseas, and it met only *ad hoc* to consider them. It was responsible neither for formulating nor for implementing any overall deception 'policy'. In the early years of the war no such policy existed.

The idea that such a policy was possible and desirable owed its origin to one man: General Sir Archibald Wavell, C in C Middle East between 1939–41. We shall see in due course* how he applied his ideas to the conduct of the campaign in the Middle East, building up a special deception section ('A' Force) on his staff at Cairo under the guidance of Lieut Col Dudley Clarke. From December 1940 onwards 'A' Force had proved its worth, growing from a body concerned purely with tactical deception in the Western Desert to one masterminding strategic deception throughout the Middle East. In October 1941 the Chiefs of Staff Committee took advantage of Lieut Col Clarke's presence in London to summon him to give them an account of his operations.[6] Clarke proved persuasive. The Joint Planning Staff examined his ideas and recommended, on 8 October, that an organisation along the lines he had created in Cairo should be established in London.[7] They considered that, like that of 'A' Force, such a body should operate as an intrinsic part of the operational planning staffs. Its success however would depend, like that of 'A' Force, not on the effectiveness of its organisation but on the personality of its head, who would, they pointed out, need to be a man of 'considerable ingenuity and imagination, with an aptitude for improvisation, plenty of initiative and a good military background'. He would have to function as a commander with a staff, and not as chairman of a committee. This 'Controlling Officer', as they christened him, would be responsible both for preparing plans

---

* See Chapter 2 below.

to cover intended operations and for executing them, using existing machinery. There should be no separate 'deception staff'. The services of the intelligence and security authorities, of the Political Warfare Executive, and of the armed forces themselves would all be available to implement such executive action as was necessary to give artistic verisimilitude to his schemes.

The Chiefs of Staff approved this boldly imaginative proposal on the spot,[8] and made an equally imaginative choice for a Controlling Officer. Colonel Oliver Stanley, M C, was eminent both as a social and as a political figure. After a distinguished military career in the First World War he had entered politics, becoming President of the Board of Trade in Mr Chamberlain's administration from 1937 until January 1940, when he had succeeded Leslie Hore Belisha as Secretary of State for War; an office he held until the formation of the Churchill administration four months later. He commanded the confidence of the Services and had wide experience to reinforce it. His appointment was camouflaged under the title of Head of the Future Operational Planning Section of the Joint Planning Staff. Unfortunately his distinguished background was not enough in itself to enable him to operate effectively in the Whitehall bureaucracy. The clandestine nature of his role in itself made it difficult to convince the Services of its importance. He was given a single staff officer and a secretary, but the representatives from each of the three Services needed to provide his office with even minimal effectiveness were not forthcoming. He was not even told of the existence of the double agents; only that MI5 had 'special means' of conveying information to enemy intelligence if required.

Under the circumstances, and given the complete absence in Whitehall of any experience of strategic deception, there was very little Colonel Stanley could do. His appointment coincided with the darkest days of war, when the checking of the British offensive in the Western Desert and the Japanese attack in the Far East rendered any offensive operational planning out of the question and made it difficult to indicate to the most credulous enemy that there might be any. But he did not waste his time. In December 1941 the Chiefs of Staff approved his proposals for a notional attack on the Norwegian coast, Operation *Hardboiled*; the first of many such feints which were to be mounted over the next three years. For this, forces were actually nominated and trained; plans were drawn up with Stavanger as the objective; billeting requisition forms were printed in Norwegian; supplies of Norwegian currency were earmarked; the Norwegian General Staff in London was consulted, and enquiries were made about the availability of Norwegian interpreters. The operation was freely gossiped about in London, and the double agents retailed some of the gossip in their traffic. It would be claiming too much to assert that all this activity was in itself the cause of the rumours of a British operation which began to circulate in Stockholm in January 1942 and in the German Press the following March, or in the reinforcement of the German garrison in Norway which took place in April and May. Hitler was himself abnormally sensitive about his northern flank and needed no prompting to take extraordinary precautions for its defence. But whether or not it served its strategic object, Operation *Hardboiled* gave the deception authorities some useful practice and encouraged the patient case-officers of the double agents with evidence that the misinformation which they fed to the Abwehr could on occasion be taken seriously by the German military authorities.[9]

The units notionally training for *Hardboiled* were in fact used for an amphibious attack successfully mounted against Madagascar in May 1942. This operation provided the deception authorities with an opportunity to put into effect a cover plan which involved the co-operation of both London and Cairo. The expedition, consisting of an infantry brigade, a commando and supporting troops, sailed from England on 23 March and called at Durban on 22 April. At Durban briefings were given to the officers of the force and maps were distributed which indicated that the objective of the attack was the Italian-occupied Dodecanese Islands in the eastern Mediterranean. At Alexandria arrangements were made for the reception of the expedition and staff officers gossiped freely about its notional destination – gossip, again, retailed by the double agents at the disposal of 'A' Force. The Italians were sufficiently impressed to reinforce the garrisons of Cos and Leros and certainly when the expedition arrived off Diego Suarez on 4 May, it achieved complete surprise. Here again the deception authorities could not claim a proven success. It can be said only that if the sailing expedition had come to the attention of the enemy, they were provided with an alternative and no less plausible explanation of its intentions; and if reports of its true destination reached them this would have been quite likely itself to have been considered a deception rather than the truth.[10]

But during this period the deception authorities had another and more chastening experience. In December 1941, after General Auchinleck's forces in the Western Desert had successfully expelled the Axis forces from Cyrenaica in the aftermath of Operation *Crusader*, operational planning had begun for a further advance westward to Tripoli. 'A' Force covered this with the notional plan that no further advance would take place, but that Auchinleck would now build a strong defensive flank in Libya and transfer substantial forces to Persia and Iraq; to reinforce the Russian forces in the Caucasus who were threatened by the German advance in south Russia, and to provide encouragement to the Turks.

Stanley himself saw weaknesses in this deception and pointed them out in a memorandum to the Chiefs of Staff dated 5 January 1942.[11] It was not yet certain that the advance to Tripolitania would take place;

such rumours would disturb the neutral Turks; while anyhow the story seemed unnecessarily elaborate when the obvious and urgent need to send reinforcements to defend Malaya against Japanese attack would provide a far better cover if any was wanted. Rommel's successful attack at El Agheila in January 1942 in any case pre-empted British plans, but not before 'A' Force had flooded the Middle East with reports of the strength of British defensive capabilities in the Western Desert.

At the same time, unfortunately, the Press and the BBC in London were being encouraged by the military authorities to emphasise the strength of the reinforcements which were being sent to Malaya, in the hope that this would act as a deterrent to Japanese attack. The revelation of actual British weakness both in the Western Desert and in Malaya, coming on top of these encouraging reports, was not good for allied morale. It was clear that manipulation of the Press for deception purposes was a highly dangerous and potentially self-defeating process.[12] As a result the Chiefs of Staff issued a directive on 11 February 1942 to the effect that in future all major deception plans should be referred by Commanders-in-Chief to the Chiefs of Staff Committee for approval; and that directives to Directors of Public Relations should be devised by the Joint Planning Staff, in consultation with the Foreign Office and with Colonel Stanley, 'to enable them to give confidential guidelines to the Press in harmony with our operational intentions'.[13]

These and other difficulties may have made the Chiefs of Staff less optimistic about the potentialities of strategic deception than they had been the previous October. Clearly Colonel Stanley himself felt increasingly frustrated, and in May 1942 he asked the Prime Minister to release him so that he could return to a career in active politics. Permission was granted – in November of that year he became Secretary of State for the Colonies – and on 21 May the Chiefs of Staff approved his replacement as Controlling Officer by Lieut Col J H Bevan, an officer with considerable experience in military intelligence who had been involved in tactical deception activities in Norway in April 1940.[14] Also so involved had been the well-known author and traveller Lieut Col Peter Fleming; and Fleming had been summoned by General Wavell to head his deception staff in India when he had assumed command in that theatre in July 1941. As it happened, Fleming could not leave England until February 1942. The reports which he then carried about developments, or lack of them, in Whitehall may have been influential in convincing Wavell that the seed sown the previous October when Dudley Clarke had visited London had not as yet borne much fruit. For whatever reason, on the very day that Bevan took up his post as Controlling Officer Wavell sent a signal to London, this time addressed personally to the Prime Minister.

'I have always had considerable belief (this ran) in deceiving and disturbing enemy by false information. C in C Mideast instituted Special Branch Staff under selected officer charged with deception (of the) enemy and it has had considerable success. I have similar branch in India and am already involved in several deception plans. These however can have local and ephemeral effect only, unless part of general deception plan on wide scale. IHQS (sic) can only be provided from place where main strategical policy is decided and Principal Intelligence Centre located. Coherent and long term policy of deception must be centred there. [I] fully appreciate value of work done by ISSB and Controlling Officer but have impression the approach is defensive rather than aggressive and confined mainly to cover plans for particular operations. May I suggest for your personal consideration that policy of bold imaginative deception worked between London, Washington and Commanders in the field by only officers with special qualifications might show good dividend, especially in case of Japanese'.[15]

This message was supremely fortunate in its timing. Its arrival coincided not only with Bevan's appointment but with the first serious plans being laid, in association with the United States Joint Chiefs of Staff, for the invasion of continental Europe. The Prime Minister circulated it to all members of the Defence Committee of the Cabinet and the Chiefs of Staff referred it to the Joint Planning Staff, which on 18 June put forward a strong supporting recommendation.[16] The text of this document showed how much had been learned during the past few apparently sterile months.

'Experience [suggested the JPS] has shown that to achieve its object the deception plan must –
(i) simulate intentions which are plausible
(ii) reach the enemy through as many possible of his normal channels of information
(iii) to this end be backed by real evidence of troop movements, shipping, signal traffic, etc. Moreover it is impossible to develop strategic deception on a large scale unless our general strategy is clearly defined and likely to be adhered to. In the absence of firm strategic policy, any deception plan entails the grave risk of drawing the enemy's attention to a move which may in fact prove to be one we really want to make when the time comes'.

The JPS proposed that the existing deception section 'which we suggest might be known in future as "The Controlling Section", should be responsible for strategic deception on a global scale. Deception specifically to cover the forthcoming operations against the continent of Europe should be the responsibility of a staff attached to the Supreme Commander. The Controlling Section should concentrate on broad deception policy and co-ordination of theatre deception plans. Finally, the Americans should be invited to set up a parallel organisation in Washington, which should maintain close liaison with their colleagues in London'.

The Chiefs of Staff approved these suggestions in their entirety.[17] Lieut Col Bevan's section was now to be named 'the London Controlling

Section' and Bevan himself received a directive of wide scope.* He was to 'prepare deception plans on a world-wide basis with the object of causing the enemy to waste his military resources'. He was to co-ordinate the deception plans proposed by Commands at home and abroad and the cover plans prepared by the ISSB for specific operations. He was to watch over the execution by the armed forces or other appropriate bodies of the deception plans he had prepared, and control the support of Service deception schemes by leakage and propaganda. Finally, his work was 'not to be limited to strategic deception alone but [was] to include any matter calculated to mystify or mislead the enemy wherever military advantage may be so gained'.

It will be noted that the Controlling Officer was given no executive authority commensurate with these broad responsibilities. His function was to plan, to co-ordinate and to supervise. His effectiveness would lie in the closeness of his co-operation with the Joint Planning Staff, with whose offices his own were located in the War Cabinet Offices at Storey's Gate, and in the direct access he would enjoy to the Chiefs of Staff. There was no 'deception staff' as such. Deception was seen as being unequivocally an operational responsibility, both notional and factual plans being made and implemented by the same authorities. Lieut Col Bevan was directed to keep in close touch with the Joint Intelligence Sub-Committee, the Political Warfare Executive, the Special Operations Executive, the Secret Intelligence Service and similar arcane bodies, but his base was firmly established among the operational planners of the Service staffs.

Psychologically this was to be of profound importance. The military of all three Services always tend to be ambiguous in their attitude towards their colleagues who are concerned with intelligence, subversion and in general the less orthodox aspects of warfare. While respecting their abilities and recognising the value of their contribution, they sometimes find it difficult to treat directives or advice emanating from such sources with quite the same respect as they do instructions coming down through normal operational channels of command. This was something that Bevan realised the moment he took up his new and vast responsibilities. He would be able to implement these only if he gained the confidence of the senior military commanders who controlled the resources he would have to use; and this could be done only by emphasising the essentially operational nature of his activities.

The Chiefs of Staff also accepted the recommendation of the JPS that they should enlist the co-operation of their United States colleagues. The United States Joint Chiefs of Staff, on 28 July, agreed in principle to co-operate along the lines suggested by the British, and instructed their own secretariat to work out an appropriate scheme.[18] The Ameri-

---

* See Appendix 3. COS (42) 184th Meeting. Annex I.

can system developed slowly, and co-operation was at first very much *ad hoc*. The Joint Chiefs did not yet possess the kind of joint service secretariat which provided so convenient a framework for the London Controlling Section; while traditionally their military and naval commands enjoyed a degree of autonomy which made any central direction extraordinarily difficult to impose. But in August 1942 a body was set up, known as Joint Security Control, consisting of two members only: Major General G A Strong of the United States Army and Captain George C Dyer of the United States Navy. This focus enabled the London Controlling Section to obtain the kind of co-operation, information and guidance from the United States that it needed for its own activities.

Bevan's directive of 20 June was drafted on the assumption, first that large-scale planning for an Allied invasion of Continental Europe was about to begin, and second that deception for this would be the responsibility of the Supreme Commander of that operation. But almost immediately the British Chiefs of Staff came under heavy pressure to prepare plans for an immediate assault on the French coast by British forces – Operation *Sledgehammer* – and Bevan's first task was to produce a cover plan for this. He had time to do no more than point out the huge complexity of this task[19] when the assignment was cancelled. The Chiefs of Staff unanimously declared the operation unfeasible; the Prime Minister and the War Cabinet supported them; and President Roosevelt instructed his Chiefs of Staff to accept the alternative proposed for the invasion of north Africa, Operation *Torch*. Although a Supreme Commander, Lieut General Dwight D Eisenhower, was nominated for this operation, Lieut Col Bevan was made responsible for the management of all deception in connection with it. On 27 July he received instructions from the Chiefs of Staff to prepare two major plans. The first had as its object the containment of the largest possible number of enemy forces in North-West Europe during the coming autumn. The second was to provide cover for the armada which would soon be converging from the United Kingdom and the east coast of the United States on the coast of French North Africa.[20]

The measures taken by the LCS to carry out these instructions and the success which attended them will be examined in due course. It remains to describe the relations established between that Section, with all its new responsibilities, and the Twenty Committee, which had so valuable an instrument under its control and was, as we have seen, so impatient to use it.

It will be recalled that on 15 July 1942 the W Board had considered a memorandum in which MI5 had claimed that it now controlled the only German intelligence network of any consequence in the United Kingdom, and had pointed out the possibilities which this opened up for positive deception of the enemy on a very large scale. What was now needed was a deception policy, which this could be used to implement. Lieut Col Bevan had now been given responsibility by the Chiefs of Staff for the working out of just such a policy, and the W Board agreed that he must be put '100 per cent in the picture': informed, that is, not only about the double agents but also about Sigint. There was no question but that he should join the Twenty Committee. It was even suggested that he should become its Chairman, but to this BıA demurred. Although operational deception was a major function of the double agents, the Chairman of the Twenty Committee pointed out in a minute to Liddell on 5 September, it was not their only role, and the delicate business of running them and controlling the flow of appropriate information was one which the security authorities ought to keep in their own hands. 'I am convinced' he wrote 'that the Security Service alone is in a position to run X X agents; but at the same time, the running of them depends upon retaining the good will and the full support of all the Services'.

Bevan himself did not favour the idea of chairing the Committee. It did not, as he explained to the W Board when he attended its meeting on 24 September, fit in with the directive he had received from the Chiefs of Staff, and it would make too heavy demands on his time. There may also have been in his mind a certain fear lest too close an association with the Twenty Committee might distort, or be seen to distort the operational nature of his work on which he laid such proper stress. He was happy to be simply a member of the Committee and to be kept in close touch with its work. What really mattered, however, was the close and continuous informal liaison between Bevan's small staff at Storey's Gate and Robertson and his associates in BıA. Thereafter, as Masterman himself expressed it, the Twenty Committee saw it as its business 'not, as it had been in the past, to promote and press through small plans of our own but to provide channels for deception according to the plans of the Controlling Officer'.[21] The instrument had been created. Now it was to be put to the test.

REFERENCES

1. J C Masterman, *The Double-Cross System in the War of 1939 to 1945* (Yale University Press 1972), p 66.
2. ibid, p 64.
3. ibid, p 65.
4. ibid, p 71.
5. ibid, p 104.
6. CAB 121/105, SIC file A/Policy/Deception/1, COS(41) 344th Meeting, 7 October.
7. ibid, JP (41) 819 of 8 October.
8. ibid, COS (41) 348th Meeting, 9 October.
9. ibid, JP (41) 1101 of 27 December.
10. CAB 154/2, 'A' Force War Diary Vol II, p 60.
11. CAB 121/105. COS (42) 8(0) of 5 January.
12. ibid, COS (42) 94 of 6 February.

13. ibid, C O S (42) 47th Meeting, 11 February.
14. ibid, D M I to Ismay, 11 May 1942, C O S (42) 153rd Meeting, 18 May, Controlling Officer to Ismay, 20 May C O S (42) 157th Meeting, 21 May.
15. ibid, Wavell telegram to the Prime Minister 12461/C of 21 May 1942.
16. ibid, J P (42) 619 of 18 June.
17. ibid, C O S (India) 60 of 21 June 1942; C A B 79/21, C O S (42) 184th Meeting, 20 June.
18. C A B 88/6, C C S 96 of 20 July 1942; Joint Chiefs of Staff (6–23–42), Record Group 218, National Archives of the United States, C C S 334, J C S 26th Meeting, 28 July 1942.
19. C A B 121/105, C O S(42) 208(o) of 20 July.
20. Ibid, Controlling Officer memo C/O/22 of 1 August 1942.
21. Masterman, op cit, p 55.

CHAPTER 2

'A' Force: The Middle East
September 1939–August 1942

WHEN WE consider the development of deception policy in the Middle East we have to take account of certain fundamental differences from the position at home. For whereas in the United Kingdom the possibilities for misleading and misinforming the enemy in the early years of the war far outran the operational requirements for their use, in the Middle East the need for operational deception was from the very outset urgent and continuous, while the environment for satisfying it was highly unfavourable.

From the moment Italy entered the war in June 1940 the British forces in Egypt had to deal with an enemy far superior to them in numbers, hemming them in from south and west. But so far from possessing the advantages of a besieged fortress such as the security authorities in the United Kingdom were able to turn to such good account, the British were based on countries whose populations were largely indifferent to their fate where they were not actively hostile. These populations were elements in a Levantine society extending around the shores and throughout the islands of the eastern Mediterranean, bound together by commercial and family links dating back over millennia; a society whose complexity foreign security authorities could barely comprehend, let alone control. Thus although individual Axis agents might be detected, eliminated or 'turned round', there could be no question of imposing, in British-occupied territories, the complete control over sources of information which was possible at home. Reports from double agents were liable to be contradicted by others; either from undetected enemy agents or from the numerous freelances who abounded in Cairo, Alexandria and Beirut.

The British, having occupied Egypt for over fifty years and Palestine for twenty, were under no illusions about the problems which faced them at the outbreak of war. The region might be described as an intelligence officer's paradise and a security officer's hell. British intelligence-gathering activities do not constitute part of our story, but two events may usefully be noted: the establishment in Cairo in June 1939 of a Middle East Intelligence Centre (MEIC) to co-ordinate and furnish intelligence both for GHQ Middle East and for the Joint Intelligence Committee in London; and, in November 1940, the establishment of a Combined Bureau Middle East (CBME) as a centre of all cryptanalytic activity, directly linked with the Government Code and Cypher

School at Bletchley Park.[1] As for security, that became on the outbreak of war a military responsibility. The senior representative of the British security authorities in Egypt became, with the rank of Lieut Colonel, head of a Security Section on the staff of GHQ Middle East, with a general responsibility for watching and countering the activities of hostile agents throughout the region. This section rapidly became known as SIME (Security Intelligence Middle East) and exercised many of the same functions as MI5 in the United Kingdom. Like MI5 it had its difficulties with Section V of MI6, which naturally conducted its own local counter-espionage activities and which, as in Britain, controlled the distribution of ISOS material after it became available.* These difficulties were very largely resolved by the excellent personal relations between the officials concerned. Liaison was a matter of friendly and largely informal contacts, and the system worked reasonably well for the rest of the war.

Such bodies as SIME and CBME had close affinities with comparable organisations in Britain. 'A' Force, however, was entirely indigenous to the Middle East. It was the brain child of the Commander-in-Chief Middle East, General Sir Archibald Wavell. Behind an inarticulate and ruggedly orthodox exterior Wavell concealed one of the most fertile minds ever possessed by a British senior officer. No one understood better than he the role which deception and its child, surprise, should play in all military operations – especially operations conducted by numerically inferior forces far from home. He had observed at first hand, and subsequently chronicled, the use to which his hero, General Allenby, had put deception, under very similar circumstances in Palestine in 1917 and 1918, to gain decisive victories over the Turkish Army. In November 1940 when Wavell was preparing to attack the Italian forces which had entrenched themselves within Egyptian territory at Sidi Barrani, deception measures formed an intrinsic part of his plan. It was not enough to conceal what he proposed to do: it was necessary to persuade the enemy that he was going to do something else – to have a complete 'cover plan'. The cover plan for Operation *Compass*, his attack in the Western Desert, provided for the British forces† on that front to be notionally weakened so as to build up an expeditionary force to go to the aid of the Greeks, who at that time were fighting to repel an Italian invasion of their territory. As yet no serious network of double agents existed, but certain Axis sources in Cairo had been identified and misleading information was duly planted. Diplomatic channels were also used: the staff of the consulate of Japan, still a neutral country, had especially appropriate intelligence made available

---

* ISOS traffic in the Middle East area was broken from June 1941 onwards, but the MI6 controlling section in Cairo was not set up until nearly a year later.

† Throughout this work the term 'British' will be used to designate all forces under British command, whatever their country of origin.

to them on the assumption that they would quickly pass it on to Rome and Berlin. Administrative measures were taken compatible with the imminent embarkation of a sizeable force, and dummy radio traffic indicating a withdrawal of forces from the Western Desert was engendered for the benefit of the enemy Y (tactical sigint) services. The evidence is unclear whether these measures played any part in the complete surprise which the British attack secured on the morning of 9 December, and the subsequent completeness of the victory. But the whole operation convinced Wavell that it was necessary to have a special section on his staff to initiate and to orchestrate deception measures by all the multiple means that were now available; and if possible to develop more.[2]

On 13 November Wavell sent a personal signal to London stating his intention of forming 'a special section of Intelligence for Deception' and asking that Lieut Col Dudley Clarke should be sent out to run it.* Clarke arrived the following month. His activities were kept deeply secret. Working in a converted bathroom in the GHQ building, he received his orders from Wavell in person, either verbally or in writing. He dealt only with the Chief of Staff, Major-General Sir Arthur Smith, and the Directors of Operations and Intelligence at GHQ. Only two officers assisted him – Major V H Jones, 14/20 Hussars, an expert in visual deception, and Captain Mark Ogilvie Grant of the Scots Guards – and ten other ranks. The unit was officially constituted on 28 March 1941 as 'Advanced HQ, "A" Force'. 'A' Force itself was a notional Brigade of the 'Special Air Service' – itself at this time a purely notional body which was allegedly based in Transjordan where it could be available to intervene in operations in any part of the Middle East. Eventually that spectral body became '1st SAS Brigade' and Lieut Col Clarke's unit became 'A' Force, *tout court*. Its role was defined by the War Office simply as 'the control and administration of units of GHQ Troops operating dummy weapons'. Local cover however was also provided by the work it carried out in association with MI9, the section of military intelligence concerned with assisting the escape of prisoners of war. In this capacity Captain Ogilvie Grant particularly distinguished himself, and subsequent operations, first in Greece and Crete and then in Syria, provided plenty of excuses for the members of 'A' Force to extend their connections throughout the Levant.[3]

The Special Air Service, which since then has had so varied a history, originated with the capture of an Italian officer's diary after the battle of Sidi Barrani in December 1940, whose contents revealed the apprehensions felt by the Italians about the possibility of airborne landings in their rear.[4] One of the first rules of deception is to play on real fears, and Clarke's first task was to build up the notional strength of

---

* Clarke's previous activities are described in his own book, *Seven Assignments*, (London 1948).

the forces available to Wavell; both as a deterrent to enemy attack and as an aid to deception in the offensive. No British airborne units in fact appeared in the Middle East until 1943, but the '1st SAS Brigade' notionally arrived in January 1941, followed by others; a deception implemented by rumours, leakages, bogus radio traffic and displays of dummy gliders provided by Major Jones's craftsmen. At the same time, and by the same means, the arrival of a notional '10th Armoured Division' was projected to enemy intelligence.[5] These were early days. Channels were few and uncertain and experience in using them slight. The effectiveness of these deceptions has to be judged not on the very marginal impression they may have made on the enemy but on the growing experience gained by the British which enabled them, in the latter years of the war, to mount the grandiose and comprehensive 'Order of Battle' deceptions which so facilitated the landings both in southern Europe and in North-West France.

Of more immediate significance was the activity which 'A' Force undertook in connection with the attack on Italian East Africa, which Wavell began to plan even before his attack in the Western Desert had been successfully launched. Both the real plan and the cover had already been worked out by Wavell himself when Clarke reached Cairo on 18 December 1940.[6] The attack was actually to be launched simultaneously against Eritrea from the Sudan in the north and against Abyssinia and the southern part of Italian Somaliland from Kenya in the south; coincidentally with tribal risings within Abyssinia itself. The northern attacking force, consisting primarily of 4th Indian Division with accompanying armour, was withdrawn from the Western Desert in deep secrecy on the eve of the Sidi Barrani battle and sent southwards via the Nile and the Red Sea. Clarke's task was to persuade Italian intelligence that such moves as they might detect were preparations for an amphibious attack on Italian occupied-territory from the *east*; that the target was in fact Italian-occupied British Somaliland, on which forces from Egypt and from Kenya would converge in order to establish there a base for the reconquest of Abyssinia; and that therefore Italian forces should be concentrated in the eastern provinces of Abyssinia, not worrying too much about the north and the south.

For this deception plan, *Camilla*, Wavell put all his forces at Clarke's disposal. Both naval and air raids were launched from Aden against targets in British Somaliland, and major administrative arrangements were made at Aden for the reception and dispatch of a large amphibious force. Maps and guides to British Somaliland were printed and issued to appropriate units; an elaborate radio deception plan was put into effect; while in Cairo rumours were circulated, leakages of information were arranged and appropriate documents were allowed to go astray. There is little doubt that all this activity powerfully contributed to the complete surprise which the main attacks secured when they were launched at the beginning of February. But here as elsewhere it was easier to deceive the enemy if one knew his real intentions. Throughout the East African campaign Italian signals were being regularly intercepted and 90 per cent of them were being read.

Long before the East African campaign ended with the surrender of the Duke of Aosta and his forces at Amba Alagi on 19 May 1941 the Western Desert front had flared up again when German forces recently arrived under Lieut General Rommel attacked at El Agheila on 24 March. With few forces to check them – the bulk of his fighting units were already committed to Greece – Wavell instructed Clarke on 30 March to simulate an attack on the Axis lines of communication between Tripoli and El Agheila.[7] This was to be done partly by a notional amphibious attack mounted by a commando force under Colonel Robert Laycock which had recently arrived from the United Kingdom in the hope of recapturing the Dodecanese and whose assault ships were now prominently displayed in Alexandria Harbour; and partly by an airborne landing by the still notional '1st SAS Brigade'. At the same time the equally notional '10th Armoured Division', with the help of Major Jones's dummies, was to move into the Cyrenaican desert to threaten an attack against the flank of the Axis advance; while long-distance raids would notionally be launched by Free French forces deep in the Sahara. These proposals were worked out and approved at a Commander-in-Chief's conference on 6 April, and were implemented primarily through rumours and calculated indiscretions. There is no evidence that they had any effect on the Axis plans. Not only did Rommel move too fast, but his own Y (tactical sigint) Service gave him sufficiently precise information about actual British movements for him to be able to ignore any alarming rumours which reached him through more roundabout channels.[8]

Rommel was therefore able to sweep Cyrenaica clear of British forces at the same time as the Wehrmacht overran Greece, at the end of April. A month later the Germans completed their triumph with the capture of Crete. For those operations deception could do nothing and 'A' Force was fully occupied establishing escape routes for prisoners of war. But Wavell enlisted Clarke's aid in deterring the Germans from following up their successes with an attack on Cyprus – an island held at the time by some 4,000 troops of moderate quality. 'A' Force first offered to spread the rumour that plague had broken out on the island, but Wavell thought that this, for all manner of reasons, would be unwise. So 'A' Force fell back on more orthodox tactics of inflating the notional size of the garrison. A bogus '7th Division' was brought in to hold the island, with full supporting troops and tanks provided by Major Jones's workshops. A full programme of visual deception was carried out, camps were erected, divisional signs painted, and transport displayed for the benefit of enemy air reconnaissance and agents on the spot. Movement and administrative orders were issued in quantity, and prolific radio signals were exchanged. A complete defence plan of the island together with the order of battle of its defending forces 'went astray' in Cairo. The information it contained reached Rome and was found embodied in Italian intelligence bulletins which British troops captured when they overran the Axis defences in Cyrenaica the following December.[9] And here lay the value of this particular operation. The German High Command had no intention of attacking Cyprus, so the presence of '7th Division' played no part in deterring them. But '7th Division' found its way into OKW intelligence appreciations of the British Order of Battle in the Middle East, and remained there for the rest of the war.

By the summer of 1941 'A' Force was thus well established; so well that it survived the departure of its founder and patron, General Wavell, when he left to become Commander-in-Chief in India on 21 June. Its role had expanded far beyond the provision of cover for specific operations. Clarke's responsibilities now encompassed the whole of Middle East Command from east Africa to Iraq. They included deception on the widest scale – cover for troop and convoy movements, creation and maintenance of bogus units, the engendering of misleading information about British strength and strategic intentions of every kind. Cairo provided an excellent echo chamber for rumours, but Clarke extended his channels on a visit to Turkey in April/May 1941 where he was able to establish contacts closer to the Abwehr Stellen which were operating in that country. The Military Attaché in Ankara, Major General A C Arnold and the Assistant Naval Attaché in Istanbul, Commander V Wolfson RN proved enthusiastic and ingenious assistants.[10] When a few months later, in August 1941, the speed of the German advance in south Russia aroused fears for the safety of Turkey itself, Clarke visited Lisbon, and there identified a number of channels that might be used if necessary. But it was not necessary, and Turkey remained the principal channel for 'A' Force deception until the end of the war.

At the same time 'A' Force was building up a team of double agents in Cairo, of whom the first and most successful was *Cheese. Cheese* was rather complicated. An Italian of Jewish parentage, *Cheese* had been recruited by SIS as a double agent before the war, and had been employed by the Abwehr in France until June 1940, when the Germans made him available to the Italian Military Intelligence Service to operate in Egypt. The Italians sent him out, together with a colleague to operate his radio set, through Istanbul, where the radio operator lost heart and went home. *Cheese* contacted the MI6 representative and after further adventures reached Cairo, without a radio set, in February 1941. There SIME provided him both with a radio set and with an operator – the former having been notionally constructed by the latter who, notionally a Syrian named Paul Nicosoff, was actually a member of the Royal Corps of Signals. *Cheese* then returned to Italy and no more was heard of him until 1943. He had in fact been imprisoned by the Italians, allegedly for black market activities, possibly as a result of feuds between the Italian and German Secret Services. Certainly his channel was not 'blown'. The role of *Cheese* was taken over by 'Nicosoff', who in July 1941 succeeded in making radio contact with an Axis radio control at Bari. Whatever the Italians thought of him, the Abwehr classified *Cheese* as a reliable source and eventually transmitted his reports direct to Rommel's Headquarters. By the Autumn of 1942 *Cheese* was providing a daily service, and by February 1945, when he finally signed off, he had transmitted a total of 432 messages to the Abwehr from Cairo.

The first task allotted to *Cheese* was to help in providing cover for the offensive in the Western Desert, Operation *Crusader*, which General Sir Claude Auchinleck began to prepare as soon as he succeeded Wavell in June 1941. The Eighth Army would be in no state to launch such an offensive until the autumn, and it was above all necessary to keep Rommel quiet until it was ready. This 'A' Force attempted to do by persuading enemy intelligence that an attack was imminent, and so compelling them to keep their forces on the defensive. To do this for four months was not easy, but the attack was notionally mounted and stood down three times. Throughout the late summer *Cheese* kept his employers misleadingly abreast of Auchinleck's plans with information which he notionally obtained from a disgruntled South African confidential clerk on the Operations Staff at GHQ Cairo; the rest of 'A' Force's now numerous channels in Cairo and Istanbul providing a full orchestral accompaniment.[11] D-Day was successively set for 9 August, 30 August, and 15 September; then the attack was notionally postponed until after Christmas. In fact it was launched on 17 November and secured total tactical surprise. The setbacks that followed certainly cannot be attributed to any enemy foreknowledge of the operation.

Meanwhile 'A' Force had been expanding and proliferating with consequences which, although inevitable, were not altogether happy. Lieut Col Clarke's frequent absences made it necessary to devolve further responsibility on to his subordinates. In July 1941 all activities concerned with tactical deception in the field, apart from those involving the use of camouflage and dummies, were hived off under a separate organisation, GSI(d), under Major A D Wintle, of the Royal Dragoons.* Among its other occupations this body initiated a scheme for manufacturing defective ammunition and planting it on the Axis forces – rounds which not only misfired but would be found on examination to contain subversive messages indicating sabotage in the armaments factories. Some 5,000 of these had been manufactured by the end of 1941 and half of them were planted in the enemy lines by special patrols. There

---

* An account of the career of this very remarkable officer will be found in his autobiography: *The Last Englishman* (London 1968).

is no evidence to indicate that this ingenuity had any effect whatever on enemy morale.[12]

The name 'A' Force was now used to designate simply Major Jones's organisation for the manufacture and deployment of dummy units – not only tanks and mechanised transport but aircraft and shipping – which established a special depot in Cairo. The services of this organisation were increasingly in demand. The dummy armoured units now added up to a complete notional brigade – '74th Armoured Brigade' – divided into three notional battalions of the Royal Tank Regiment. These were deployed in Cyprus and in Syria, and during the summer of 1941 they were used to help simulate the build-up in the Western Desert. The new GOC Eighth Army, Major General Sir Alan Cunningham, was particularly taken with the value of these devices for armoured warfare in the desert, and strongly recommended an increase in their numbers. They could, he pointed out to GHQ, mislead the enemy as to the location and strength of armoured reserves; they could simulate feints at enemy flanks; they could be mingled with real units and give a misleading impression of their size; and they could 'enable real Tank Units to move and be rapidly substituted by dummy units, thereby misleading the enemy as to our real strength and dispositions'.[13] Largely on Cunningham's recommendation, Major Jones was able to expand the scope of his operations, and was powerfully assisted by the ingenuity of the distinguished conjuror, Major Jasper Maskelyne.* The original dummies, folding models made of steel piping covered with painted canvas, were adapted to fit over motor chassis. (Later these were replaced in their turn by inflatable rubber models.) Conversely covers were produced, known as 'Sunshields', which when fitted over real tanks gave them, from the air, the appearance of lorries. Apparatus was devised both for making and for concealing tank tracks. A new notional unit, '101 Bn RTR', was equipped with these and other devices and played a distinguished role in the desert fighting throughout the winter of 1941/1942. The number of occasions on which its units were subjected to enemy air attack provided impressive if unwelcome evidence of their success.[14]

By the end of 1941 considerable experience had thus been gained of the operation of 'visual deception'. A beginning had also been made with 'Sonic Deception'. This also originated in an ingenious improvisation. During the course of Operation *Crusader* there was a tactical need to give the impression of large numbers of tanks massing to assault the defences of the German garrison at Halfaya, on the Egyptian frontier. To achieve this, 'A' Force arranged for an Egyptian film company to record the sound of tank movements, and then broadcast the results over amplifiers normally used by a political warfare unit. Thereafter

---

* For the numerous and valuable contributions made to visual deception by Major Maskelyne, see his book *Magic – Top Secret* (London 1949).

special apparatus was manufactured to record and broadcast every kind of useful sound, and was installed in an armoured car appropriately named 'Sonia'.[15] Sonic and visual deception units were henceforward to play their part in every major operation conducted by the Eighth Army throughout the war.

The trouble was that as the facilities for misleading the enemy increased and became more in demand, so the problems of control became greater. Gone were the days when Dudley Clarke could control everything – double agents, diplomatic indiscretions, notional units, displays of dummy tanks – from his desk in a converted bathroom at Wavell's headquarters. Now he had to spend long periods away, in Istanbul, east Africa, South Africa, Lisbon and London, arranging channels for strategic deception. In his absence GSI(d) and Major Jones's dummy units found themselves under direct requisition from the General Staff, where 'Ops' and 'I' fought a protracted battle for their control. Moreover 'A' Force personnel were still deeply involved, perhaps more than was altogether wise, in the affairs of MI9. Captain Ogilvie Grant had been captured in Greece and Lieut Col Wintle went off on an adventurous foray to Marseilles from which he did not return.[16] It was a messy situation which General Cunningham's Brigadier General Staff, Brigadier J F M Whiteley, tried to reduce to order in time for Operation *Crusader*. In October 1941 he laid down that 'Strategic Deception' – messages passed to enemy intelligence through special channels – should remain the responsibility of Lieut Col Clarke and 'A' Force; but that 'Tactical Deception', the misleading of the enemy in the field, should be controlled by an officer on the staff of Eighth Army who would have the title of Chief Deception Officer and run a Section, G(DEC) to handle 'planning and development of deception units and schemes and the control of camouflage'. Special deception officers would be attached to corps, divisional and brigade headquarters to implement these plans.[17]

All these arrangements looked neat on paper, but they made Lieut Col Clarke extremely unhappy. In his eyes strategic and tactical deception could not and should not be divorced: they were different instruments in a single orchestra for which there had to be only one composer and one conductor. Moreover to institutionalise deception so blatantly was to destroy its entire purpose: once everyone knew about it, adequate security would become impossible. The success of 'A' Force had depended on only a handful of people knowing of its very existence and an even smaller handful knowing what it did. In any case no facilities existed for training 'deception officers' in the numbers required by Whiteley's scheme in time for Operation *Crusader*. In consequence that attack was launched and conducted without any tactical deception at all.*

---

* For the subsequent strategic deception, Operation *Advocate*, see p 24 above.

The full weaknesses of the deception organisation came to the attention of General Auchinleck only in February 1942. In that month, confronted with a strong counter-attack by Rommel which threatened to drive the Eighth Army out of Cyrenaica once again, Auchinleck called on Clarke to produce a crash deception programme, with the object of misleading the enemy as to the strength of the British defences. Clarke had to make it clear that he could no longer do this: 'tactical deception' of the kind Auchinleck wanted was now the responsibility of the Deception Officer at Eighth Army HQ. Auchinleck immediately ordered all deception activities to be placed again under 'A' Force, which itself should be responsible to the Operations Branch at GHQ.[18] Clarke, with the valiant assistance of Major Jones, did his best: Operation *Bastion* was mounted, mobilising all available dummy units to swell the notional strength of Eighth Army's forces.[19] When eventually the fighting died down along the Gazala Line Clarke turned his attention to the consolidation of his new command.

All this confusion, in Clarke's view, had taught two fundamental lessons about deception:

'1. Deception will pay its best dividends when both planning and implementation by *all* methods is made the responsibility of one controlling mind.
2. Control should lie with 'Ops' rather than 'I'. 'Ops' are the user and dictate the Object, direct the tempo of the plan and decide when it must be replaced.'[20]

'A' Force was therefore reorganised on 27 March 1942. GSI(d) disappeared. So did the hierarchy of Deception Officers below the level of Army HQ. 'A' Force was subdivided into three sections: Control, with responsibility for Plans, Policy and Administration; Operations, with responsibility for physical implementation and tactical deception in the field; and Intelligence, which implemented deception schemes through the channels controlled by intelligence or security authorities.[21] These were now numerous. Colonel Clarke on his travels had built up an extensive network of executives who were now designated as 'Sub-Operators'. These were stationed in east and south Africa, in Cyprus and later on in Algiers, as well as at the headquarters of Eighth Army and of Ninth Army in Syria. These 'Sub-Operators' had at their disposal, for the planting of deceptive information, 'Special Correspondents' in Ankara, Istanbul, Lourenco Marques, Asmara, and Malta. When later during the summer of 1942 PAI (Persia and Iraq) Force was organised under Lieut General Maitland Wilson to counter any German offensive beyond the Caucasus, 'A' Force established a linked HQ there, operating mainly in Persia.[22] All these branches were kept in touch with Cairo and with one another by 'A' Force Instructions and Strategic Addenda, which Clarke had circulated throughout the theatre, to keep all his agents properly informed about new intelligence and methods. By these means he was able to re-establish the centralised control which he rightly saw as being essential to the success of his efforts, and to make effective used of his now very considerable experience.

About this time Clarke, now a full Colonel, summarised the lessons which he and his colleagues had absorbed over the past eighteen months as follows:

'1. It is important to appreciate from the start that the only purpose of any Deception is to make one's opponent ACT in a manner calculated to assist ones own plans and to prejudice the success of his. In other words, to make him *do* something. Too often in the past we had set out to make him THINK something, without realising that this was no more than a means to an end. Fundamentally it does not matter in the least what the enemy thinks; it is only what line of action he adopts as a consequence of his line of thought that will affect the battle. As a result we resolved the principle that a Commander should tell his Deception Staff just what it is that he wishes the enemy to DO ... while it is the duty of the latter to decide, in consultation with the Intelligence Staff, what he should be made to THINK in order to induce him to adopt the required line of action.
2. ... Every Deception Plan must be given time to work. It is no good telling a Deception Staff to try and influence an enemy 'at once'. The Plan must be aimed at making him act in a favourable manner only at some selected future date, when its implementation has had a fair change of exerting some effect. [This period Clarke estimated to be, in the Middle East, about three weeks.]
3. Deception should never rely on a single method, but use both 'Intelligence' (planting) and 'Physical' – the latter predominating increasingly as one became in closer physical touch with the enemy'.[23]

But the most important development for 'A' Force, as for all deception operators, was the breaking of the Abwehr Enigma cypher at Bletchley Park in December 1941. With the ISK material thus made available, the security and intelligence authorities in the Middle East were able to trace the operations and developments of the Abwehr intelligence network controlled from Istanbul and Ankara. The could identify and deal with agents controlled by the Abwehr. They could verify the credibility of their own double agents and see which of the messages they planted commanded credibility and which did not. Above all, in association with the enemy operational traffic which was being read, a reliable insight could be gained into enemy fears and expectations. As a subsequent report was to put it:

'It may be taken as a principle of strategic deception that it is neither economical in time nor productive in results to attempt to produce in the enemy anxiety over an area concerned with which the enemy himself has had no previous fear ... Knowledge of the trend of enemy anxiety was therefore of very great value ... The principal channel through which such knowledge became available was ULTRA ... On the foundation of fear, and having regard both to inherent plausibility and to contact identifications which the enemy was likely to have made, it was possible to build up a fictitious and misleading structure and to represent Allied capabilities and intentions as very different from what they really were'.

The first major strategic deception which the enlarged and re-organised 'A' Force was called upon to implement was the cover plan for the attack on Madagascar in April 1942, to which we have already referred.* It will be recalled that the notional destination of the invasion force was the Dodecanese Islands, and that the deception was successful enough to ensure that the garrisons of Leros and Rhodes were placed on full-scale alert.[24] Clearly there was a real fear here which could be exploited, and when the following June it became necessary to provide cover for a convoy which the Royal Navy was attempting to get through to the beleaguered island of Malta, this nerve was played on again. Not only were rumours of an imminent attack circulated round the Middle East, but for forty-eight hours all communications from Egypt, Palestine, Syria and Iraq with the outside world were severed. No official explanation was given. 'A' Force channels indicated that the attack on the Dodecanese was imminent. A gratifying stir was caused in enemy intelligence circles, but by Colonel Clarke's own criteria the deception failed. The enemy failed to act in the manner required. The Italian High Command diverted no forces to the defence of the eastern Mediterranean, and the convoy suffered heavy losses. Nor was 'A' Force any more successful the following month, when they tried by similar means to tie down the garrison of Crete, so as to prevent it sending reinforcements to Rommel's forces in Cyrenaica. The threats of attack were duly relayed by the Abwehr, but no action was taken on them. The reinforcements were despatched to Rommel just the same.[25]

It would indeed be difficult to identify any significant occasion on which the strategic dispositions of Axis forces in the Mediterranean were affected by the operations of 'A' Force between May 1941 and July 1942. It was a period of trial and error. But by the summer of 1942, as Colonel Clarke himself put it, 'the organ was now built, its stops were ready for us to pull at will, and all we had to do now was write the music and gain a little more practice in playing it'.[26] Above all, a sound foundation had been laid for what was to prove one of the most important measures of strategic deception of the entire war – one without which few of the others would have been possible.

Perhaps the most valuable contribution which deception can make to operational success is to mislead the enemy as to the real strength of the forces at one's disposal. When one is on the defensive a misleading appearance of weaknesses may lure him to disastrous attack; a misleading appearance of strength may deter him from attacking at all. When one is contemplating an attack, a misleading appearance of weakness may lull the enemy into unreadiness; a misleading appearance of

---

* See p 24 above.

strength may deceive him as to the direction and scope of the attack. In 1942 the British forces in the Middle East were on the defensive and were very weak indeed. The last thing they wanted was for the enemy to attack. The most important task for the deception staff was therefore to give a misleading appearance of strength, and this they began to do, in March 1942, with Operation *Cascade*.[27]

Cascade was the first comprehensive Order of Battle Deception Plan for the whole of the Middle East theatre, and from it there developed all subsequent plans on which cover for the invasion of western Europe, both from the Mediterranean and from the United Kingdom, would be based. 'A' Force, as we have seen, had already made a start in 1941 by inventing the SAS Brigades (which later achieved actuality), the '10th Armoured Division', to swell forces in the Western Desert, and '7th Division', to garrison Cyprus. This piecemeal build-up was now absorbed in a systematic plan for inflating British strength through-out the Middle East. In March 1942 that strength actually stood at five armoured and ten infantry divisions. The object of *Cascade* was to increase these, for the benefit of enemy intelligence, to eight armoured and twenty-one infantry divisions.

The task was intricate and complicated. The bogus units had to be notionally created and shipped our from their home base – the United Kingdom, India, and in one case New Zealand, in another South Africa; which meant close liaison with the staff directorates in those countries. They had to be equipped with orders of battle, divisional signs and, if they were likely to be observed by uncontrolled enemy agents, some visible evidence of their presence. If they were within range of enemy intercept services they had to engender their own radio traffic. Their movements and administration had to be credibly docu-mented. And once created, they had to stay created, or a plausible explanation be provided for their disappearance.

'A' Force created in 1942 one bogus armoured division (15th) and seven bogus infantry divisions, two of them Indian and one New Zea-land; as well as a bogus '25th Corps' headquarters. During the course of 1943 they were to add to this eight more infantry divisions (including two Polish and one Greek), three armoured and one airborne division, as well as a bogus Army (12th) and another bogus Corps Headquarters (14th). Each formation had a real core in a training or line-of-communi-cation unit. Careful records were kept, both in Cairo and in London, showing where each formation actually was, insofar as it was anywhere; where it was notionally supposed to be; the enemy's probable knowledge of the unit as gained from misinformation fed through strategic decep-tion and through direct operational contact; and the conclusions he was known to have drawn through Sigint or documents captured from him in the field. Such documents became available in quantity after the Battle of El Alamein. An analysis of them published by 'A' Force on 19 November 1942 showed that the existence of the greater number of their bogus units was now firmly credited by enemy intelligence. The armoured strength credited to the British forces was over estimated by 40 per cent, infantry strength by 45 per cent. These inflated figures were to remain in German intelligence estimates until the end of the war.

REFERENCES

1. F H Hinsley and others, *British Intelligence in the Second World War*, Vol 1 (1979), Chapter 6 passim.
2. CAB 154/1, 'A' Force War Diary, Vol 1, p 1 et seq.
3. CAB 154/100, Historical Record of Deception in the War against Germany and Italy (Sir Ronald Wingate's Narrative), Vol 1, p 44.
4. CAB 154/1, pp 8–9.
5. CAB 154/100, p 87.
6. CAB 154/1, pp 2–4.
7. ibid, p 19.
8. Lieut Gen Albert Praun, *German Radio Intelligence*, p 52 (MS No P 038, Foreign Military Studies, Historical Office, European Command, Records of US Army Commands 1942, Record Group 338, National Archives of the United States).
9. CAB 154/1, p 43.
10. ibid, p 25.
11. CAB 154/100, p 88.
12. CAB 154/1, p 37.
13. ibid, pp 35, 51.
14. ibid, p 52.
15. ibid, p 87.
16. CAB 154/2. 'A' Force War Diary, Vol II, p 19.
17. ibid.
18. ibid, p 22.
19. ibid, p 9.
20. ibid, p 22.
21. CAB 154/100, p 65.
22. ibid, p 66.
23. CAB 154/2, p 16.
24. ibid, p 60.
25. CAB 154/100, p 111.
26. CAB 154/2. p 92.
27. ibid, pp 35–44.

CHAPTER 3

The German Intelligence Services

S INCE THE purpose of all deception operations was to influence not only enemy thinking but enemy action, the ultimate target both of the London Controlling Section and of 'A' Force was the body which controlled all German operations against the Western Allies: the Supreme Command of the German Armed Forces, the Ober-kommando der Wehrmacht. Here Hitler as Commander-in-Chief of the Armed Forces reigned supreme. His principal administrative assist-ant was the Head of OKW, Field-Marshal Wilhelm Keitel, but his effective operational staff, the Wehrmachtführungsstab, had as its chief Colonel-General Alfred Jodl, assisted by General Walter Warlimont. By a curious division of responsibilities operations on the Russian Front were the responsibility of the Army High Command (OKH) alone which Hitler directed as Commander-in-Chief of the Army (after December 1941) through successive Chiefs of the Army Staff. But the Wehrmachtführungsstab depended for intelligence about its western adversaries on the intelligence services of OKH; as they depended for intelligence about the other two services on the specialists of the Naval and Air Force High Commands. The effective authority for the collation and evaluation of intelligence about the Western Allies was thus a department in the Army High Command Foreign Armies West, Fremde Heere West (FHW). It was the daily situation reports issued by this section that the operational staffs took as the basis for their plans.

FHW had been built up largely through the work of Lieut Col Ulrich Liss, who was succeeded, on his promotion to a field command in March 1943, by Colonel Alexis von Roenne. Both were highly compe-tent and experienced intelligence officers. Like all intelligence organisa-tions FHW relied on a wide range of sources; Sigint, POW interrogation, captured documents, diplomatic reports and open sources among them.[1] Only last, and normally least, did they depend for infor-mation on the agents employed by the German intelligence services. Intelligence evaluators are always sceptical about the value of agents' reports, but the Wehrmacht had more cause to be sceptical than most. Among its military colleagues the prestige of the purveyors of these reports, the German Intelligence Service or Abwehr, did not stand very high.

This may seem a little surprising. Unlike its British equivalent, MI6, the Abwehr was itself part of the Wehrmacht. Its upper ranks at least were recruited almost wholly from officers of good social background and conservative political outlook. Formally it was a section of an umbrella organisation for the gathering of military intelligence entitled the Amt Auslands Nachrichten und Abwehr, whose chief, Admiral Wilhelm Canaris, reported directly to the Oberkommando der Wehrmacht.[2] The Abwehr itself was one of three sections, of which the others were concerned with administration and with overt channels. It was divided into three parts. Abwehr I, that with which we are mainly concerned, was responsible for secret intelligence and was thus comparable to MI6. Abwehr II was the 'dirty tricks' department, dealing with sabotage and clandestine operations of every kind. Its equivalent in the British services, in so far as it had one, would have been the Special Operations Executive. Abwehr III dealt with security and counter-espionage, and roughly corresponded to MI5. Within each department there were sections dealing with naval and air force questions. Both Abwehr I and Abwehr III had sub-sections studying technical and economic affairs.

The Abwehr consisted of a network of stations inside and outside the Reich, in each of which the various specialist departments were duplicated. Those within the Reich and German-occupied territories were called simply Abwehrstellen, or Asts for short. Those in neutral countries such as Sweden, Spain and Turkey, normally operating under the flimsy cover of diplomatic consular or commercial camouflage, were called Kriegsorganisationen, or KOs. Both types of organisation developed where necessary subordinate organs, Nebenstellen. The Abwehr KO in Ankara had Nebenstellen in Istanbul and Tehran, that in Madrid had its own in Casablanca and Tangier. Within the Reich there were something over a dozen Asts, each operating within one of the military districts into which Germany was divided and most of them specialising in intelligence-gathering for a particular area. Thus, the Asts in eastern Germany dealt primarily with eastern Europe and the Soviet Union; those in Bavaria and Austria with the Balkans and the Mediterranean; those in north and west Germany with western Europe. The Ast at Hamburg had particular responsibility for the gathering of overseas intelligence, including the United Kingdom and the British Empire; while naval and shipping questions were handled by Nebenstellen in Bremen and Kiel.[3]

The activities of these Asts within the Reich were supplemented by the Kriegsorganisationen abroad. That in Stockholm was particularly busy, being well placed to gather information about both the Soviet Union and the United Kingdom. Those in Lisbon and Madrid were strategically placed to monitor events in the United Kingdom, the Atlantic and north Africa, the latter through the Nebenstellen in Casablanca and Tangier. A KO in the Argentine collated information about the western hemisphere; another in Shanghai covered the Far East and liaised with the Japanese. Before the summer of 1941 KOs in the neutral states of south-east Europe covered the Soviet Union and the eastern

Mediterranean. The Middle East, curiously enough, was neglected until the military events of 1941 drew the German armed forces into that theatre, when a KO was established at Ankara with Nebenstellen at Tehran and Istanbul. At the extreme end of the line the Abwehr maintained a Nebenstelle at Kabul, monitoring events in India.

It first became possible to follow the activities of the Abwehr when early in 1940, as we have seen, the Radio Security Service happened to intercept and began to monitor the encyphered traffic of an Abwehr control vessel in the North Sea, communicating with its agents in the Low Countries. Although unable to read the traffic, they accumulated enough data for a team at Bletchley Park led by Mr Oliver Strachey to be able to break the cypher in December of that year.* The material which then became available (called, as we have seen in a previous chapter, ISOS) consisted mainly of the hand cyphers used by the Abwehr Asts and KOs for communicating with individual agents, or with stations not yet equipped with the *Enigma* machine. A year later, as we have also seen, the relevant *Enigma* keys were also broken, and a flood of new information became available. Certain communications, of course, remained secure throughout the war. All internal communications within the Reich that went by land-line, as did those between the Asts and Abwehr HQ, and between Abwehr HQ and OKW, fell within that category. But the Abwehr stations abroad, particularly those in such key neutral capitals as Stockholm, Lisbon, Madrid and Ankara, communicated with Berlin by *Enigma* cypher, while the situation reports produced daily by FHW, communicated over the air to such out-lying military headquarters as Rome, Tripoli and Salonika, were read by the British almost before they had reached their German destination.

Once the *Enigma* keys were broken and the ISOS material was reinforced by the machine cypher material of ISK and ISOSICLE† it became possible for the Radio Intelligence Section of the Radio Security Service to build up a full picture of the Abwehr's activities; and the more of the picture that emerged, the more encouraging it became.

On paper the German intelligence-gathering apparatus appeared formidable. The very fact that the Abwehr was an intrinsic part of the Wehrmacht, and that the intelligence and security services were part of the same organisation and responsive to the same head, might appear to give it an important initial advantage over the sprawling committees, part military, part civilian, all created very much *ad hoc*, of its British counterparts. In fact all was far from well. In so centralised an organisation, everything depends on the personality of its chief. Admiral Canaris,

---

* See p 14 above.
† See p 15 above.

an officer of the old Imperial Navy who had seen active service in the First World War, was a man who commanded the deep loyalty of his intimates but who beyond their circle remained an enigmatic, even a suspect figure. Even before the war several of his closest associates had been involved in the resistance to the Nazi regime. His own loyalty to it was at best lukewarm, and turned to hostility once it became clear (as with the sources available to him it rapidly did after 1942) that Germany was going to lose the war. His own interests centred upon Spain, where internment during the First World War and close involvement during the Civil War had enabled him to build up a useful network of influential friends, including General Franco himself. In consequence German intelligence operations in this key area were highly effective; in particular the observation posts established by the Abwehr at Algeciras and Tangier, on either side of the Straits of Gibraltar, provided a flow of accurate and valuable information. But elsewhere – in the Middle East, for example, and the United States – Canaris showed little enterprise or initiative in building up Abwehr activities, and his efforts against the United Kingdom were, as we have seen, pathetic. Canaris's immediate subordinates, particularly his second-in-command Hans Oster, were men who shared his political views and devoted an increasing amount of their time, as the war went on, to political intrigue. The Abwehr as a whole became notorious as a haven for dissidents from the regime, 'a group of men' as a defector from the organisation was to describe them, 'who do not like the Nazis and do not want to go to war'. One of these was the head of Abwehr I himself, Colonel Hans Pieckenbrock, an anti-Nazi officer of the old school who not only tolerated but appeared positively to encourage extreme inefficiency in his subordinates. Under his genial and relaxed regime posts were left unfilled, officers were encouraged to take extended leave, files got lost, reports, if made, were seldom read and even more seldom checked. There was some consternation when in March 1943 Pieckenbrock was replaced by an expert from FHW, Colonel George Hansen. Hansen tightened things up and cleared out a great deal of dead wood. So good an impression did he make indeed that when in March 1944 Canaris was eased out of office and the work of the Abwehr was gradually taken over by his rival Heinrich Himmler, Hansen was left for some months effectively in charge of all Abwehr activities. But behind the facade of efficiency Hansen was, to a far greater extent than either Canaris or Pieckenbrock, an active conspirator in the 20 July plot. In spite of his show of activity the Abwehr dissidents had in consequence nothing to fear from him.[4]

As a result the Abwehr increasingly came to show the weaknesses which beset all clandestine services unless they are continually and rigorously supervised. It recruited agents with little concern either for their loyalty or for the accuracy of their information. Abwehr officials, enjoying life in the oases of Lisbon, Madrid, Stockholm or Istanbul, fiddling their expenses and running currency rackets on the side, felt that they were earning their keep so long as they provided *some* kind of information. This explains why for example *Garbo* was able to get away with his early fantasies, and *Tricycle* could run such outrageous risks. The information gathered by the spymasters in Madrid, Lisbon or Hamburg was passed on raw to the departmental heads in Abwehr I, who made little attempt to evaluate or collate the reports which passed over their desks. All was dumped, largely unsorted, in the in-trays of the unfortunate officers at OKH's FHW.[5]

The shortcomings of the Abwehr, their failure to provide advance warning of the El Alamein offensive, or the landings in French north Africa, or the landings in Sicily or the landings at Anzio, would have aroused unfavourable comment under any circumstances. As it was, they played into the hands of Canaris's rival Heinrich Himmler, who had justifiable doubts not only about the effectiveness but about the loyalty of the Abwehr and who worked patiently to absorb it into his own satrapy, the SS. The SS ran its own security service, the Sicherheitsdienst (SD) whose responsibility was the detection and elimination of political dangers to the regime. Within this organisation one department, Amt VI, under the young and ambitious Walter Schellenberg, was responsible for foreign intelligence, and maintained its own network of agents independent of the Abwehr. In principle this office was concerned purely with political matters and communicated anything of military significance to its Abwehr colleagues; in practice relations at every level were marked by mistrust if not outright hostility. In France in particular, where the SD acquired a great deal of valuable information about Allied intentions through their penetration of Resistance units and failed to communicate it to the Abwehr, the rivalry of the two organisations played into the hands of the Allies.[6] In neutral capitals the representatives of the SD observed the weaknesses of their Abwehr colleagues and reported them to an attentive Himmler, who had accumulated by the end of 1943 a devastating dossier on the shortcomings of the rival organisation.

Matters came to a head in February 1944, when an Abwehr official, Erich Vermehren, defected with his wife to the Allies, triggering off a whole sequence of further defections. This, in combination with the Abwehr's dismal record of failure to foresee Allied intentions in the Mediterranean, provided Himmler with a cast-iron case against Canaris; whose sources in Spain had dried up once the Allies, in the autumn of 1943, established effective dominance in the western Mediterranean and begun to bring heavy pressure to bear on Madrid. The process of the absorption of the Abwehr by the SS began. Canaris was removed, Hansen becoming his *locum tenens*. But the efficiency of the service was not improved. Experienced if indolent Abwehr officials were replaced by SS men whose loyalty to the Führer in no way compensated for their ignorance of intelligence operations. The entire intelligence service was thrown into a state of confusion just at the moment, in the early summer of 1944, when its efficient functioning was vital to the survival of the Third Reich. The July plot and its aftermath was to compound that confusion, and for the last six months of the war the intelligence services were to find themselves virtually leaderless.

The relations between the Abwehr and the SD, were of less direct significance to the British deception authorities than were those between Abwehr and the officers in FHW, who had the task of evaluating the raw material which the Abwehr provided. These were also uneasy. FHW may have had good reason to consider its Abwehr colleagues to be unreliable, but the Abwehr in its turn regarded the staff of FHW as inexperienced and inefficient. This did not apply to its leaders, Liss and von Roenne, who brought to their work expertise of a very high calibre, but among their staffs there was a rapid rate of turn-over, and few officers occupied a desk at FHW for long enough to become a real expert on his topic. Officers seconded to FHW had no special training in intelligence work. In the German, as in other armies, it was assumed that a General Staff training enabled a staff officer to fulfil any staff appointment required of him, and – again as in other armies – there was a general reluctance among German staff officers to become pigeon-holed as intelligence specialists. In consequence they brought to their work no special knowledge, and by the time they were beginning to acquire any they were moved on to other posts.

Neither within the Abwehr nor at OKW, therefore, was adequate provision made for evaluating intelligence. So far as British deception operations were concerned, however, this cut both ways. On the one hand it made it easier to get misinformation accepted at its face value. On the other it meant that the carefully orchestrated signals that the deception authorities were feeding into the enemy intelligence systems were usually swamped by the 'noise' generated by the mass of rumours, gossip, diplomatic indiscretions and garbled reports that the Abwehr Asts and KOs collected and forwarded, largely unfiltered, to their head offices. Confronted by the amorphous mass of unsorted information provided by the Abwehr (and its bewildered and inexperienced successors of the SD) the overworked officers at FHW learned to pay little attention to anything emanating from that source unless it was backed by more solid evidence such as air reconnaissance or Sigint. Fortunately in the later years of the war these were hard to come by, but until the summer of 1942 the Germans were monitoring the communications of the British armed forces, at least in the Western Desert, quite as efficiently as the British were monitoring the German; and the solid information they gained from their intercept services was not likely to be counteracted by any stray agents' reports.[7]

As a result the British deception authorities repeatedly had the frustrating experience of successfully planting misinformation, seeing it reported up the various Abwehr channels to Berlin, and waiting in vain to see it repeated in the FHW bulletins. But here as elsewhere the tide was gradually to turn. The German sources of radio-interception were, as we shall see, to dry up. Their capacity for air reconnaissance was to be drastically reduced. The British channels for deception were to multiply, and gradually FHW came to rely on the Abwehr agents, especially for information about the United Kingdom, as the only sources available.

There was one respect however in which FHW showed extraordinarily little scepticism with regard to the misinformation which the Allied deception authorities fed them, and that was the most important of all: the strength of the Allied armed forces. Every single bogus unit dreamed up by 'A' Force and the London Controlling Section eventually found its way on to the Order of Battle maintained by FHW, and stayed there. In the case of an intelligence officer so experienced as von Roenne this was indeed remarkable, and it is not surprising that it has been attributed to deliberate treachery. Von Roenne was certainly privy to the July 20 plot, and was one of those executed in its aftermath; but there is every indication that till the very end he performed his work with the dedication of a non-political technician, as did the overwhelming majority of his colleagues on the General Staff. Another explanation which has been offered was that he deliberately inflated his figures, knowing that they would be halved by the SD before they were seen by Hitler. But von Roenne worked, not to the SD, but directly to the Wehrmachtführungsstab, where the officer responsible for evaluating his reports was not a member of the SD but a close associate of Warlimont's, Colonel Friedrich-Adolf Krummacher.* It was not until the summer of 1944, after von Roenne's own fall, that Krummacher's activities were taken over and re-organised under the auspices of the SS.[8]

A more probable explanation of the credulity of FHW with regard to the Allied Order of Battle lies in the continuing tug-of-war between the demands of the Eastern Front, which were so urgent and unremitting, and those of the West, for which FHW had a direct responsibility. However much they may have tried to discount their own interest in the matter, von Roenne and his associates must have felt constantly anxious lest the forces available to deal with the threat from the West, when it came, had been reduced below the margin of safety. This anxiety would have done something to mitigate the rigour with which

---

* The intelligence evaluation branch at the Wehrmachtführungsstab (*Wf/st/Ic*) was established in January 1943 and enlarged in the spring of 1944. Krummacher was head of one of its three branches, (Abt II), the others being concerned with Front Reconnaissance and Counter-Intelligence.

they scrutinised the evidence which the Allied deception authorities provided of a continuing build-up of forces in the Mediterranean and the United Kingdom; and once a bogus unit had been accepted by the evaluators at FHW, it was extraordinarily difficult to remove it from their files. If the Abwehr showed a certain readiness to co-operate in accepting the credibility of the double agents foisted on them by MI5, since they provided them with *some* material to justify their existence, FHW was no less co-operative in believing in the existence of units whose imminent threat provided them with good reasons to prevent yet more German formations being sucked into the fighting on the Eastern Front, leaving the West totally vulnerable when its critical moment came. Deception can never be effective either in love or in war, unless there is a certain willingness to be deceived, and the London Controlling Section could never have succeeded as well as it did had it not possessed, at the highest level of the German Command, its unconscious sympathisers.

REFERENCES

1.   The range is well described in David Kahn, *Hitler's Spies* (1978), passim.
2.   A good account of this organisation is given in Gert Buchheit, *Der Deutsche Geheim-dienst* (Munich 1966), and in Paul Leverkuhn, *German Military Intelligence* (1954), especially 27–33.
3.   Buchheit, op cit, pp 111–112.
4.   ibid, p 425; Kahn, op cit, p 237.
5.   In addition to the sources quoted this account draws heavily on the confidential report by H R Trevor-Roper, *The German Intelligence Services and the War* (1945) filed in CAB 154/105.
6.   Buchheit, op cit, p 344.
7.   Lieut Gen Albert Praun, *German Radio Intelligence* (MS p 038, Foreign Military Studies, Historical Office, European Command, Records of US Army Commands 1942, Record Group 338, National Archives of the United States).
8.   Kahn, op cit, pp 397–398.

PART II

The Tests, August 1942–December 1943

CHAPTER 4

The Turn of the Tide

(i) *Torch*: The United Kingdom, August–December 1942

NO SOONER had the London Controlling Section been reconstituted under Lieut Col Bevan in the summer of 1942 than it was subjected to as gruelling a test as could be conceived. From the viewpoint of the British Chiefs of Staff, the Section could hardly have been established at a more opportune moment. The months of June and July 1942 witnessed the discussions between the political and military leaders of Great Britain and the United States out of which developed the plans for the first major allied offensive of the war – Operation *Torch*, the landing on the coast of French north Africa. The decision to mount this operation was the result of the assessment by the British that an attack on the coast of north-west France was not yet a feasible military operation, combined with the determination both of Mr Churchill and of President Roosevelt that an offensive must be mounted somewhere in the European theatre before the end of 1942; partly to relieve their Russian allies at a critical moment in the campaign on the eastern front, and partly to counter American pressures for abandoning the strategic priorities agreed the previous December and concentrating resources, not on the war against Germany, but on that against Japan.

The British and American Combined Chiefs of Staff, with varying degrees of reluctance, agreed on their recommendations on 24 July 1942, and these received the immediate approval of the Prime Minister and the President.[1] The full details of the operation continued to be debated for several weeks, but its outlines were clear and formidable. A landing on a supposedly hostile coast had to be mounted from two widely separated bases, each thousands of miles from the objective. One British and US assault force was to sail from the United Kingdom, a voyage of some 2,760 sea miles. A US assault force was to sail from the United States, a distance of some 4,500 miles. In the oceanic stretches over which the convoys would have to pass German submarines were active and successful; in June 1942 their sinkings had reached a peak of 700,000 tons. The arrangements for combining the land, air, naval and amphibious elements of the operation, and the liaison in all these elements between Allied armed forces with different operative procedures, were highly complex and the necessary communications involved would in consequence be massive. To maintain the secrecy of the operation presented as a result unprecedented problems of security. But if secrecy were *not* preserved; if the alerted enemy were able to attack the convoys at sea and reinforce the defences of the threatened coasts; the operation could easily turn into an irretrievable disaster.

It was no doubt more for this reason than because deception operations had as yet shown any notable degree of success that deception was made so intrinsic a part of the planning for *Torch*. The London Controlling Section received its instructions within a few days of the decision to launch the operation; on 27 July to be precise, before any detailed operational planning had commenced at all.[2] Their task was twofold. First, although the Allies had now decided not to attack north-west Europe that summer, everything possible had to be done to conceal that decision. German forces in that theatre had to be so effectively pinned down by the appearance of an imminent assault that no troops would be transferred either to the Russian front or to the Mediterranean. Second, a 'cover plan' had to be prepared for *Torch* itself, concealing the real destination of the invading armadas by the indication of a plausible alternative.

Lieut Col Bevan and his colleagues had their plans ready within a week and they presented them to the Chiefs of Staff on 5 August.[3] For the first assignment given them they proposed a feint at the Pas de Calais; effectively a continuation of the planning for the operation, *Sledgehammer*, which the Chiefs of Staff had had under consideration since April and had only just definitely abandoned. For the second they proposed, as the alternative destination for the *Torch* forces, the coast of Norway; a theatre where the Germans were known to be abnormally sensitive and for which plans for an attack, Operation *Jupiter*, were already being examined, on the peremptory instructions of the Prime Minister, by Lieut General McNaughton of the Canadian Army.[4]

To implement these gigantic deceptions Bevan had a staff of three. He had brought with him from his previous post at Western Command his GSO 2, Major H L Petavel, and they were now joined by Major Sir Ronald Wingate. He had inherited from Colonel Stanley one officer, Flight Lieut D Y Wheatley, better known as Dennis Wheatley, one of the best-known mystery novelists of his generation, who had been feeding stimulating and unorthodox ideas into the Joint Planning Staff since 1940.[5] Both Wheatley and Wingate, who has recently concluded a career of great distinction in the Indian Civil Service which took him to many parts of the Middle East, were men of the world with a wide range of contacts, as indeed had Bevan himself; and the LCS was to some extent able to compensate for the small number of its members by their sparkling inventiveness and their skill in cutting corners. But no plans could be effective if no one would implement them. Later in the year the Admiralty allocated to them a naval officer, Commander J Arbuthnot, RN, and ultimately the Section reached a total of ten.[6] But when on 2 September after a month of work Bevan complained to the Chiefs of Staff of the absence of machinery to implement his ideas, he was told simply that he was to be 'directly responsible to the Directors of Plans who would thus be charged with the task of assisting him with securing the implementation within their respective departments of such plans as might be approved by the Chiefs of Staff'.[7] This laid a heavy burden on Bevan's personality and persuasiveness; no heavier, fortunately, than they were able to bear.

Bevan's proposal for a feint across the Channel, approved by the Chiefs of Staff on 18 August, was named, with unconscious foresight, Operation *Overthrow*. It was implemented partly through visual displays, partly through the spreading of rumours, partly through messages passed through the 'special means' controlled by BɪA. The first medium was the least satisfactory. A little could be done with assemblies of shipping, the construction of 'hards' for the loading of landing craft and the embarkation of vehicles, and photographic reconnaissance sorties flown over the French coast. The LCS had set its greatest store by an amphibious exercise, Operation *Cavendish*, which was due to be held in the Channel in October. Unfortunately the administrative problems which this raised proved insuperable and eventually it had to be cancelled. More effective were the double agents, especially *Garbo*, who sent ominous accounts of troop movements in the south of England and whetted the appetite of their controllers for more. *Garbo* warned his employers on 16 September that 'rumours which are circulating that the English cannot invade for lack of tonnage are put out with the intention of confusing you and so that you do not suspect the improvised plan which they have to use every sort of transport'. He was pressed for further details: 'It is of the greatest importance' his Abwehr controller told him in a letter of 14 September 1942 'that you should intensify all your efforts to try to get extensive information and transmit it here quickly by air mail on concentration of troops and material, motorised units, aviation and airfields, as well as bases of departure in the south of England and especially the Isle of Wight and regions of Wales'. *Garbo* did his best to oblige.

The German military authorities, as we have seen, were not in general impressed by Abwehr agents' reports, but Hitler himself was less sceptical. On 5 October, 'on the basis of numerous reports from agents' he drew the attention of the Wehrmachtführungsstab to the threat in the west, ordering that the coast should be put in a state of alert and coastal defences be strengthened.[8] Four days later the Führer's intuition indicated Cherbourg as the most likely target, and measures were ordered for its defence. These instructions were received at the headquarters of Field Marshal von Rundstedt, Commander-in-Chief West, with less irritation than might have been expected. Ever since the raid on Dieppe on 19 August, von Rundstedt had been on the alert. 'The general situation [is] in no way altered by that operation' he reported on 24 August.[9] 'Commander-in-Chief West anticipates various enemy operations for prestige reasons precisely in the near future. There is every possibility of renewed large-scale landing attempts based on the experience gained in that operation, which may be considered a "dress rehearsal".' With this expectation firmly fixed in their minds, von Rundstedt's intelligence officers snatched at every crumb that the London Controlling Section put in their way, and discounted the absence of Sigint to back them up. On 14 September they reported that changes in ship positions and movements in the Poole–Southampton area 'would seem to indicate continual landing practice. Wireless intelligence was unable to establish changes in the disposition of troops in England; landing practice on the other hand [has occurred] on a fairly large scale since 9 September in the land and water area of the northern outlet of the Bristol Channel. This enemy activity in conjunction with the concentration of troops already known to us in the Isle of Wight ... confirms C-in-C West in his opinion that further enemy operations are imminent'. The point of main effort was as yet indeterminate but there was a possibility of 'several simultaneous operations at different points'.[10]

By mid-September the London Controlling Section had thus already achieved their object, and they succeeded in keeping von Rundstedt on the alert for another two months. On 12 October he reported 'enemy attack possible at any time and in different places, Normandy and the north coast of Brittany appearing the most likely enemy point of departure'.[11] A week later he had to admit that the evidence was obscure and contradictory, but held firmly to his opinion 'that British are trained and in complete readiness for landing operations on a fairly large scale'. And even on 2 November he reported that 'from various sources of information operations similar to Dieppe seem likely in November under still favourable weather conditions'.[12] Not until December did he admit that such conditions were now unlikely.

Operation *Overthrow* must therefore be judged a major success. Throughout the summer and autumn, up to the eve of the *Torch* landings, German forces in north-west France remained on the alert in expectation of an imminent Allied attack, and the fears of von Rundstedt and of Hitler reinforced one another. No 'substantial forces were removed either to the Russian front or southward towards the western mediterranean; and the German lack of suspicion about the real intentions of the Allies can be attributed at least in part to the success of the London Controlling Section's activities in covering them.

The notional attack on Norway – *Solo I* – was only part of the protective web which the LCS wove around Operation *Torch*. A subsidiary deception – *Solo II* – was practised on the assault forces themselves, among whom rumours were spread that their real destination was the Middle East, but that they were being practised in assault techniques and equipped for an opposed landing in order to seize the port of

Dakar, in French west Africa, in the course of their voyage.[13] For the assault forces sailing from the United States a different story was necessary, implemented in co-operation with the American Joint Security Control. They themselves were told that they were embarking for a destination in the Carribbean, to train for warfare in tropical conditions. Information fed to German intelligence suggested that their convoys were bound southward round the Cape, to reinforce the British in the Middle East. Finally there were operations *Townsman*, to cover the all too visible preparations in Gibraltar, and *Kennecott*, to deceive the enemy as to the real destination of the convoys once they had put to sea.

The London Controlling Section already had some experience of deception operations directed towards Norway: Operation *Hardboiled*, it will be recalled, had occupied them – or rather their predecessors – during the early months of the year. These activities were now developed still further. The notional objectives were the ports of Trondheim and Narvik, where the British had landed briefly in the spring of 1940. The RAF mounted reconnaissance sorties over these areas. The Royal Navy sent out minesweepers to clear a passage for the invasion. The Army issued mountain-warfare equipment to a select number of units. A large quantity of radio traffic was simulated around ports and airfields in the north of Scotland. The double agents reported troops to be training for mountain warfare, the purchase of snow-chains and anti-freeze in large quantities, and a subtle rumour that Lascar seamen on vessels in the Merchant Navy were being offered large bonuses if they agreed to serve in waters north of latitude 60°N – something which contractually they were not obliged to do.[14]

In Norway, as in the case of north-west France, the LCS found themselves pushing at an open door. Hitler's anxiety about the Norwegian defences was continual and notorious. 'The constant threat of an enemy invasion' was cited by Admiral Raeder in August as a major reason for maintaining a substantial part of the German fleet in northern Norway.[15] On 19 October Hitler ordered an additional infantry battalion to be sent to that theatre, and demanded special protection for the approaches to Narvik.[16] On 2 November the whole of central and northern Norway was put on a state of full alert.[17] Like Operation *Overthrow*, *Solo I* fully achieved its object.

The real difficulty arose however once the *Torch* convoys were at sea and once it became evident from the activity at Gibraltar that something was brewing in the Mediterranean. The dimensions of this latter problem can be gauged from the diary of Colonel Dudley Clarke, who naturally co-operated to the full wherever his Mediterranean channels were able to do so:

'The scene in Gibraltar on the first day of November was a memorable one. On the aerodrome aircraft were stacked in closely-packed ranks as if for the flying-deck of some gigantic carrier, leaving only a single narrow runway down the centre; while solid walls of stores and supplies flanked the streets leading into the town. Inside the startled population of the Rock rubbed shoulders with crowds of staff officers, airmen and supply-personnel of both Britain and America, straining the packed quarters of the fortress as never before. It seemed amazing that German agents across the narrow frontier-line to Spain could not have given Berlin a proper account of what was in store'.[18]

The account which the LCS wished to have given, and which they floated in Operation *Townsman*, was that Gibraltar was being used as a base for a massive relief of the beleaguered island of Malta.[19] The Governor of Gibraltar, Lieut General Mason Macfarlane, gave all the forces on the Rock this information, naturally in the strictest confidence, and paid a notional visit to Malta to co-ordinate arrangements. While this story accounted for the aircraft and the accumulation of stores, it did not cover the landing craft and other evidence of amphibious operations; but these, it was rumoured, were intended for the attack on Dakar. To reinforce this story maps of the coast of west Africa and tropical kit were issued to appropriate units.

But the LCS was unwilling to indicate Dakar too firmly as the objective of the *Torch* convoys. If the Germans did decide that Dakar was the objective they might easily decide to move naval and air forces into that general area and alert French defences throughout north and west Africa.[20] Indeed the amount of diplomatic speculation during September and October that was being read at GC and CS and firmly indicated Dakar as the Allied objective was slightly alarming. Instead therefore the LCS decided, in concert with 'A' Force, to suggest that the convoys were aiming for Sicily and Italy. This would have the advantage of playing on the fears of the Italians and also of preserving the cover of the convoys even when they were inside the Mediterranean. To reinforce this story, diplomatic channels were brought into play. British diplomats in Cairo and Ankara were ordered to enquire into the probable reactions of the Italian communities in Egypt and in Turkey if the Allies were to land in Italy. In Barcelona and in the Vatican indiscreet questions were asked about the political and ecclesiastical situation in Sicily. The former British Consul in Palermo was ordered to stand ready to report to Gibraltar at short notice. And on 31 October all available channels to the Abwehr passed urgent warnings of an imminent Allied landing on the Sicilian and Italian coasts.[21]

As it happened, the convoys miraculously evaded enemy detection until they were inside the Mediterranean on the afternoon of 6 November.[22] 'Given a maximum speed of 14 knots' ran the OKW situation report, when news of the sightings came in, 'the enemy could still be at Cap Bon by about 1600 hours on the 8th. If it is intended to break through the Sicilian Channel, having regard to the strength and make-up of the formation, we must take into account the possibility of a landing being made on the Tripoli–Benghazi area, in Sicily or Sardinia, apart from supplying Malta'. The Maltese hypothesis was thus taken almost for granted. The Italian objective was also regarded as entirely credible – Rome radio already warned the populations of Sicily and Calabria to expect enemy landings – but the destination considered most likely was that about which the Germans were most sensitive, but which the LCS had considered too improbable even to be suggested: the rear of Rommel's army, whose front had already been broken at El Alamein a few days before.[23] As it was, the assault forces landed at Oran and Algiers in the early hours of 8 November and achieved complete surprise.

All these deceptive operations were carefully orchestrated by the LCS. Timing was everything, and a timetable was drawn up at the beginning of August indicating the nature and the purpose of stories to be put out through various channels.[24] During August emphasis was to be placed on the rumours and signals indicating the forthcoming relief of Malta, for which supplies would be accumulated at Gibraltar. Early in September the emphasis was to switch to activities in Scotland – the troop concentrations, the calls for Norwegian interpreters, Norwegian guide-books and Norwegian currency, the manufacture of snow-chains and anti-freeze liquid for vehicles. In mid-September the Assault Forces for *Torch* were to be warned to prepare for a long sea voyage, given lectures about tropical hygiene, vaccinated against tropical diseases and issued with mosquito nets and anti-malarial prophylactics. At the same time attention was to be focused on south-east England. Tank movements were to be reported in Kent and Sussex, hards for invasion craft were to be displayed in the Thames and the Medway and hards for embarkation built along the south coast, anti-aircraft guns were to be deployed in their defence, and the story put about that the Dieppe raid had been simply a rehearsal for an attack on a large scale – which as we have seen was exactly what von Rundstedt himself believed. About the end of September there was to be a crop of diplomatic indiscretions dealing with increasing British interest in Scandinavia, the improvement of the British government's relations with de Gaulle, and the intention to relieve the desperate position of Malta. Then in October matters were gradually to be brought to a head. In Scotland mountain clothing was to be issued to selected units. In Kent reports were circulated of civilians being evacuated from the south coast, of large numbers of hospital beds being prepared, and of army convoys practising driving on the right of the road. At the same time reports were put into circulation about the demand for Italian interpreters and guide-books, the printing of Italian money, the attachment of Roman Catholic chaplains to units on the strength of their knowledge of Italy, and the imminence of heavy air raids on Italian cities.

Meanwhile the LCS was getting enough 'feed-back' from Sigint to assess the success of their efforts as they went along. This showed that they were almost too successful: rumours proliferated in Europe, and were duly reported by the Abwehr, of imminent Allied attacks everywhere along the Atlantic coast from Narvik to Dakar, as well as on the northern shores of the Mediterranean. At Vichy, predictably, fears centred on Dakar and Casablanca, and though there were a few references to Algiers these were lost in the general 'noise'. The most accurate accounts came from the Vatican, from which Abwehr agents reported in mid-September that in October the Americans would land at Dakar and the British at Algiers; an alarmingly good guess, if indeed it was a guess, but fortunately one that was not followed up. When the convoys were sighted on 6 November, an intercepted message from the German Military Attaché in Madrid to Berlin reported Spanish opinion as believing that their objective was to relieve Malta and go on to land behind the lines of Rommel's Panzerarmee. Suggestions that their destination might be either Italy or French north Africa were explicitly discounted.

It must be admitted that by far the greater part of these misleading rumours consisted of self-inflicted wounds, compounded of the obsessions of local commanders and the inventions of Abwehr agents anxious to keep on the pay roll. Even if the LCS and the Twenty Committee had not existed the enemy might have blinded himself with his own fears. But then again he might not. What mattered was that von Rundstedt's forces in north-west France remained paralysed for four months by their belief in the imminence of Allied landings, and that two great armies were ferried across thousands of miles of ocean in conditions of total secrecy to land at the very last place the enemy had foreseen. Not even the most sceptical of critics can deny to Lieut Colonel Bevan and his colleagues the credit for their substantial part in this remarkable achievement. It was the first major success for strategic deception, and it was to foreshadow many more.

In the whole of this operation the double agents played a leading part. The LCS maintained intimate liaison with BıA and the Twenty Committee, weekly meetings being held to approve traffic and assess progress. *Tricycle* was in the United States for the whole of this period, but *Tate*, settled in a 'safe house' in north London with a radio set, was notionally able to see and report on troop movements in south-east England; *Gelatine* reported gossip from her friends in the armed forces; two Norwegian refugees, unkindly named *Mutt* and *Jeff*, observed activities in Scotland; and *Garbo* began to enjoy full scope for his inventive genius.

One of *Garbo*'s greatest skills in this direction lay in giving birth to notional sub-agents. Eventually he had nearly thirty of these, dispersed in strategic locations throughout the United Kingdom, all providing prolific information and many of them having to be paid. They included a garrulous officer in the RAF; an official at the Ministry of Information of extreme left-wing views; another who obtained for *Garbo* part-time work at the Ministry where he could see useful documents; a Venezuelan businessman living in Glasgow; a communist Greek sailor operating in eastern Scotland; a Gibraltese waiter working in Service canteens; an Anglophobe sergeant with the US Army Service of Supply; a whole clutch of Welsh nationalists in the Swansea area; and many more.* This Dickensian cast of characters was only just beginning to develop in 1942, but enough of them were in existence to keep *Garbo* informed about Canadian, Scottish and Norwegian troops undergoing mountain warfare training in the north of Scotland; while his Ministry of Information contacts advised him to discount the rumours of a forthcoming attack on Dakar as officially-inspired 'cover' for something else – an attack on France, perhaps, or on Norway. On 29 October *Garbo* urgently informed his controller in Madrid 'I do not wish to make further predictions about the future objective only I can assure you that an operation of great importance is imminent and I think I fulfil my duty by advising you of this danger'. At the same time he reported, correctly, the sailing of a convoy from the Clyde. Three days later, on 1 November, he passed on a hot tip that he had picked up at the Ministry of Information, that the Allies were about to invade French north Africa. Unfortunately for the Germans the letters carrying these two vital pieces of information were somehow delayed in the post, and reached Lisbon only on 7 November, after the convoys had already been spotted by German reconnaissance and a few hours before the landing took place. The evidence was incontrovertible, however, that *Garbo* had discovered the correct destination six days before the landings occurred, and had communicated it to his masters as quickly as possible. The Abwehr were almost pathetically grateful. 'Your last reports are all magnificent' they told him on 26 November, 'but we are sorry they arrived late'.

(ii) Alamein and Beyond: The Mediterranean, August 1942–January 1943

By the summer of 1942 'A' Force had, as we have seen, at last solved its organisational problems; Colonel Clarke had built up his network of agents throughout Africa and the Middle East for passing misinformation to the enemy; and at least one trusted double agent, *Cheese*, was sending traffic from Cairo which was relayed almost daily to Rommel's headquarters. All this now made it possible for 'A' Force to engage in a range of activities extending from tactical deception in the battles in the Western Desert to co-operation with the London Controlling Section over strategic deception for *Torch*; especially in successfully misleading the enemy as to the significance of the build-up at Gibraltar (Operation *Townsman*) and the destination of the *Torch* Convoys (Operation *Kennecott*).

---

* A full account of this network will be found at Appendix 2.

When the decision was taken in London to launch Operation *Torch*, at the end of July 1942, the Eighth Army was fighting at bay on Egyptian territory along what was to become known as the El Alamein Line. As soon as Allied grand strategy was settled the Prime Minister visited the Middle East *en route* for Moscow, and replaced the Commander-in-Chief, General Sir Claude Auchinleck, by General Sir Harold Alexander, Lieut General Sir Bernard Montgomery arriving a few days later to assume, on 13 August, command of the Eighth Army.[25] 'A' Force meanwhile had implemented a cover plan, *Grandiose*, to confuse enemy intelligence about the Prime Minister's movements. It was felt that to conceal the visit of so scintillating a collection of notables to Cairo would be impossible, so it was decided to disseminate information about his itinerary which would be by and large accurate, but which reported each of his movements two or three days late. The deception channels thus enhanced their credibility, but no effective action could be taken on the information they passed on.[26] As is so often the case there is no evidence to indicate whether this contributed to the safe travel and return of the Prime Minister, but the fact is that he came to no harm.

General Montgomery summoned Colonel Clarke within a few days of his arrival, on 19 August, and gave him his first instructions. He was to do everything possible to delay the Axis attack which 'Special Intelligence' had revealed to be imminent. 'A' Force was already trying, with little evident success, to divert reinforcements from the Panzerarmee by mounting a notional threat against Crete (Operation *Rayon*), by rumours, bogus radio traffic and displays. Dummy landing-craft were assembled in Cyprus harbours to simulate an amphibious threat, dummy gliders were displayed on Egyptian airfields to suggest airborne support, and the Greek forces in the Nile delta were put on stand-by. These activities were now intensified.[27] In addition, a dummy support line was constructed behind the main British positions, manned by two of the notional divisions created as part of Operation *Cascade*. Plentiful visual evidence was provided for curious observers in the way of minefields, trenches and tracks, and the rumour was put about that this was to be the main line of defence, the Alamein line being no more than an outpost. The inflated strength of the British forces was accepted by German intelligence, but this had no effect on Rommel's plans. He attacked as soon as he had enough fuel to do so, on 31 August. But he was at the limit of his resources, as the British, thanks to Sigint, knew very well. Montgomery refused to be drawn from his carefully-sited positions on Alam el Halfa ridge, the Desert Air Force maintained complete command of the air and the Panzerarmee was forced to withdraw finally on the defensive.

The value to the British of the Sigint now being passed to them from Bletchley Park – information, the more prolific since the Panzerarmee was wholly dependent on radio communication with Tripoli, Rome and Berlin – was now all the greater since as from the end of July the main leaks in Britain's own security had at last been located and plugged. One of these came from the traffic of the American Military Attaché in Cairo, Colonel Fellers; to whom military intelligence was made freely available at GHQ and who communicated it in detail to Washington in a cypher which had been broken by the Germans.[28] The second leak came from lax signal security within the Eighth Army and the Desert Air Force, whose traffic had been freely read by the German radio intercept service under its chief, Captain Alfred Seebohm, since the early months of 1941. These two sources had given Rommel such reliable insights into the intentions and movements of the British during the past year that it was hardly surprising that 'A' Force had failed to chalk up any major deception successes.[29] On 10 July, however, Seebohm's intercept unit was overrun in the course of an offensive by Australian units. Seebohm himself was killed. A large quantity of material was captured which revealed the extent of both leaks – and by implication the extent to which the Germans were reading British military traffic elsewhere, including the United Kingdom itself. The necessary changes in signal procedure were made, and Rommel was denied a vital source of intelligence. Colonel Fellers henceforth communicated in a new and unreadable cypher. A number of minor Axis agents in Cairo were 'blown' and arrested. From now on *Cheese* had the field very much to himself.

It was with these advantages therefore that 'A' Force was able to play its part in the preparations for the Battle of Alamein. The Eighth Army had to attack a short and heavily defended front whose flanks rested, in the south, on the Qattara depression, which both sides held to be impassable, and in the north on the sea. General Montgomery's plan, as described in the official history:[30]

'was for the infantry of 30 Corps with massive artillery support, to breach the enemy's defences in the north. The bulk of the armour (10th Corps) would pass through the breach and position itself "on ground of its own choosing astride the enemy supply-routes". This would force the enemy's armour to attack and the more powerful British armour would destroy it. The Axis infantry would then be rounded up.

The secondary attack in the south by 13 Corps would be more than a mere demonstration; it would be real enough to prevent the enemy from moving troops to reinforce the northern sector ...'.

To complement this, 'A' Force devised a closely related strategic deception (*Treatment*) and a tactical plan (*Bertram*). Briefly, whereas Eighth Army was actually to launch an attack on 23 October concentrated on the north part of the front, the enemy was to be led to expect one a fortnight later, on 6 November, concentrated on the south. That an attack was pending could not be concealed, but the enemy could be misled as to the place, the time, and the object. According to *Treatment*, the British did not intend to launch a major offensive in the Western Desert at all, so long as they felt their rear to be threatened by the German advance towards the Caucasus. The object of Montgomery's operations would be simply to improve his tactical positions and to test his forces under battle conditions. The major offensive intended by the British was still directed towards Crete.[31] It was hoped by 'A' Force that this would slow down the rate of reinforcement for Rommel's Panzerarmee in north Africa. At the same time everything was done to divert enemy attention from the last week in October as a likely moment for the attack. A notional conference was arranged in Tehran to take place on 26 October to be attended by the Commanders-in-Chief of the Middle East, Persia and Iraq and India Commands – Alexander, Tedder, Maitland Wilson and Wavell. Complete preparations were made for their travel and accommodation; the conference was cancelled only when the Alamein attack was well under way. For Eighth Army the last week in October was scheduled as a leave period: rooms were booked for senior officers in Cairo hotels and units were encouraged to organise a round of social and sporting engagements.[32] The success of this deception can be gauged from the fact that not only was Field Marshal Rommel still on sick leave when the attack opened, but that Hitler ordered him to return only at midnight on 24 October, more than 24 hours after the battle had begun. Not until then did he regard the situations as 'serious'.[33]

For the tactical deception plan, *Bertram*, most of the implementation was visual, backed up by bogus radio traffic. In the south, where the major attack was to be simulated, an entire dummy logistical network was created, with pipe-lines, pumping stations, reservoirs, supply dumps and camps; all carefully but not too carefully camouflaged, and constructed at a pace to suggest completion not before early November. In the north the situation was more difficult. So far as possible, all dumps were concealed, their contents being brought up at night and either buried or camouflaged as ordinary camps and vehicle parks. The concentration of X Corps armour could not be hidden, but it could be camouflaged. Before the guns and fighting vehicles arrived, their concentration areas were occupied by 'soft-skinned' vehicles, to suggest ordinary transport parks. By cover of night these were gradually replaced by guns and armour which were then concealed by day under the covers, 'Sunshields' and 'Cannibals', designed by Lieut Col Jones's section to make tanks and guns look from the air like harmless trucks. Altogether 722 Sunshields and 360 Cannibals were used, while the bogus concentration in the south absorbed 550 dummy tanks, 150 dummy guns and 2,000 dummy vehicles of all kinds.[34]

There can be no doubt of the success of this deception. On 7 October Rommel's deputy, General Stumme, told his Corp and divisional commanders that the main axis of the forthcoming offensive would be between Ruweisat and Himeimat which he confirmed on 20 October as 'the northern part of our southern sector'; together with an advance in the north along the coast road. Montgomery's plans were thus misperceived exactly as he intended. The Germans were too skilled to concentrate the bulk of their forces at any single area of the front, but the 21st Panzer and Ariete armoured divisions were left watching the southern sector while the 15th Panzer and Littorio divisions watched the north. Tactical surprise was complete. Not until the evening of 26 October, after three days of battle, did Rommel feel sufficiently confident that the Schwerpunkt of the British attack lay in the north to move up 21st Panzer Division to that area.[35] By then the British forces were established deep within the Axis lines.

Colonel Clarke could not witness the consummation of his plans, since in addition to his responsibilities in the Western Desert he was deeply involved in the various schemes masterminded by the London Controlling Section for providing cover for *Torch*. The implementation of *Treatment* had therefore been left very largely to Lieut Col H N Wild, and that of *Bertram* to Lieut Col C L Richardson, who continued to mount minor tactical deceptions as the Eighth Army advanced from Alamein to Tripoli. Meanwhile Clarke used his channels, particularly *Cheese*, to suggest that both Italy and Crete were threatened by imminent attack, the latter probably enjoying priority. ISOS decrypts between 2 and 9 November showed that the Abwehr was passing on these suggestions as coming from a 'highly reliable' source. Hitler himself reacted strongly to the threat to Crete. As early as 23 September he had ordered the garrison to be reinforced, and the order was reiterated on 21 October[36] (the OKW War Diary for this period reveals no hint of anxiety about the Western Desert); and on 9 November, the day after the *Torch* landings, General Warlimont reported him as still demanding the rapid reinforcement of Crete, insisting that 'the Crete transports are just as important as the Africa transports'.[37]

Throughout the following winter ISOS decrypts revealed increasing anxiety on the part of the Germans about Crete and Greece. Something of the tortuousness of German channels of information can be gathered from a message which the German Commander-in-Chief South East sent to Berlin on 29 November, transmitting a report from Prague that a Swiss official had heard from 'a well-informed source' that the British (sic) would land in Spain, Greece and Italy on 5 December; a message which OKW thought worth repeating to Rome the following day. On 16 December the Abwehr Stelle in Athens reported that preparations in Cyprus for an attack on Greece were far advanced, and eight days later the German Air Force was urged to carry out daily reconnaissances of the island. The results of these were presumably negative, for on 30 December a report from Bucharest said that investigations had discovered no extraordinary activity in Cyprus. But on 3 January 1943 the Naval High Command in Rome informed the Naval Command in Athens that they had heard from a 'reliable source' that the Allies would open major operations against Crete between 15 and 20 January. On 4 February Berlin forwarded to the Abwehr K O in Istanbul a report from an agent 'considered reliable' that the British had taken up shipping for the occupation of Rhodes. And on 25 February the Japanese Ambassador in Rome reported to Tokyo that considerable assault forces were accumulating in Malta, Alexandria and Cyprus, and that a large-scale attack would be launched on Crete once the Allies had cleared the north African shore. All these messages were read by G C and C S and duly forwarded both to the L C S and to 'A' Force.

Clearly the Abwehr was gathering information from many sources other than those controlled by 'A' Force, but it is significant how many of the 'reliable sources' referred to in the above messages were telling the tale devised by Colonel Clarke and Lieut Col Wild. *Cheese* still remained the most successful channel at their disposal, but others were becoming available. With the elimination of the unfortunate Colonel Fellers as a source of prolific and reliable information the Abwehr tried to infiltrate more agents into Cairo – agents whose progress could be tracked through I S O S decrypts and who on arrival were put under control. Such was *Quicksilver*, an officer in the Greek Air Force, who arrived in October 1942 with a useful radio set; *Rio*, a Greek sailor, and *Gala*, a lady tactfully described as a secretary, all of whom gave themselves up on arrival. There was a group of three low-grade agents collectively termed *The Pessimists*, and two other groups infiltrated into Cyprus, christened the *Lemons* and the *Savages*. All played their part in maintaining the illusion, after the main struggle had moved to the western and central Mediterranean, that the Middle East remained a powerful *place d'armes* garrisoned with numerous formations preparing attacks on Crete, the Aegean islands and the Balkan peninsula.[38] While 'A' Force could never, as could BịA, make the proud claim that they controlled the entire enemy espionage network in their theatre of war, they certainly disposed of enough channels for their misinformation to predominate in the cacophony of voices from whose conflicting evidence the luckless officers of Fremde Heere West had to build up a picture of Allied strategic intentions. It is not surprising that for the rest of the war the record of those officers was to be one of unredeemed failure.

REFERENCES

1. Michael Howard, *Grand Strategy*, Vol IV (1972), Prologue p xxiii.
2. C A B 121/105, S I C file A/Policy/Deception/1, Controlling Officer memo C/O/22 of 1 August 1942.
3. ibid, C O S(42) 228th Meeting, 5 August.
4. J M A Gwyer and J R M Butler, *Grand Strategy*, Vol III (1964), p 646.
5. Dennis Wheatley, *Stranger than Fiction* (1959).
6. C A B 121/105, C O S(44) 201 of 6 October.

7. ibid, COS(42) 253rd Meeting, 2 September.

8. Helmuth Greiner and Percy F Schramm, *Kriegstagebuch des Oberkommandos der Wehrmacht* (Frankfurt am Main 1965), Vol II, p 794.

9. CAB 154/101, Historical Record of Deception in the War against Germany and Italy (Sir Ronald Wingate's Narrative), Vol II, Appendix B, p 380; Imperial War Museum, AL 17/04, OBW Lagebeurteilung of 24 August 1942.

10. CAB 154/101, pp 380–381; Imperial War Museum, AL 17/04, Lagebeurteilung of 14 September 1942.

11. CAB 154/101, p 381; Imperial War Museum, AL 17/04, Lagebeurteilung of 12 October 1942.

12. CAB 154/101, p 382: Imperial War Museum, AL 17/04, Lagebeurteilung of 2 November 1942.

13. CAB 81/76. LCS(42) 1 of 8 August.

14. CAB 154/100, Historical Record of Deception in the War against Germany and Italy (Sir Ronald Wingate's Narrative), Vol I p 103.

15. Anthony Martiensen (ed), Führer Conference on Naval Affairs, 26 August 1942 (Imperial War Museum AL 721/1).

16. Greiner and Schramm, op cit, Vol II, p 841.

17. ibid, p 893.

18. CAB 154/2, 'A' Force War Diary, Vol II, p 106.

19. CAB 154/100, p 104.

20. CAB 81/76, LCS(42) 6 of 26 November.

21. ibid, LCS(42) 5 of 23 October; CAB 154/100, pp 106–109.

22. CAB 154/101, p 383, Fremde Heere West Lagebericht for 1800 hours, 6 November 1942.

23. CAB 154/100, p 100.

24. CAB 154/70.

25. ISO Playfair, *The Mediterranean and Middle East*, Vol III (1960), pp 369, 402.

26. CAB 154/100, p 115.

27. CAB 154/2, p 79.

28. David Kahn, *Hitler's Spies* (1978), p 193.

29. Lieut Gen Albert Praun, *German Radio Intelligence* (National Archives of the United States), p 55; Hans Otto Behrendt, *Rommel's Intelligence in the Desert Campaign* (1985), p 168 and passim.

30. Playfair, op cit, Vol IV (1966), p 19.

31. CAB 154/2, p 108 et seq.

32. ibid, p 110.

33. B H Liddell Hart (ed), *The Rommel Papers* (1953), p 304.

34. CAB 154/2, p 113.

35. Liddell Hart, op cit, p 308; Playfair, op cit, Vol IV, p 51.

36. Greiner and Schramm, op cit, Vol II, p 846.

37. ibid, p 927.

38. Accounts of the operations of these and other controlled agents in the Middle East are to be found in David Mure, *Practice to Deceive* (1977) and *Master of Deception* (1980).

CHAPTER 5

The Mediterranean Strategy

(i) *Cockade*: The United Kingdom 1943

THE VERY success of the cover and deception plans for Operation *Torch* created new problems which had to be promptly solved if a similar standard of excellence was to be maintained in future. Pressure of events had made it necessary for the London Controlling Section to assume virtually sole responsibility for Operation *Torch*, co-ordinating its operations with 'A' Force and co-operating with US Joint Security Control very much *ad hoc*. These largely improvised arrangements had been highly successful, but they would not do for the kind of sustained deception, interlocking over every operational theatre and lasting perhaps for years, that it was now Colonel Bevan's task to maintain.

In October 1942 the simultaneous presence in London of Colonel Dudley Clarke from 'A' Force and Colonel Peter Fleming from India, together with Lieut Cdr Cook and Major General Strong of US Security Control, made it possible not only to perfect the cover and deception plans for *Torch* but also to work out an Allied organisation for future deception activities. In December Colonel Bevan visited the United States, and these arrangements were given definitive form. From now on, the London Controlling Section (LCS) was to be responsible for Europe, north Africa, the Middle East and India. United States Joint Security Control would be responsible for the western hemisphere including Canada, the Pacific including Australia and New Zealand, and China except for one or two channels established from India by Colonel Fleming. Liaison would be maintained by an LCS representative with the British Joint Staffs Mission in Washington.[1] The British thus retained full responsibility for deception in the Mediterranean theatre after the north African landings. The manner in which 'A' Force was re-organised to handle these wider responsibilities will be described in due course.

At the end of December 1942, for want of any further directives from the Chiefs of Staff, the LCS put forward its own proposals for a deception policy to fill the remainder of the winter. Deception operations cannot be switched on and off to order. The flow of messages through double agents had to continue. The enemy had to be kept in a state of mind receptive to any further misleading information that, in due course, it might be necessary to pass to him. On December 27 therefore the LCS proposed to the Chiefs of Staff that it should occupy itself by maintaining the threat which had been built up against Norway; by exaggerating the strength of Allied forces in the United Kingdom and their state of readiness for an assault on the continent; and by keeping on foot the threat in the eastern Mediterranean against the Aegean and Greece. In addition, to deter U-boat attacks against convoys in the north Atlantic the LCS should indicate that there had been a major reinforcement of escort vessels on those routes; and to keep Japanese naval forces at a distance, it should indicate the presence of an aircraft-carrier task force in the Indian Ocean and of minefields in the Persian Gulf.[2]

The Chiefs of Staff had no time to consider this paper before they were summoned to the conference at Casablanca which charted the next stage of the war, but every one of the items suggested by the LCS was to find a place in its later activities.

The decisions reached at Casablanca in January 1943 imposed heavy tasks on the deception staffs, and within a few months they were to become yet heavier. It would not be too much to say that by the summer of 1943 responsibility for pinning down German forces in north-west Europe and preventing them from despatching reinforcements either to the eastern front or to the Mediterranean rested overwhelmingly with Colonel Bevan and his colleagues on the staff of COSSAC, the organisation set up after Casablanca to plan the Allied invasion of northern France.

This was not foreseen at the Casablanca conference. The Combined Chiefs of Staff there agreed that the principal operation in the European theatre during the ensuing summer should be the invasion and occupation of Sicily. But they agreed also (under heavy pressure from Mr Churchill) to launch from the United Kingdom 'such limited offensive operations as may be practicable with the amphibious forces available' and to assemble there 'the strongest possible force ... in constant readiness to re-enter the continent as soon as German resistance is weakened to the required extent'. They intended that preparations should be made for three types of amphibious operations against the French coast: raids with the primary object of provoking air battles and causing enemy losses; operations 'with the object of seizing and holding a bridgehead and, if the state of German morale and resources permit, of rigorously exploiting successes'; and a return to the continent, should the opportunity present itself, to take advantage of any internal disintegration of the Third Reich. The second of these operations was the most significant, and was to take the form of an operation against the Cotentin peninsula, with target date 1 August 1943.[3] These decisions were communicated by the Chiefs of Staff to Colonel Bevan on 29 January, with instructions 'to prepare, as a matter of urgency, for their approval, general strategic deception plans for those areas which are a British responsibility and to co-ordinate with the American authorities concerning the world-wide plans'.[4]

Within a week the LCS presented its proposals.[5] Little alteration, in fact, was needed in the outline drawn up a month earlier, but the separate items in that outline could now be put together in a coherent whole. The cover story proposed was that the Allies had decided to make their main assault in 1943 against France, with attacks both across the Channel and against the Mediterranean coast. A subsidiary thrust would be launched through the Balkans. The threat against Norway was also to be maintained.

The main problem of course, was that attacks across the Channel were, at this stage, actually intended. How could a threat be simulated that would not alert the enemy to the operations that were really being planned? In the solution which the LCS found to this problem lay the secret of the success which was to attend the assaults and the deception of 1944. The fact of an attack could not be concealed, but its scale and its timing could be. The first essential was to exaggerate the strength of the forces available to the Allies for the cross-Channel attack, and to use every means available – especially visual means – to emphasise their state of readiness. The second was to threaten as many targets as possible. In the absence of any precise plans for actual landings it would not be possible – as it became the following year – to give any specific deception target. The LCS could only suggest that 'actual sectors threatened should accord with real plans but extend beyond them'. Thirdly, deception must extend to timing; the enemy must be caught unprepared when the real assault came. So since the real attack was projected for August, preparations should be seen to come to a climax in July and the operation should then be notionally 'stood down' until September. The air battle called for by the Casablanca directive, suggested the LCS, could be brought about by the simulation of a large Combined Operations raid on the French coast.

As for the Mediterranean, the threat against the south of France could be mounted by the forces preparing for the invasion of Sicily, reinforced, to add verisimilitude, by the French forces in north Africa which were now being re-armed and re-equipped under the command of General Giraud. The threat from the Middle East against Crete, Greece and the Dodecanese should be sustained. As for Italy, the impression should be given that it had been written off as a strategic dead end, and would be simply neutralised by attack from the air.

The Chiefs of Staff had no difficulty in approving these plans when they considered them on 9 February.[6] Then there was a long pause. No serious measures of deception could be undertaken until operations themselves had been determined, and about those operations nobody, with the exception of the Prime Minister, was enthusiastic. The Chiefs of Staff had always maintained that the opening of a front in the western Mediterranean in 1942 ruled out any attack in north-west Europe before 1944. The US Chiefs of Staff took the Casablanca decisions as warrant for diverting so substantial a proportion of their resources to the Pacific that the build-up of American forces in the United Kingdom (*Bolero*) came to a virtual halt. It had been agreed at Casablanca that a staff under a British commander should be set up in Britain to plan for a cross-Channel attack pending the appointment of a Supreme Allied Commander, and Major General Sir Frederick Morgan had been designated as the Chief of Staff (COSSAC). But as a result of all these uncertainties, Morgan did not receive his final directive from the Combined Chiefs until April. By then it was clear that the lack of resources in the United Kingdom, and in particular the lack of landing-craft, rendered any cross-Channel operations out of the question.

This was reluctantly agreed by the Prime Minister on 13 April.[7] Five days later Mr Churchill redefined COSSAC's tasks as being to –

'(a) Prepare an amphibious feint to bring on an air battle "and make the strength of the Metropolitan Air Force count in general process of attrition".
(b) Camouflage and pretence on a most elaborate scale to help (a) above and to pin down the enemy in the west by keeping alive the expectation of invasion'.

COSSAC was also to carry on with preparations for attack in 1944 and to exploit any signs of German collapse. But, concluded the Prime Minister, 'If it gets about, as I fear it must, that any *Sledgehammer* is off for this year, it should be insinuated that this is part of our cover, and that the real preparations are going forward. Very large preparations should be made at the embarkation ports, and the assembly of the greatest amount of barges and invasion craft should be made, culminating in July and August'.[8]

The Prime Minister's minute did little more than endorse the conclusions reached at a meeting between Generals Ismay, Hollis and Morgan on 14 April, and the next day Hollis circulated an account of their discussions.[9] 'Now that major deception has assumed such importance for 1943', he wrote, 'consideration has been given to the precise procedure and machinery which shall be established to enable a deception policy to be pursued effectively'. Deception plans would be drawn up by COSSAC, but they would have to be implemented by senior Service commanders who might be reluctant to give them priority over operational or training requirements. In order to convince those commanders of the importance of deception he suggested that the situation should be explained to them at a Chiefs of Staff Conference, perhaps with the Prime Minister in the Chair: The Chiefs of Staff did not agree with this proposal. Instead they ordered, on 27 April, that COSSAC should simply request the commanders concerned to co-operate in the preparation of a workable deception plan. When this plan had received Chiefs of Staff approval, the Service ministries should be 'invited to take the necessary executive action'.[10] Channels of command would thus be preserved intact.

By now COSSAC had at last received his directive from the

Combined Chiefs of Staff. Issued on 23 April, three months after Casablanca, this instructed him to plan for a full-scale attack on the continent as early as possible in 1944 and to prepare 'an elaborate camouflage and deception scheme to pin down the enemy in the west and keep alive his expectations of attack in 1943'.[11] General Morgan had by this time assembled the bulk of his senior staff, and one of them, Lieut Col J V B Jervis Read, was given responsibility for deception operations as head of a section entitled 'Ops. B'. In close co-ordination with the London Controlling Section details of these were now drawn up. They received the composite name of Operation *Cockade*, and consisted of three distinct operations.[12] The first, *Starkey*, was a notional attack by fourteen British and Canadian divisions to establish a bridgehead on either side of Boulogne between 8 and 14 September. Three weeks later, when it was assumed that all German reserves in the west wou 'd have been drawn in, an American Corps would notionally sail from the United Kingdom to capture Brest, and a further US Corps would follow direct from the United States to exploit this attack (*Wadham*). Ultimately for various reasons this operation would be called off. In its place an attack against Norway would be mounted, five divisions strong, to seize Stavanger and exploit inland as far as Oslo (*Tindall*).

Before any of these operations could be set on foot, however, the Germans had to be persuaded that forces were available to carry them out; which, as we have seen, they were not. In June 1943 there were only some 22 British and 4½ Canadian divisions, few of them yet operational, in the United Kingdom, and the bulk of the US troops available were still administrative and logistical units. Since the beginning of the year however the LCS had been quietly building up a notional order of battle and feeding it to the Germans; first for the British and British-controlled forces (*Dundas*), and then for the American (*Larkhill*).

Dundas eventually became very ambitious. In its final form, in July,[13] it provided for an expeditionary force 15 divisions strong, with a 'Home Forces Field Army' of 24 divisions as a follow-up force; together with a 'Static Home Force', including the Home Guard, of two million men. It was feared however that the plan could not be implemented on this scale, since the signalling equipment was not available to simulate the radio traffic of so large a number of formations. Subsequently the LCS found that it had been unnecessarily cautious. German intercept services were indeed active, and up to the end of 1942 they had been highly accurate, but absence of radio traffic did not deter Fremde Heere West (FHW) from accepting the existence of a formation once it had been identified by other – usually 'special' – means. Nevertheless *Dundas* was reconstructed on more modest lines, making use primarily of existing forces but imposing on them non-existent or rudimentary operational formations. Three armies were still found for an expeditionary force and were given, somewhat prematurely, the title of 21st Army Group. For the Home Forces Field Army, two armies were found by dignifying

Scottish Command with the title of Fourth Army and Eastern Command with that of Sixth Army.[14] The strength of the Home Guard remained at the not inaccurate figure of two million (in fact it was nearer one and a half million), great stress being laid on the active and offensive nature of their training.

The implementation of *Larkhill*, the exaggeration of the size of the United States forces in the United Kingdom, was more complicated, since it had to be tied in to what the enemy could be expected to know about the raising and training of divisions in the United States and the sailing of Atlantic convoys. It was agreed with US Joint Security Control that this deception should rest on a solid basis of truth. Formations which were actually destined for the United Kingdom were reported as arriving several months before they had really landed, and the numbers carried in each convoy (whose safe arrival would be reported by double agents too late for anything to be done about it) would be considerably exaggerated. A number of bogus formations were quietly built up as having arrived in the United Kingdom at an earlier date. Thus in June, when there were only 107,000 United States troops in the United Kingdom, 300,000 were reported. By August, when 330,000 had arrived, 570,000 were reported.[15]

All these reports, which went mainly through double agents, were treated as credible by FHW. In October it reported that the Allies had available for a landing in north-west Europe a total of 43 divisions, comprising 26 infantry, 14 armoured, 3 airborne, of which 15 could be used as assault formations.[16] In a lecture delivered in Munich on 7 November, Jodl was still more generous in his estimates.[17] He reckoned the Allied forces in the United Kingdom at 40 infantry and 9 armoured divisions with 4 independent infantry and 11 armoured brigades, 2 airborne divisions and 7 parachute battalions.* As has been noted earlier, once a bogus formation had found its way on to the order of battle which German military intelligence maintained for the Allied armed forces, it was likely to remain there. By the summer of 1943 the hopes expressed two years earlier by MI5, that they might be able to use their double agents to fill the files of the enemy with a mass of appropriate misinformation, had been fully realised.

All the double agents at the disposal of B1A were enlisted to put across various aspects of *Cockade*. From the beginning of May a stream of messages passed through more than a dozen sources, reporting rumours, government announcements and regulations and observed troop movements. *Bronx* and *Gelatine*, two sociable and vivacious ladies with a wide range of friends, the one among the diplomatic service, the other among the armed forces, reported back high-level gossip.

---

* The correct figures, for the British Army in the United Kingdom for 30 September 1943, were 12 infantry divisions, 4 armoured and 1 airborne.

Two business men, *Mullet* and *Puppet*, passed on reports from the City and government circles. The two Norwegians whom the Abwehr had infiltrated by dinghy in April 1941, *Mutt* and *Jeff*, specialised on the threat to Norway. *Brutus*, a Polish Air Force officer who had reached England via the French Resistance in 1942 under Abwehr auspices and had promptly turned himself over to the British, reported back at length to the Abwehr about preparations which he observed in Scotland in March, along the south coast in April, and in the south-east in June. *Balloon*, the former Army officer, notionally cashiered, now a dealer in armaments, was prepared to sell any information that came his way, and a remarkable amount did.* But the double agents who proved of greatest value were those whose early history has already been recounted: *Tricycle* and *Garbo*.

We have seen how *Tricycle* had been extricated from his unproductive sojourn in the United States in the' autumn of 1942, and returned to London via Lisbon with his cover still intact. But although the Abwehr did not suspect him of being a double agent, they were beginning to believe that he was more trouble than he was worth. He had provided no intelligence for them from the United States, and during the winter of 1942–1943 he had not done much better in London. This of course was hardly his fault. He was now being pressed by his sceptical employers in Berlin to send specific information about military units and new weapons which his employers in London were naturally unwilling or unable to provide, and his instructions were becoming increasingly per-emptory and pressing. The mounting of *Cockade* now provided a flood of calculated misinformation which floated him back into the Abwehr's favour. From May onwards he reported the offensive concentrations of troops which were beginning to assemble in various parts of the United Kingdom: a group of British divisions in the south Midlands, an Anglo-Canadian force on the south coast, the Americans in the west country and the forces in Scotland preparing for the attack on Norway. Landing-craft, he reported, were being manufactured in inland centres and their parts sent to warehouses on the coast where they could be rapidly assembled. In July he paid a visit to Lisbon, taking with him a mass of information gathered on notional visits to south coast towns, where he reported not only intensive troop movements but such civilian measures as the preparation of great numbers of hospi-tal beds for expected casualties. On his return he continued to receive detailed questionnaires about orders of battle, troop and landing-craft concentration areas as well as such long-term measures as tank and aircraft production; which he was now able to provide in a detail which did much to restore him to favour in Berlin.

But the most effective channel of mis-information was *Garbo*, and

---

* *Balloon* it will be recalled had been notionally recruited by *Tricycle*.

the large network of notional sub-agents under his control.* From the beginning of June his control in Madrid was bombarding him with questionnaires about allied preparations for an invasion of north-west Europe, demanding precise and frequent information about troop movements. Obediently he forwarded reports of exercise and troop concentration in south Wales, and in August visited Scotland to report on the scope of military preparations and training going on there. While he was in the north, however, he received alarming reports from his notional agents about concentrations in southern England. Great camps were reported around Southampton. Assault barges were concentrating at Dover and Folkestone. 'There is talk', he reported, 'of large-scale aerial attack and bombardments over the Channel intended to destroy your defences and at the same time facilitate large concentrations of barges and small boats there'. So *Garbo* himself sped to the south coast, and duly discovered in the region of Brighton no less than seven divisions assembled as the spearhead of an attack, with aircraft and amphibious vessels to match. *Garbo* warned that the whole thing might be simply a practice for a major operation not intended to take place that year, and like a good agent he submitted the evidence that might support such an idea: the amount of publicity these movements were receiving, the lack of precautions taken by the authorities to prevent speculation, and the 'lack of that nervousness in official circles which existed when other military operations were about to be realised'. The easy collapse of the Italians in Sicily, he suggested, might have led to a last-minute change of plan. But he drowned out these messages with other, excited warnings of imminent action. 'I have received a long and formidable report from Agent 3 (the notional deputy-chief of his network)', he radioed on 5 September, 'which indicates from a very certain source that operation will take place at dawn of the 8th, it being possible that the embarkation may be delayed a day or so on account of the weather'. And on 8 September he reported that troops had been confined to barracks, were removing their identification insignias and receiving four-day ration packs, while large numbers of small landing-craft were concentrating in the region of Hythe, Folkestone, Deal and Walmer. Next day however he radioed 'Reports that troops have again disembarked ... It appears that the operation has been suspended. Troops surprised and disappointed'.

All these reports had a certain basis of truth. Beginning on 25 August, XII British Corps did assemble 2½ divisions between Dover and Newhaven, and I Canadian Corps a comparable force around Southampton and Portsmouth. Security regulations, not very strictly enforced, were applied in these areas from the beginning of August. Dummy gliders were displayed on airfields in East Anglia and dummy fighters

---

* See Appendix 2 below.

in Kent. Dummy camps and hards were displayed in appropriate locations, dummy landing-craft appeared in the appropriate ports in early August, and a radio network appropriate to an amphibious force was set up and activated. From June onwards, air operations over the Pas de Calais were intensified, being almost doubled between 25 August and 8 September. Unfortunately bad weather forced the cancellation of half the proposed attacks. Moreover, it had been hoped that a substantial proportion of Bomber Command might be diverted from targets inside Germany, but in the event this could not be arranged. Nevertheless, in the expectation that the 'invasion attempt' would force the German Air Force into the air, 9 medium squadrons and 72 fighter squadrons were earmarked for the projected battle, and 500 heavy bombers were made available for the climactic day, 9 September.

Just before that day the troops were marched to their allotted embarkation points, and the motor transport of the assault formations was actually embarked. Three flotillas of minesweepers had already cleared a passage across the Channel from Dungeness towards Le Touquet. Early in the morning of 9 September a convoy of 30 vessels assembled off Dungeness and sailed to within 10 miles of the French coast. Then, under cover of a smoke screen, it turned for home. At the same time a convoy of landing craft laden with MT sailed eastwards from the Solent towards Newhaven, and returned after three hours to their home ports.[18]

The Germans did not rise to the bait. The British preparations had been duly noted both by OKW and by the intelligence staff of General von Rundstedt, Commander-in-Chief West. The reports of *Garbo* in particular about the disposition of Allied troops and shipping, found their way, as 'unconfirmed but credible' into the situation reports of the Wehrmachtführungsstab.[19] But OKW was not deceived as to Allied strategic intentions. As it informed von Rundstedt on 11 July, 'the Schwerpunkt of the enemy attack on the mainland of Europe lies in the Mediterranean and in all probability will remain there'.[20] As a result, over von Rundstedt's protests, OKW ran down the forces under his command from 45 divisions in May to 35 at the end of August; building them up again however in October, after the Allies had shown their hand in the Mediterranean and the situation in Italy was under control. But as a result, von Rundstedt watched developments in the United Kingdom with all the greater anxiety. 'Stimulus for a major [enemy] operation is given by the removal of further major [German] formations', he pointed out on 20 July: 'sufficient shipping space and air forces are at the enemy's disposal'.[21] A month later, on 31 August, he was yet more anxious, reporting air-drops to resistance movements in France and movement of men and supplies in southern England on an unusual scale. 'The tension continues, with the constant possibility of far-reaching surprise operations with the object of securing at least a bridge-head on the Channel'.[22] And on 6 September, while admitting that 'it could not be laid down with certainty' that a major attack across the Channel was imminent, he reported that he had taken all necessary measures to meet it.[23]

The Germans did indeed have reservations about some of the information they received. Von Rundstedt's staff noted on 30 August that 'the general make-up and number of agents' reports gives rise to the suspicions that the material was deliberately allowed to slip into the agents' hands'.[24] A week later they wrote of the 'somewhat too obvious preparations for attacking the Channel front, which are at the same time conspicuously slow in reaching completion'. But this implied that the real attack might be coming somewhere else in North-west Europe – Normandy and Brest, the Netherlands, or even the Heligoland Bight; and these 'somewhat too obvious preparations for attacking the Channel front' might be intended 'to entice German reserves there and to pin them down'.[25]

This caution may do something to explain why, although the German defences in the Pas de Calais were fully alerted by 9 September, they did not report the movements of the convoys as anything remarkable. Indeed the only Allied activity on that day that von Rundstedt's headquarters regarded as worthy of note was that in the air, but even that was not sufficient to activate the German Air Force.[26] The landings simultaneously occurring in the Bay of Salerno naturally monopolised all attention. Learning as they immediately did from Sigint about the complete absence of German reaction, the British were, naturally and understandably, very disappointed. But this very failure to elicit any response in itself solved a problem which had always perplexed the British planners; how to prevent the Germans from claiming that the Allies had attempted a landing and been successfully repulsed. Arrangements had been made to give the Press a confidential briefing in advance, informing them that the whole affair was simply a rehearsal, and to issue an official statement to that effect afterwards,[27] but these precautions proved unnecessary. The Germans had independently come to the same conclusion, but they neither used it to obtain a propaganda advantage nor assumed that the danger was now over. On the contrary: von Rundstedt's staff, on 13 September, drew highly alarming conclusions from the whole experience:

'OB West considers the British measures of the previous week to have been a large scale preliminary rehearsal for a genuine attack to be launched against our west coast. By these measures the enemy has got to know the weaknesses of our artillery coastal defences and of our air force and air defences and will be able to turn that experience to his own advantage. Judged by the methods employed by the British it is very probable that they have gone through a performance of single phases of a large-scale attack on the Channel coast in the form of a rehearsal, involving naval units, embarkation of troops and other movements, whereas other phases, as for example minesweeping and the throwing of the air force into action against us were carried out in full operational employment. It is certainly possible that the enemy has thus launched a large-scale invasion manoeuvre timed to a nicety ... All the same, the transition to a real invasion attack is possible at any time ... Relief from this state of tension will only come when the autumn gales are due, and with an easing of the situation in the east'.[28]

Von Rundstedt in short did not believe that the Allies had shot their bolt with the completion of Operation *Starkey*, and the Allies did not intend him to believe it. Operation *Wadham*, the American invasion of Britanny, was projected for late September, while *Tindall*, the attack on Norway, was always projected as an alternative to *Starkey*, to be mounted only if that direct assault on the French coast was called off. *Wadham* involved an attack by five (largely notional) United States divisions from south-west England and seven sailing directly from the east coast of the United States. The British contribution consisted largely in providing their channels for the passing of misinformation. The Americans provided the dummy displays of aircraft, gliders and landing-craft, most of the air reconnaissance and striking forces against the Brest peninsula, and all the staff planning. Only a very small number of the American officers involved knew of the deceptive nature of the operation, and as the notional D-day of 22 September approached, a wave of despair swept over the unfortunate planners who realised only too well the impossible nature of the job they were being asked to do.[29] In the United States the situation was even worse. A report has survived from the Officer Commanding VII Corps, the formation notionally responsible for the trans-Atlantic invasion, describing the difficulty, in the time available, of training the necessary transportation personnel; of manufacturing, crating, and camouflaging the material that was needed; and in co-ordinating the communications systems of the Army, the Navy and the Air Force. His staff could not find out what supplies were needed, nor what would be available. No co-operation was possible with the Navy until two weeks before the notional D-day, and no co-ordination with the Air Force was possible at all. Not one of the units assigned to the operation was amphibiously trained; many of them were in no condition for operations of any kind, and one had not been known at its alleged address for two years. Neverthe-less, the report concluded stoically, 'regardless of actual deception results attained, the operation is considered not only worthwhile from the point of view of training, but exceptionally valuable'.[30]

Tindall, the notional attack on Norway, was less ambitious in its scope and demands. Clearly the first step in any real operation would have to be the capture of an air base, and the only one within range of air attack from the United Kingdom and sufficiently near the coast to be vulnerable to amphibious assault was Stavanger. Stavanger, in the words of the COSSAC appreciation, was 'in fact the key to Nor-way'. A sufficient threat to this area should therefore pin down the German forces in Norway.[31] So Stavanger was to be seized, by four divisions from the sea and an airborne division. It was not necessary to create many bogus formations for the operation: four divisions, including a mountain division, were already on hand in Scotland. There was no lack of naval vessels, including aircraft-carriers already in northern waters, and there were plenty of aircraft available in the United Kingdom that could be notionally earmarked for the operation. An order of battle for the forces involved was established, and complete operational orders were drawn up; first for reconnaissance, then for neutralisation from the air of enemy airfields and coastal batteries, then for the assault itself, for the consolidation of the bridgehead with anti-aircraft and maintenance units, for the landing of the main force, and finally for exploitation inland.

The deception was put over by shipping movements and troop deployment reported by double agents, by airfield displays, and by a certain amount of radio traffic.[32] It was initiated in July by a conference of senior officers at Largs, (General Sir Bernard Paget, GOC Home Forces, Lieut General Sir Kenneth Anderson, and Air Marshal Sir Trafford Leigh-Mallory, the notional land and air commanders of the operation) and came to a climax at the end of August; being stood down, before it became necessary actually to take up shipping or begin the preliminary bombardments, allegedly to release forces for *Starkey*; and reactivated after that abortive operation as a threat in being, until the onset of winter weather made it clearly impracticable.

It never took much to make Hitler believe in a threat to Norway, and at the beginning of September German Headquarters in Oslo reported that agents' reports led them to expect a landing – for which air and beach reconnaissances had already begun – between 6 and 12 September.[33] It was a view reinforced by FHW whose appreciation of 29 August estimated the threat, very accurately, at between 4 and 6 divisions, with 'all the evidence indicating an early beginning'.[34] In spite of the demands of the Mediterranean and the eastern front, the strength of the German garrison in Norway never fell below 12 divisions. The four British divisions training in Scotland during the autumn of 1943 certainly earned their keep.

As for von Rundstedt, his expectations of an invasion of north-west France were in no way lessened by the failure of Operation *Starkey* to materialise. True, Operation *Wadham* failed to make any impact whatever on von Rundstedt's intelligence staff, let alone on OKW; Britanny remained practically denuded of troops. But the fears of an imminent cross-Channel attack initiated by *Starkey* took a long time to die down. On 30 October OKW reported that 'forces and shipping in south England are sufficient for a major operation, and on account of Russian pressure we must reckon with this being brought forward'.[35] On 8 November von Rundstedt reported that, even making allowance for possible deception, a major landing must be expected soon;[36] and as late as 30 November he was insisting that such an attack must still be reckoned with, a view which the Wehrmachtführungsstab endorsed and which the Führer himself completely accepted, as we shall shortly see.[37] But by now deception was beginning to blend into reality. With the completion of the Allied landings in Italy, preparations for the real cross-Channel attack in 1944 were at last under way.

(ii) *BARCLAY*: The Mediterranean, 1943

We have seen how closely 'A' Force had worked with the London Controlling Section in implementing the deception plans which contributed so much to the success of Operation *Torch*. During the course of that collaboration, longer term plans had been made. In October 1942 Colonel Clarke had visited London and in consultation with Colonel Bevan had worked out a framework of co-operation which effectively geared the machinery for deception in the Mediterranean theatre into the organisation centrally controlled from London. 'A' Force continued to function, both at the strategic and at the tactical level, according to the principles which it had developed over the past two years. The London Controlling Section passed on to it only the broadest of directives. The autonomy of the deception staffs in the Mediterranean theatre (as in the Far Eastern theatre, as we shall see in due course) was made all the more necessary by the principle, constantly re-affirmed by Colonel Bevan, that the officers engaged in deception should not constitute a separate group set apart from their colleagues responsible for planning, intelligence, logistics and operations. They had to be fully integrated into the operational staffs of the appropriate commanders in the field. Obviously they had the right to deal directly with their colleagues in London over strictly technical or highly secret matters, but ultimately they were responsible to their own local operational commander. It was his plans that they had to implement, and his resources that had to be used in implementing their own.

This created an immediate problem in the Mediterranean theatre. Obviously, 'A' Force should now be responsible to the Supreme Allied Commander in that theatre, General Eisenhower, and work closely with his staff at Allied Force Headquarters in Algiers. But the whole apparatus for deception which Colonel Clarke had been building up since 1940 was based on Cairo. It was from there that all his links ran to the eastern Mediterranean, the Middle East, Turkey, Greece, the Balkans and Italy. The maintenance of these contacts and their nourishment with a prolific flow of plausible misinformation was all the more necessary once the centre of gravity of Allied operations had moved westward. The maintenance of a credible threat in the eastern Mediterranean remained a constant and highly successful factor in Allied deception plans well into 1944.

Main HQ of 'A' Force therefore remained in Cairo, controlling its 'sub-operators' and 'special correspondents' throughout the Middle East and north-east Africa. A so-called 'Rear HQ' at Nairobi similarly supervised activities in east and South Africa. At Algiers an 'Advanced HQ' was established with a substantial US element, working directly with General Eisenhower, and controlling out-stations in Malta and north Africa. This was headed jointly and amicably by Lieut Col M H Crichton from 'A' Force, Cairo, and Colonel E C Goldbranson of the US Army. Tactical deception in the field became the responsibility of a new 'Tactical HQ' under Lieut Col D I Strangeways; who worked directly under General Alexander when the latter set up his 18th Army Group, to which all British, French and US forces fighting in Tunisia were subordinated, at Constantine in Algeria in February 1943. This Tactical HQ was later to accompany General Alexander to Italy and implement tactical deception in that theatre for the remainder of the war.

After November 1942, however, 'A' Force did not have to rely entirely on its established channels through Cairo. Once Admiral Darlan had aligned himself with the Allies, the French intelligence service in north Africa, the redoubtable Deuxième Bureau, placed its resources at General Eisenhower's disposal, and these included an impressive array of double agents, most of them wireless agents, allegedly working for the Abwehr.[38] These included *Ram*, a French NCO notionally employed in the communications branch of French Army HQ in Algiers. There was *Whiskers*, a Spanish officer working to the Abwehr Stelle in Spanish Morocco, who (like *Garbo* in England) built up so impressive a network of notional agents that he was eventually appointed head of the Spanish Secret Service in Algeria. Most impressive of all was *Gilbert*, a regular French Army officer who was slipped into Tunis by the Abwehr in December 1942 as a stay-behind agent, who at once placed himself at the disposal of the 2me Bureau, and who as soon as Tunis fell began a series of communications to the Abwehr which acquired, in the eyes of German military intelligence, a level of authoritativeness second only to those of *Garbo*.[39] There were a dozen or so others, including a useful Italian stay-behind agent left at Tripoli, *Llama*, who communicated prolific false order-of-battle information until the Italian surrender.[40] These joined the east Mediterranean orchestra directed from Cairo, led by the ever-reliable *Cheese*. But it is important to remember that although 'A' Force controlled an impressive number of enemy agents in the Mediterranean, it did not, unlike BiA in Britain, control them all. A certain amount of true information inevitably filtered back to the Abwehr. Thus although it succeeded in so thoroughly confusing enemy intelligence that the German High Command was never able at any subsequent stage in the war to develop any clear picture of Allied intentions in the Mediterranean, 'A' Force was never quite able to convince the enemy of the unambiguous truth of the notional stories with which it so assiduously fed him.

The misinformation passed through double agents was controlled, on the analogy of the Twenty Committee in London, by a number of 'Thirty Committees' established throughout the Mediterranean and Middle East, increasing in number as Allied operations extended in scope. Eventually there were to be twenty-one of them, extending from Lisbon to Baghdad and from Nairobi to Florence. Each consisted of a triumvirate, with an 'A' Force officer as chairman, an MI6 officer as secretary, and a third member from MI5. 'A' Force was responsible for general policy and for the text of the messages to be passed. MI5, as in Britain, 'ran' the agents, providing case-officers and developing new channels. MI6 provided staff, communications, cyphers, and finance, and ran those agents who operated in territories not under the control of Allied forces. In Algiers, where the 2me Bureau played so significant a part in the provision and running of the agents, a French representative joined the triumvirate and the body became known as the Forty Committee. All these bodies worked as harmoniously together as could be expected. The misunderstandings and rivalries of the early war years had been very largely obviated, and co-operation came more easily when it was aimed at an immediate operation goal.[41]

The overall Mediterranean deception plan for 1943, *Barclay*, was worked out by 'A' Force within the general framework devised by the London Controlling Section and approved by the Combined Chiefs of Staff.* The main Allied operation approved at the Casablanca conference, it will be recalled, was the invasion of Sicily, Operation *Husky*. The object of *Barclay* therefore was to secure the greatest possible surprise for *Husky* by posing credible threats which would pin down enemy forces in the south of France and the Balkan peninsula; to weaken the garrison of Sicily and retard its reinforcement, especially by German troops; and to reduce to a minimum air and naval attacks on the shipping being assembled for the assault on Sicily from Britain, north Africa and Egypt.[42]

Much of the material for this deception already lay to hand. Ever since the Battle of El Alamein the previous October, 'A' Force had been sustaining a notional threat to Crete (Operation *Warehouse*) with the object of containing Axis forces in the Balkans and the Aegean and preventing both the despatch of reinforcements to Rommel's Panzerarmee in north Africa and the opening of a new front in Turkey and Persia.[43] In January 1943 this was reinforced by a further plan, *Withstand*. This projected the story that the Allies were so anxious about the danger of a German invasion of Turkey through Bulgaria that they were planning a pre-emptive attack via Crete against the

---

* 'A' Force received the LCS plan on 27 February. It produced *Barclay* on 21 March. This was approved by General Eisenhower on 10 April and issued by the LCS as LCS(43) 44 on 24 April.

Dodecanese. A further object of this plan was to emphasise to the Turks the degree of Allied concern about the possibility of a German attack on their country, and make them the more inclined to accept the help which was being offered and which Mr Churchill was to urge on them so insistently when he visited Adana after the Casablanca conference, a visit which was, fortuitously, of enormous value to 'A' Force.[44]

So, in addition to the visual displays of amphibious forces mounted in Cyprus and east Mediterranean ports, British armoured units, judiciously reinforced with dummies, manoeuvred in Syria, within easy range of the Turkish frontier, from January well into May. Thanks to the inflated British Order of Battle which had been fed into their appreciations, FHW assessed in February 1943 that there were 4½ divisions available in the Middle East for an attack in the Aegean and a further 4½ poised for an invasion of Turkey.

Through Sigint it was possible to monitor the success of the rumour factory based on Cairo. On 3 January the Italian Naval High Command in Rome informed their colleagues in Athens and Cagliari that according to 'a reliable source' an amphibious attack would be launched against Crete between 15 and 20 January. On 4 February the Abwehr in Berlin informed their station in Istanbul that according to an agent 'considered reliable' the British had taken up shipping for an attack on Rhodes. On 15 February the Japanese Ambassador in Rome reported back to Tokyo that considerable assault forces were gathering in Malta, in Alexandria and in Cyprus, which would be used to attack Crete as soon as the situation in Tunisia had been cleared up. 'A' Force indeed perhaps overdid it, for on 26 February OKW issued a general warning that the reports of Allied landing intentions showed that the Allies were practising deception on a large scale. Even so they concluded that major landing operations would take place in March, beginning with attacks on, in order of probability, Sicily, Crete, Sardinia and Corsica.

In the eastern Mediterranean therefore *Barclay* had only to prolong the anxieties already stirred up by *Warehouse* and *Withstand*. The 'story' was that the British, with their notional 'Twelfth Army' based on Egypt, intended to invade the Balkan peninsula through Greece during the early summer.[45] This, they hoped, would bring Turkey into the war on the Allied side. Substantial forces would then be moved up through Turkey to open a front against Bulgaria in Thrace and to join hands with Soviet forces advancing through south Russia. The first move would be an assault on the Peloponnese by two Army Corps, while a diversionary attack was launched against western Crete.

This according to the scenario, was to be the main Allied effort for 1943, the real 'Second Front'. But in order to pin down German forces in western Europe diversionary attacks would be launched, shortly after this front opened, against the coasts both of north and of south France. The attacks on the south of France would be carried out by an Army Group under General Alexander, consisting of the

British Eighth Army as the assault force and a French Army to exploit up the Rhone valley. Simultaneously an American force under General Patton would attack Corsica and Sardinia. Sicily and Italy would be by-passed and neutralised by heavy bombing for which purpose the Allied air forces in north Africa were being strongly reinforced. 'We had firmly rejected', it was stated in the plan, 'the prospect of a long and laborious advance through the mountainous terrain of Italy's mainland, where considerable resistance by the civil population might be expected and with the formidable barrier of the Alps at the far end'. Given that the attack on Sicily was actually planned for the first half of July, enemy expectations of an Allied offensive were to be prematurely aroused some five weeks earlier; around 25 May for the attack against Crete and the Peloponnese, and against Sardinia, Corsica and the Riviera around 5 June. On 20 May these notional attacks were to be postponed for a month – until 25 June and 3 July respectively. On 20 June, they would be postponed for another month. Total surprise, in time as well as place, would thus, it was hoped, be achieved.[46]

'A' Force was under no illusions about the difficulties that faced it. Sicily was so very much the obvious target. Until it was in Allied hands, passage through the Mediterranean could never be regarded as secure, and it must have seemed unlikely that the Allied forces being mustered in Tunis and Bizerta were intended for more distant and less fruitful destinations. Matters were made worse by the reluctance of Allied air force commanders to diversify their attacks on the scale 'A' Force regarded as necessary. They did not feel able, out of their limited resources, to provide the intensity of 'cover bombing' against the notional targets of Corsica, Sardinia and France for which 'A' Force had hoped. The concentrated air attack on and subsequent capture of Pantellaria on 11 June pointed all too clearly to Sicily as the next objective; especially since during the next four weeks targets in Sicily were bombed twenty times and Sardinia was only visited once.[47] But photographic reconnaissances were mounted against all the cover targets. Naval reconnaissances and beach raids were also carried out to alert their garrisons. To feed the rumour factory, actual amphibious training was carried out by Greek troops in Egypt and by French troops in Algeria. Appeals were circulated for Greek interpreters, and for fishermen familiar with the bays and inlets of southern France, Corsica and Sardinia. Greek drachmas in large quantities were purchased in Cairo and Alexandria. Pound notes surcharged 'France', 'Greece' and 'Bulgaria' were printed; and pamphlets about Greece, leaflets about Axis forces in the Balkans and maps of the cover objectives were distributed to units training for the invasion of Sicily.[48]

Radio deception ranked high among 'A' Force's priorities. Since the great bulk of traffic engendered at the Allied command posts at Tunis and Malta would have provided a clear indication of Allied concentrations, as much as possible of this was carried by land-line, while an elaborate programme of bogus traffic was initiated at 'Twelfth Army' HQ at Cairo.[49]

Great care was also taken to sow confusion about the date of the operations. General Eisenhower ordered that no leave should be granted after 20 June, and then on 15 June countermanded the order. Permission was given by the occupation authorities for an Arab medical conference to be held in Beirut, but on condition that all the delegates should have left by 16 June; which meant that the meeting had to be postponed, to general annoyance and acrimony. It was ordered that frontiers of all Middle Eastern countries under Allied control should be closed from 16 June – an order cancelled on the 15th. Arrangements were made for General Montgomery to stay at Government House, Jerusalem, between 3 and 6 July – that order also being cancelled at the last moment.[50] Finally, to conceal the actual D-day for *Husky* from all the polyglot workers at the ports where the invasion fleets were assembling, an X-day was nominated as their target for completion; 24 July; – the notional D-day for the third stage of *Barclay*,[51] but two weeks after D-day for the real operation *Husky*.

In addition to all this, a really massive display of dummies was erected in the Western Desert for the benefit of German aerial reconnaissance: Operation *Waterfall*.[52] Colonel Jones created, out of his 74th Armoured Brigade, a bogus '8th Armoured Division'. This was conveniently deployed within reach of such Cyrenaican harbours as Bomba and Tobruk, which were gradually filled with dummy landing craft. Eleven fighter squadrons were displayed on nearby air-fields. When the first notional postponement of the operation took place, these forces were 'dispersed'; to be reconcentrated early in June, this time with the addition of glider squadrons. At the beginning of the third week in June these forces were brought to maximum readiness and began to move down to the harbours for embarkation. Then on 17 June came the second postponement. All this of course was reflected in radio traffic, the simulation of which was brought to a new pitch of sophistication after the arrival, in May 1943, of Major S B D Hood at 'A' Force in Cairo and a team of American experts in Algiers.[53] To encourage local agents, a real anti-aircraft Brigade was deployed in the area of Tobruk and real workshops and fuel installations were established. A total of 700 men were engaged full time on the project. Unfortunately so complete was Allied command of the air that few German reconnaissance flights were able to approach the area, and of those that did the majority were shot down on their return journey. Still, as Colonel Clarke reflected afterwards, 'we could never have afforded to do without it even had the air reconnaissance shrunk to negligible proportions ... The risk always remained that a single visit from a single photographic reconnaissance unit aircraft on a single day would have vitiated the whole of the rest of the deception effort'.[54]

It was against this background that there took place what was certainly the best known and perhaps the most successful single deception operation of the entire war: Operation *Mincemeat*. The idea of planting on the enemy the body of a courier carrying misleading plans of future operations is probably as old as war itself. Credit for its application to Operation *Husky*, or rather Operation *Barclay*, must be shared between Lieut Cdr Ewen Montagu, RNVR, who was later to write a deservedly popular account of the operation,* and Flight Lieut Charles Cholmondley, RAF.

On 29 September 1942 a British aircraft had crashed into the sea off the coast of Spain. A body had been washed ashore carrying documents which the Spanish authorities had made available to the Abwehr. In this case the documents had been unimportant. But what if they *had* been important? Flight Lieut Cholmondley of BiA suggested how a deception might be worked. 'A body is obtained from one of the London hospitals (normal peacetime price £10). It is then dressed in uniform of suitable rank. The lungs are filled with water and the documents disposed in an inside pocket. The body is then dropped by a Coastal Command aircraft at a suitable position where the set of the currents will probably carry the body ashore in enemy territory ... While this courier cannot be guaranteed to get through, if he does succeed, information in the form of the documents can be of a far more secret nature than it would be possible to introduce through any other normal BiA channel'. Lieut Cdr Montagu made enquiries of the London coroner, Mr Bentley Purchase, and of the pathologist, Sir Bernard Spilsbury, both of whom were encouraging; and on 4 February Cholmondley and Montagu reported to the Twenty Committee that a suitable cadaver had been procured and would be fit for use any time within the next three months.

Operation *Mincemeat* was then set on foot. Cholmondley's original idea was modified to the extent of transferring the documents from an inside pocket of the courier's uniform, where they might not be found, to a briefcase chained to the body. It was also decided to despatch the courier by submarine rather than aircraft, and to float him ashore at Huelva, on the Spanish coast, where the currents were favourable and the Germans were known to have a highly competent Vice-Consul. The body was provided with the notional identity of a Major Martin of the Royal Marines, serving on the staff of the Chief of Combined Operations, Vice Admiral Lord Louis Mountbatten. In his briefcase he carried three documents: a letter of introduction from Admiral Mountbatten to Admiral Sir Andrew Cunningham; the proofs of a manual on Combined Operations sponsored by Mountbatten, to which General Eisenhower had agreed to contribute a foreword, the size of which explained the use of a briefcase; and a personal letter, dated

---

* *The Man Who Never Was* (London 1953).

23 April from the Vice Chief of the Imperial General Staff, Lieut General Sir Archibald Nye, to General Alexander.

This letter was carefully drafted, finally approved by the Chiefs of Staff Committee on 13 April, and will be found printed in full at Appendix 4. As will be seen, it indicated that the Allies were planning an assault-landing in Greece, code-named *Husky*, at Kalamata and Cape Araxos; that the idea of using Sicily as the cover target for this operation had been rejected in favour of using it as cover for another operation *Brimstone*,* for which the target was unspecified. A jocular reference in Mountbatten's letter to sardines, however, would enable the Germans to make a very good guess. It suggested that General Maitland Wilson, the notional commander of the landing in Greece, should use the Dodecanèse as his cover target.

The submarine, HMS *Seraph*, sailed with its grisly cargo on 19 April, but 'Major Martin' carried in his pocket the stubs of two West End theatre tickets for the evening of 22 April, to indicate that he could not have left London before 23 April at earliest and so must have been travelling by air. The body was floated ashore at Huelva, together with a capsized rubber dinghy, in the early hours of 30 April, and was discovered by local fishermen at 09.30. All then happened as planned. The corpse was impounded by the Spanish authorities, pending investigations. The British Naval Attaché in Madrid, who had been briefed by Lieut Cdr Montagu, made urgent representations for its return. Spanish officials friendly to the Germans opened the briefcase, extracted the documents, photocopied and replaced them, and gave the photocopies to the Abwehr. The body and its possessions were then turned over to the British authorities, who gave it Christian burial after its long unhappy pilgrimage. The contents of the documents were sent to Berlin. Their subsequent progress was traced through Sigint and followed in London with interest.

The *Mincemeat* documents did not tell the Germans anything they did not already expect. The danger of a landing in Crete and Greece had been stressed by the German commanders responsible for that area throughout the winter, and it was known through Sigint that at Axis staff conversations in Rome in February, Greece had been regarded as the most vulnerable target once the Allies had captured Tunisia. The full scale of the threat which 'A' Force tried to project was not taken very seriously, for the simple reason that the experts at FHW had a very shrewd idea of the total shipping available to the Allies in the Mediterranean. However much the Allies might successfully inflate the number of their notional divisions or display dummy landing craft, shipping was the factor that effectively limited the scale of their

---

* *Brimstone* was in fact the code-name for a plan for an invasion of Sardinia, which had been considered and rejected at the Casablanca conference.

major offensives across the water, and the Germans knew it. They expected therefore a British attack with limited objectives in the eastern Mediterranean: possibly against Crete, possibly the Dodecanese, possibly the Peloponnese. An attack on either Sicily or Sardinia however seemed equally probable, and the Italian authorities understandably thought it very much more likely. The possibility of an attack on the south of France was not, at this stage, taken very seriously.

The Abwehr forwarded the *Mincemeat* documents to OKW with a careful explanation of the grounds for their credibility.[55] The corpse had died from swallowing sea water, and had been immersed between 5 and 8 days. It corresponded to the photograph on the identity card carried on the body. The absence of other flotsam from the crash did not surprise local fishermen, in view of the strong currents in that area. The Abwehr authorities also emphasised the importance of their find. The British were not now likely to change their plans; and the revelation of their intentions in the east Mediterranean was all the more valuable in that 'on account of the geographical situation, there has up to this time been considerably less news about preparations than from the area of Algiers'.[56]

For once FHW were convinced by its Abwehr colleagues. On first receiving the report, on 9 May, FHW pass it on to the Wehrmachtführungsstab with the cautious comment that 'the genuineness of the report is held as possible'.[57] Two days later, on receiving further details from Madrid, FHW described it as 'absolutely convincing'.[58] And on 12 May a general message was sent by the Wehrmachtführungsstab to all commands ordering that 'all German commands and HQs concerned with the preparation of defences in the Mediterranean, in close and rapid co-operation, will make available all forces and all means in the greatest possible quantity to strengthen the defence of these particularly threatened areas in the briefest foreseeable time. Measures for Sardinia and the Peloponnese to have priority over everything else'.[59] The Commander-in-Chief, South East was particularly warned that 'an absolutely reliable source' had indicated that Allied landings in the eastern Mediterranean would be in the areas of Kalamata and Cape Araxos.

Throughout the next two months, OKW continued to give priority to the defence of Greece. The Abwehr in particular made careful preparations for the evacuation of its stations, the planting of 'stay-behind' agents and the sabotage of installations; all revealed by Sigint.[60] Hitler himself regarded Greece as the most threatened area, and on 25 July sent Rommel in person to take command there; only to recall him the following day on learning of the fall of Mussolini. Even after the capture of Pantellaria, which the British deception authorities had feared would give the game away altogether, the Japanese Chargé d'Affaires in Rome reported that Sardinia was still regarded as the favourite target and that there was intense alarm about the possibility of a landing in the south of France.

As a postscript to this account of *Mincemeat*, it is worth printing a report from FHW of 25 July, after the landing in Sicily had already occurred:

'According to captured document, the operation in Sicily is given the code-name *Husky*. As our earlier documents [the "Kurierfund"] showed, this code word stood for the British operation planned against S. Greece (Kalamata and Araxos) in which forces at this moment engaged in Sicily were to take part. The carrying over of this code-name to the whole Sicilian operation underlines the alteration, also reported by other sources, of the earlier enemy plan for a simultaneous two-pronged operation in the Western and Eastern Mediterranean in favour of the operation in Sicily. We may imagine the reasons for this to be the fear that the Americans, if committed alone, might suffer a defeat, and the expectation that the operation against Sicily, as the nearer objective, would be more certain to succeed. The conclusion to be drawn from these statements seems to be that, at present at any rate, the attack planned against the Peloponnese has been given up, and at the same time the invasion of Sicily is regarded as the main operation, to be followed by an attack on Southern Italy presumably with the further aim of proceeding to the Dalmatian Coast and an attack on the Balkans'.[61]

It must not be assumed that these deception operations were solely responsible for the fact that, when Allied forces landed in Sicily on 10 July, only two German divisions were available to assist the Italian Sixth Army in repelling them; both of them formations (15th Panzer Division and the Hermann Göring Division) which had been seriously mauled in Africa. By this time Hitler's lack of confidence in his Italian ally had developed into positive and well-founded suspicions about her willingness to remain in the war at all, and he was naturally reluctant to commit German forces in an area where they might be lost in the chaos of a general surrender. This reluctance reinforced his congenital obsession with the Balkans, and led him to discount the very accurate Italian intelligence appreciations which made their High Command complain bitterly about the refusal of the Germans to reinforce them at the point of maximum danger. The *Mincemeat* documents in short, together with all the misinformation provided by 'A' Force, gave Hitler additional reasons for a disposition of forces to which he was already strongly inclined.[62] Thus although the consensus of OKW appreciations after the capture of Pantellaria indicated Sicily as the most probable of Allied objectives, no measures were taken to reinforce the island, while the build-up of German formations in the Balkans under the command of the Commander-in-Chief South East steadily increased. Between 9 March and 10 July the number of German divisions in the Balkans as a whole rose from 8 to 18, those in Greece from 1 to 8. Only two divisions during the same period were sent to Corsica and Sardinia.

The assault on Sicily did not lead OKW to reassess Allied strategic intentions. On the evening of 9 July, a few hours before the landings occurred, Keitel had sent a 'Most Immediate' message to German commands in the Mediterranean. This credited the Allies with 40 divisions capable of taking the offensive – about double the real figure – and stated that 'the enemy forces concentrated in French north Africa after the capture of Tunisia are so powerful that they exceed what would be required for a large-scale landing in Sicily and Sardinia. Therefore a part of these forces has been transferred to the eastern Mediterranean to be prepared for the landings in Greece. The enemy's first aim is probably the capture of Sicily and Sardinia, and subsequently of Corsica ... A subsequent large-scale landing on the mainland of Italy is less probable than a landing on the mainland of Greece ... A landing in central and northern Italy or the French Mediterranean coast is for the time being more than improbable'.[63] Orders were therefore issued for a daily reconnaissance by the German Air Force of the whole Greek coast from Corfu to Cape Matapan.

The Allied deception authorities had better cause to congratulate themselves, not least over their careful Order of Battle deception (*Cascade*) which laid the foundation for all their subsequent successes, than had the strategists whose true intentions it was their task to conceal. The Germans would certainly have found it very difficult to believe the reality of the Allied situation after the invasion of Sicily. No plans existed for subsequent operations because British and American leaders had been unable to agree at the Casablanca conference what to do next. At the Washington conference in May (*Trident*) Mr Churchill had vainly urged that an invasion of the Italian mainland should follow the attack on Sicily as a matter of course. His American allies, led by General Marshall, had resisted any such extension of the activities in the Mediterranean theatre on which they had embarked so unwillingly the year before. Within a few days of the invasion of Sicily, however, the total collapse of the Italian Army persuaded even General Marshall that the extension of the campaign to the mainland as far north as Naples was both feasible and desirable. The fall of Mussolini on 24 July confirmed this impression, and on 26 July General Eisenhower was ordered by the Combined Chiefs of Staff to mount an attack on Naples with such forces as were available to him. As a result Eisenhower prepared two operations; one by the British Eighth Army across the Straits of Messina to free the straits for Allied naval use and pin down Axis forces in Calabria (*Baytown*); and one by the U S Fifth Army, with British X Corps under command, to land in the Bay of Salerno as a preliminary to seizing the port of Naples (*Avalanche*). *Baytown* was launched on 3 September, *Avalanche* six days later.[64]

General Eisenhower's staff had been planning for *Avalanche* as early as 20 July, and the associated deception plan (*Boardman*) was approved two days later.[65] The task allotted to 'A' Force was to weaken enemy forces in Italy, especially in the south and the centre, and to contain the greatest possible number of enemy forces in the southern Balkans, especially on the Greek mainland. It was now a fundamental principle of deception that no hurriedly-mounted operation stood much chance of success: the seeds had to be planted early in the mind of the enemy, and given time to germinate. But since nothing had yet occurred to weaken the belief of the German High Command, and particularly of Hitler himself, that the long-term objective of the Allies was the Balkans, and since this belief was well-known to British intelligence, the task of 'A' Force was less difficult than it might appear. *Barclay* led into *Boardman* without any perceptible shift of gear.

The 'story' for *Boardman* went through many vicissitudes, but eventually postulated an attack by X British Corps (actually destined for Salerno) against Sardinia, and one by a combined Franco-American force against Corsica. The possibility of an attack on the south of France, or on the coast of north-west Italy between Genoa and Leghorn, was also kept in play. An attack by the notional British Twelfth Army on the Peloponnese was kept to the fore, but a notional British III Corps was alleged, in addition, to be mounting a subsidiary attack against Apulia, in the 'heel' of Italy, to open the straits of Otranto. This last attack merged into a tactical deception plan, *Boothby*, which called for the simulation by all the usual methods – air and naval feints, radio deception and intelligence plants – of an attack from Sicily against Crotone, on the 'ball' of the Italian foot by XIII Corps; the formation which in fact was to attack across the Straits of Messina in Operation *Baytown*.[66]

One interesting aspect of *Boardman* was the part played in it by a new double agent in Tangier, codenamed *Guinea*. This was an Englishman who built up in that small and gossiping community the reputation of being a drunken and unreliable spendthrift.[67] At the beginning of September, having enticed the local Abwehr agents into his confidence, he offered to sell them the plans of the forthcoming Allied operations for 150,000 marks. These operations, he told them, would begin on 12 September with simultaneous landings by British forces on the Italian coast at Genoa and Leghorn. The original intention to land on the Peloponnese, he added for good measure, had just been abandoned by the Combined Chiefs of Staff at the Quebec conference. All this was reported to Berlin on 8 September by the Abwehr station in Tangier with the comment that the possibility that this might be a deception was considered 'very slight'.[68]

But the Mediterranean was buzzing with contradictory rumours. Six days earlier the Abwehr station in Madrid had reported that French circles believed, on the authority of General Giraud himself, that no further major attack on Europe was planned, and that the Allied concentration of troops and shipping, both in the United Kingdom and north Africa, were only standing by to take advantage of any massive withdrawal of German forces in the theatre to check a collapse on the eastern front. Plans for both landings at Naples and at Genoa had been abandoned. Landings were planned in Sardinia by US forces, but this was not expected to involve heavy fighting. General Eisenhower's major concern would be the landings in Apulia, at Brindisi and Otranto, by British forces, in preparation for an assault on Albania.[69]

At the same time Abwehr agents in the south of France were forwarding reports of imminent landings at numerous points on that coast.[70] There seemed virtually no point on the Mediterranean shores of Fortress Europe that was *not* threatened by an attack, and in the general noise produced by these rumours, the signal which 'A' Force was trying to project was very largely drowned. Alerts were ordered in the south of France and in the Balkans, and during the latter half of August the German commanders in Leghorn and Genoa were ordered to exercise special vigilance. In any case during the whole of this period German strategic dispositions in Italy were being planned with a view rather to dealing with Italian treachery than to repelling an Allied assault. OKW intelligence appreciation throughout August considered an attack on southern Italy as a virtual certainty, with Corsica, Sardinia and the Balkans as very secondary objectives. Kesselring himself placed Corsica and Sardinia first, Salerno and the Gulf of Gaeta second;[71] but General von Vietinghoff's 10th Army had three mobile divisions available to meet a threat in either of the latter areas. So although the Salerno landings secured immediate tactical surprise, German formations were well placed to take immediate counter-action, and did so very effectively, in spite of the simultaneous need to disarm and put out of action the forces of their erstwhile Italian allies. The Germans do not seem to have taken the threat to Crotone particularly seriously, but that to Apulia kept the bulk of one first-class German formation, 1st Parachute Division, pinned down until the crisis at Salerno was over. But this was due to the actual landing which the British 1st Airborne Division improvised at Taranto on 9 September, turning that aspect of the deception plan into something like reality.

The invasion of Italy, mounted as it was in circumstances of the utmost haste and confusion against an opportunity target, did not in fact provide 'A' Force with the same kind of opportunities as did the long-matured plans for the invasion of Sicily, and it is doubtful whether its activities in this instance added much to the difficulties of the German intelligence authorities. But if they failed to mislead the Germans seriously about immediate Allied intentions, they succeeded in maintaining their illusions about Allied long-term objectives. Even the landings in Italy did not shake the conviction of the German High Command that General Eisenhower's eyes were still fixed on the Balkan peninsula, whose defences had been gravely weakened by the Italian collapse. Hitler's decision to continue to defend the Italian peninsula, rather than to pull back to the Appenine barrier to the north as he had originally intended, was very largely determined by this belief. German situation reports in September and early October showed far more concern about the threat to the Balkans than about the situation in Italy, and the operations which General Maitland Wilson's forces improvised against Cos, Leros and Samos reinforced these fears; which accounted for the speed and effectiveness of the German counter-measures in the Aegean.[72]

The failure of the British attacks on the Dodecanese provided sad but incontrovertible evidence of the success of 'A' Force in concentrating German attention on the Balkans and the Aegean throughout 1943. The unexpected decision to open a real front on that area made the task of 'A' Force even more difficult. For the strategic deception plan (*Fairlands*) introduced to succeed *Boardman* after the Salerno landings naturally continued to deploy the threat posed by the notional British Twelfth Army in Egypt against south-east Europe. The overall object continued to be to pin down the largest possible number of German forces in the Mediterranean theatre, and now that the Allies had shown their hand with the invasion of Italy this had become considerably more difficult. The presence of large, as yet uncommitted 'notional forces' in the Middle East and north Africa was now more than ever the basis of any successful deception plan, and the quiet build-up of these according to the *Cascade* plan remained the most important of all 'A' Force activities. The bulk of these notional formations were in the Middle East, and from there, according to *Fairlands*, assaults were planned against Rhodes for 26 October and against Crete for 8 November. Since the object was to persuade the Germans to evacuate those islands rather than to pin them down it was indicated that these attacks would be in overwhelming force, an Army Corps being allotted to Rhodes and eight divisions to Crete.[73]

OKW intelligence summaries throughout the first half of October faithfully reported all this military activity, lamenting their inability through lack of air reconnaissance to assess, by surveying the available landing craft, on what scale the assault was likely to be. Rhodes and Crete were forecast by OKW on 7 October as the most probable objectives.[74] But meanwhile the deception had become a reality. General Maitland Wilson had actually been ordered to mount an attack on Rhodes. 'A' Force therefore attempted instead to indicate that the objectives of 'Twelfth Army' lay further west, in Cephalonia and Xante on the west coast of the Greek peninsula. But the German recapture of Cos on 3 October and Leros on 12 November, neither operation provoking any counter-measures, gave an embarrassingly clear indication of the true weakness of British forces in the eastern Mediterranean, and German air reconnaissances in December could find little sign of the military activity reported there through Abwehr channels.[75] Towards the end of 1943 therefore German anxieties about Greece and the Aegean began to abate, and 'A' Force thought it best not to try artificially to prolong them.[76] Increasingly the German Commander-in-Chief South East was to be concerned rather with the problems of Partisan activities within his command than with the prospects of invasion.

The other half of *Fairlands* involved a continuation of the threat to the Italian coast in the region of Leghorn, with the object of preventing German forces in that region from being transferred as reinforcements for their colleagues fighting south of Rome.[77] This plan merged, in mid-November, into another, *Oakfield*, which was to become the basis for all Allied strategic deception plans in the Italian theatre for the next nine months. *Oakfield* postulated simultaneous landings on the Ligurian coast in the west and on the Adriatic coast at Rimini in the east by forces which would then join hands to seal off the Germans in the Italian peninsula.[78] The fact that Sardinia and Corsica had passed into Allied hands at the end of September made the former operation, in particular, appear especially plausible. As early as 22 October an OKW intelligence summary had suggested that 'active sea-traffic between Corsica and Sardinia, an increased use of the harbours there and the ferrying of French troops to Corsica point to vigorous preparations for later operations in the Ligurian sea approaches'.[79] A further summary on 15 November emphasised that 'the fact that Seventh American Army and First English Army have some 15–20 large formations available in the western Mediterranean [an overestimate of 100 per cent] must be kept firmly in mind ... the likelihood of large-scale planning of landing operations on the Italian coast in the Tyrrhenian sea deserves our close attention'.[80] And on 25 November, just after the British Eighth Army had opened its offensive across the Sangro south-east of Rome, the summary warned that although the enemy was seeking a decisive breakthrough, 'we must also reckon with the possibility of further simultaneous outflanking landings, especially on the Tyrrhenian coast, for which purpose sufficient forces and coastal space are at his disposal'.[81]

Kesselring himself was not particularly impressed by these warnings, and it cannot be said that they did anything to ease the painful progress of the Allied armies through the mountains of southern Italy towards Rome. The Germans had in fact correctly appreciated that the Allies would take no new initiatives in the Mediterranean until the New Year; and then, as the intelligence summary of 25 November put it, 'the heaviest fighting ... must be expected in the Atlantic area (i.e. western Europe) for which the continued withdrawal of landing craft from the Mediterranean ... is a new proof'.[82] In this appreciation they were doing no more than echoing Hitler's own words in the Directive No 51 which he had issued on 3 November. It was in the west, he insisted, that 'the enemy must and will attack, and where, unless all indications are misleading, the decisive invasion battle will be fought'. So it was there that German forces had now to be concentrated and preparations made.

REFERENCES

1. CAB 154/100, Historical Record of Deception in the War against Germany and Italy (Sir Ronald Wingate's Narrative), Vol I, p 128.
2. CAB 121/105, SIC file A/Policy/Deception/1, LCS (42) (P) 1 of 27 December.
3. Michael Howard, *Grand Strategy*, Vol IV (1972), pp 621, 625.
4. CAB 121/105, COS (43) 7th Meeting (O), 29 January.
5. CAB 81/83, LCS (43) (P)2 (Final) of 2 February; CAB 121/105, COS (43) 44 (O) of 7 February.
6. CAB 121/105, COS (43) 16th Meeting (O), 9 February.
7. Howard, op cit, Vol IV, p 362.
8. CAB 121/105, COS (43) 202 (O) of 18 April (PM's Minute to COS, No D 81/3).
9. ibid, Hollis to COSSAC, 15 April 1943.
10. CAB 79/60, COS (43) 86th Meeting (O), 27 April.
11. L F Ellis, *Victory in the West*, Vol I (1962), p 10.
12. CAB 121/373, SIC file D/France/6/2, COS (43) 288 (O) of 5 June.
13. CAB 81/77, LCS (43) 9 of 13 July.
14. CAB 154/100, p 140.
15. ibid, p 139.
16. Helmuth Greiner and Percy F Schramm, *Kriegstagebuch des Oberkommandos der Wehrmacht* (Frankfurt am Main 1965) Vol III, p 1219.
17. Imperial War Museum, MI 14/120, General Jodl's Lecture on the Strategic Position at the Beginning of the Fifth Year of the War, November 1943; also in CAB 120/562, PM Registered File 412/24/11
18. CAB 154/14; CAB 154/100, p 151.
19. Greiner and Schramm, op cit, Vol III, pp 1432, 1442.
20. ibid, Vol II, p 770.
21. ibid, p 809.
22. ibid. Vol III, p 1037.
23. ibid, p 1057.
24. ibid, p 1037; CAB 154/101, Historical Record of Deception in the War against Germany and Italy (Sir Ronald Wingate's Narrative), Vol II, p 399.
25. Greiner and Schramm, op cit, Vol III, p 1061.
26. ibid, pp 1083, 1087.
27. CAB 154/100, p 150; CAB 154/14.
28. CAB 154/101, pp 402–404.
29. CAB 154/100, p 154.
30. Letter OC VII Corps to CG Ops Divn Washington, 24 September 1943 (Records of Army Staff, Record Group 319, National Archives of the United States, Folder ff 69).
31. CAB 154/65, COSSAC (43) 16 of 30 June.
32. CAB 154/15.
33. Greiner and Schramm, op cit, Vol III, p 1075.
34. ibid, p 1024.
35. ibid, p 1232.
36. ibid, p 1264.
37. ibid, p 1321.
38. CAB 154/3, 'A' Force War Diary, Vol III, p 117.
39. ibid, pp 126–136.
40. CAB 154/100, p 165.
41. CAB 154/3, p 59.
42. ibid, p 69.
43. CAB 154/2 'A' Force War Diary, Vol II, p 124.
44. CAB 154/3, p 26.

45. ibid, p 70.
46. ibid, p 176.
47. ibid, pp 66, 79.
48. ibid, p 83.
49. ibid, p 82.
50. ibid, p 84.
51. ibid, p 97.
52. ibid, p 86.
53. CAB 154/100, p 72.
54. CAB 154/3, p 88.
55. CAB 154/101, p 385, for particulars of the relevant documents, including the reports from the Abwehr station in Madrid, from Abwehr HQ to Fremde Heere West (FHW) and from FHW to the Wehrmachtführungsstab between 11 and 20 May 1943.
56. ibid, telegram from Captain Ulrich, 15 May 1943.
57. ibid.
58. ibid.
59. Greiner and Schramm, op cit, Vol III, p 1429.
60. CAB 154/96, LCS Summaries 5, *The Abwehr and Allied Intentions*, May 1943.
61. Imperial War Museum, MI 14/522/2, Kurze Feind Beurteilung West (KFW) 982 of 25 July 1943.
62. Howard, op cit, Vol IV, pp 461–466.
63. CAB 154/100, p 186.
64. Howard, op cit, Vol IV pp 502–511.
65. CAB 154/100, p 189.
66. CAB 154/3, p 155.
67. CAB 154/100, p 36.
68. G O Kent (ed), *A catalog of Files and Microfilms of the German Foreign Ministry Archives 1920-1945* (Hoover Institute) Vol 3 (1966), p 41, Messages from Rener and Reith in Tangier for Fremde Heere West, 25 August 1943 (79/888), 2 September (79,898) and 8 September (79/901).
69. Imperial War Museum, AL 1828/2, Ab. Nr 52 429/43g I H West I, 2 September 1943.
70. ibid, Transcript of telephone reports, 15 September 1943.
71. C J C Molony and others, *The Mediterranean and Middle East*, Vol V (1973), p 266.
72. Imperial War Museum, MI 14/522/3, Lagebeurteilung West (LBW) 1035 of 27 September, LBW 1045 of 7 October 1943.
73. CAB 154/3, p 164.
74. Imperial War Museum, MI 14/522/3, LBW 1045 of 7 October 1943.
75. ibid, KFW 1111 of 12 December 1943.
76. CAB 154/3, p 166.
77. ibid, p 164.
78. ibid, p 168.
79. Imperial War Museum, MI 14/522/3, KFW 1060 of 22 October 1943.
80. ibid, KFW 1084 of 15 November 1943.
81. ibid, KFW 1094 of 25 November 1943.
82. ibid.

PART III

The Climax; Bodyguard 1944–1945

CHAPTER 6

Fortitude: The United Kingdom, December 1943–June 1944

ON BALANCE it cannot be said that during the course of 1943 the deception staffs had achieved all their goals. They had not succeeded in deceiving the German High Command (OKW) as to Allied strategic intentions: the Germans had early appreciated that the Allied Schwerpunkt for 1943 lay in the Mediterranean, and had in consequence reduced the garrison of north-west France far below the point that General von Rundstedt considered compatible with safety. At the tactical level they had failed to persuade the Germans that the feint attack across the Channel on September 9th was a serious venture, and as a result the great air battle, to bring about which had been the object of the whole exercise, never took place. Operation *Wadham*, the feint attack against Brittany, never seriously registered with the Germans at all; and Operation *Tindall*, the threat against Norway, although held by OKW to be entirely credible, did not persuade them to despatch any more troops to that theatre. As a result OKW did not find it necessary substantially to reduce the strength of the forces fighting on their eastern front,* and they were able to find enough formations to hold the Allies, once they landed in Italy, with comparative ease. The German success in doing so was to confront the Combined Chiefs of Staff with the necessity of maintaining their forces in the Mediterranean at so high a level as seriously to disorganise plans for the cross-Channel attack in 1944, and thus created some of the bitterest inter-Allied disputes of the entire war.

Nevertheless the deception staffs could look back over 1943 with some satisfaction. It was thanks largely to their efforts that so large a measure of surprise had been achieved for the landings in Sicily; and that, even after that operation was completed and Allied forces had established themselves on the mainland of Italy, the Germans remained expectant of further landings in the south of France and, even more strongly, in the Balkan peninsula. Deception activities in the United Kingdom had convinced at least von Rundstedt of the probability, even the imminence, of an invasion attempt, and he remained so convinced until late November. Although the Germans were increasingly alert to the possibility of deception, and respectful of British skill in this respect,

---

* At the end of 1943 German forces on the eastern front totalled some 182 divisions as compared with 56 in northern and western Europe, 16 in Italy and 15 in the Balkans and Aegean theatres.(1)

they were not yet remotely aware of the scale of the measures being used against them, nor of the priority attached to such measures by the Chiefs of Staff. Not a single double agent had been 'blown', and the reports of *Garbo*, in particular, were treated with great respect not only by the Abwehr but by the more cautious military assessors at Fremde Heere West (FHW). Finally, and most important of all, the German High Command had accepted almost without hesitation the inflated figures of available Allied strength both in the United Kingdom and in the Mediterranean, which had been carefully fed to them over the past two years. These were to provide the solid foundation on which the successes of 1944 were to be based.

The London Controlling Section (LCS) and its colleagues on COSSAC's staff, Ops B, were able to gauge the success of their measures with a fair degree of accuracy, thanks to the information they derived from Sigint. Nonetheless when, in the late summer of 1943, they began to contemplate the problem of providing cover for what was to become Operation *Overlord*, the Allied invasion of north-west France in 1944, they were seized with a despondency bordering almost on despair.[2] For the past six months they had been trying to persuade the Germans that they faced a major invasion threat from the United Kingdom, when in fact they did not. Now they had to persuade them that they did not face such a threat, whereas in fact they did. The first task, 'to induce the Germans to make faulty strategic dispositions during the period November–February 1944 by weakening their overall strength in the Low Countries'[3] was the object of Operation *Jael*, to which COSSAC and the LCS began to direct their thoughts in July 1943.

The first suggestion of the deception staffs was that the Allies should let it be known that the strength of German defences, and the logistical problems revealed in preparing the operation, had led them not only to cancel the invasion they had projected for 1943, but to abandon any intention of reviving it in 1944. They intended now to fall back on the idea of compelling Germany to surrender by bombing alone, while continuing operations only in Italy and the Balkans. The main thrust of Allied operations for 1944 would thus continue to be in the Mediterranean, where a new front would be opened in the Balkans. The growing Allied build-up in the United Kingdom could not be concealed, but the American forces there should be depicted as consisting mainly of air ground-crews. It would be emphasised that few Allied troops were trained in amphibious operations, and the presence of such large concentrations in Britain should be explained by the Allied intention to seize limited bridge-heads on the continent, once German resistance had been sufficiently weakened, for further operations the following year.[4]

Plan *Jael* was completed in October, and the Chiefs of Staff suspended judgement on it until after the conference which had been convoked at Tehran in November to chart the next phase of Allied operations as a whole. But it did not impress even its authors and the Americans found it totally unconvincing.[5] In any case it was recognised that by the spring of 1944 the size of troop concentrations in the United Kingdom would have entirely destroyed its credibility. Deception on the level of grand strategy would then no longer be possible. It would be evident that the Allies were planning a cross-Channel operation on the largest possible scale. All that could then be done was to deceive the enemy as to the time, the place, and the strength of the assault.

As has been frequently emphasised in these pages, deception becomes possible only when operational intentions have been determined. The early deception plans for *Overlord* were thus linked to the early ideas for the actual landings. By the late summer of 1943 these had been clarified by COSSAC and his staff. The need to provide continuous air cover over the landing operations, to land over beaches of manageable gradient, and to capture a major port at an early stage of the proceedings (although provision for maintenance over beaches with the aid of artificial harbours would delay the need for this), all indicated the coast of Normandy in the region of Caen as the most appropriate target. From there it was hoped that the Allies would be able to establish their left flank securely on the Seine estuary, to seal off the Cotentin peninsula and capture the port of Cherbourg, and so establish a firm base from which to advance.[6] But since at this stage it was assumed that shortage of landing-craft would confine the scale of the initial landings to three assault and two follow-up divisions, it became an intrinsic part of the plan to reduce German capacity for resistance by tying down German forces elsewhere to the greatest possible extent. Fortunately the decision to land in Normandy left available, for deception purposes, the highly plausible area of the Pas de Calais which, with its short sea passage, its excellent air cover and the possibility of rapid exploitation under naval flanking protection along the coast to Antwerp and the Scheldt, might seem a far more obvious point of attack.

In the same way as these preliminary ideas for the actual operations were to develop into the final plan for *Overlord*, so did this deception proposal ultimately ripen into *Fortitude*; perhaps the most complex and successful deception operation in the entire history of war. But at this stage, like the operational concept itself, it remained tentative and indefinite. It was not even given a code name, being referred to simply as 'Appendix Y'. The directive ran as follows:[7]

'a. To induce the German Command to believe that the main assault and follow up will be in or east of the Pas de Calais area, thereby encouraging the enemy to maintain or increase the strength of his air and ground forces and his fortifications there at the expense of other areas, particularly of the Caen area.

b. To keep the enemy in doubt as to the date and time of the actual assault.

c. During and after the main assault, to contain the largest possible German land and air forces in or east of the Pas de Calais for at least fourteen days'.

In order to do this it would be necessary to persuade the enemy of the existence of forces available for amphibious operations over and above those actually committed to the landings in Normandy. Eventually this was to be successfully done on an enormous scale, but the initial proposals were very modest. They were to indicate, by dummies, radio traffic and 'special means' that the Allies had enough assault-craft available for one more assault division and one more follow-up division than was actually the case. These notional divisions were to be deployed with their craft around the Thames Estuary, and there would also be a notional concentration of fighter aircraft on air-fields in south-east England. All this would be assisted by a camouflage policy ranging from total concealment in Southern and Western Commands to 'discreet display' in the east and south-east; and since it was assumed, at this stage, that the enemy might have uncontrolled agents operating on the ground and be carrying out active reconnaissance from the air, real troop movements would be needed to make all this convincing. By all these means it was hoped that 'for about 14 days after D-day, a force of not less than one assault, one follow-up and four build-up divisions will be represented in Eastern and South-Eastern Commands'.

This plan was drafted and redrafted some seven times between its first appearance on 4 September and 20 November, when it was first presented to the Chiefs of Staff.[8] Once again the Americans were deeply sceptical. General Jacob J Devers, commanding American Forces in the European Theatre of Operations (ETOUSA) had allocated two officers, Colonel William A Harris and Major Ralph A Ingersoll, to collaborate with COSSAC over deception questions, and the report which they produced on 'Appendix Y' was so unfavourable that General Devers made clear his unwillingness to go along with it. With the Tehran conference imminent the Chiefs of Staff were in any case reluctant to do more than approve the plan on a tentative and provisional basis. Once firm decisions about future strategy had been taken at that conference, however, serious planning could at last begin.

At the conferences which the Combined Chiefs of Staff held in Cairo and Tehran in November and December 1943 the final decision was taken to launch Operation *Overlord* in May 1944. At the same time it was agreed that an attack, Operation *Anvil*, should be launched against the south of France. General Eisenhower was nominated as Supreme Allied Commander of the Allied Expeditionary Force; an appointment which in itself put an end to any lingering hopes of deception on a grand strategic scale. The Allies could hardly have made more explicit their intention of initiating a major operation in north-west Europe; the only hope was that sceptical Germans might take it as a rather clumsy cover for an operation being launched somewhere else. But the importance of deception as an intrinsic part of all major operations was now fully understood at the highest level. It was in the course of discussing this question with Stalin at Tehran that Churchill made his famous observation 'In wartime, truth is so precious that she should always be attended by a bodyguard of lies'.[9] On 6 December, as part of the final conclusions of the Cairo conference, Colonel Bevan was instructed to prepare the necessary deception plans. So Operation *Bodyguard* was born, and appropriately named.

Work began at once, and the London Controlling Section presented the outline plans for *Bodyguard* to the Chiefs of Staff Committee on Christmas Eve 1943.[10] The object laid down at Cairo had been 'to induce the enemy to make faulty strategic dispositions in relation to operations by the United Nations against Germany agreed at *Eureka* (Tehran)'. The problem was seen as two-fold: strategic, to 'persuade the enemy to dispose his forces in areas where they can cause least interference with Operations *Overlord* and *Anvil* and with operations on the Russian front'; and tactical, 'to deceive the enemy as to the strength, timing and objective of *Overlord* and *Anvil*'. The first implied that as many German forces as possible should be held down in the Mediterranean. As for the Russian front, it would help if the Germans could be led to believe that no major assault would be launched before late June, and that no Allied offensive would be undertaken in the west until it had begun.

With these principles as a basis, the notional Allied intentions for 1944 to be projected to the enemy were defined as follows—

'a. It was still hoped that the Combined Bomber Offensive would be sufficient to bring about the complete collapse of the enemy, so its reinforcement by United States' bombers would receive the first priority* in Allied logistic arrangements.

b. The Western Allies were preparing simply to exploit any German weakening or withdrawal from Western Europe.

c. In the spring, an attack would be launched on Northern Norway, in co-operation with the Soviet Union, to open a direct route to Sweden. Thereafter, once Swedish acquiescence had been assured, an assault might be launched against Denmark from the United Kingdom, air cover being provided from air-fields in Southern Sweden.

d. No cross-Channel operation would be possible until late summer anyway, largely because of delays in the construction of landing-craft in the United States.† As a result the main Allied effort would be directed against the Balkans: from Italy against the Dalmatian Coast, from the Middle East against Greece, and from the Soviet Union against Bulgaria and Rumania. Pressure would be brought on the Turks to provide facilities for these assaults, and strong diplomatic pressure would be brought against Germany's Balkan satellites to persuade them to follow the Italian example and leave the war.

e. Amphibious operations would be launched against the coasts both of North

---

* The Chiefs of Staff modified this phrase to: 'such a high priority that ground force build-up in the United Kingdom has been delayed'.

† Misinformation about this was the responsibility of US Joint Security Control.[11]

East and of North West Italy, the former leading to an eastward thrust through Istria in support of the general Balkan offensive.

f. No major Soviet offensive would be launched before the end of June.

g. A minimum of 50 divisions, including twelve assault-trained divisions, would be required for OVERLORD, and these would not be ready until the late summer even if the bottleneck of landing-craft could be overcome. The available British divisions were under strength, the American division under-trained. Only cadre formations were returning from the Mediterranean, to train new units. Allied strength in the Mediterranean theatre remained high and was constantly being reinforced from the Far East, from the United States and by the creation of new French formations'.

The object of *Bodyguard*, in short, was to persuade the enemy that although a cross-Channel operation on a very large scale was indeed being prepared, it was not the only stroke the Allies were planning, and in any case it would not be launched until late in the summer. It was an ingenious attempt to solve an impossible problem, and it cannot be said that it succeeded.

Without ignoring other threats, particularly in Scandinavia and the eastern Mediterranean, the attention of the German High Command, from Hitler downward, was now focussed on north-west France. This had been the case ever since Hitler had issued his Führer Directive No 51 on 3 November, which had designated that as the theatre to receive top priority in 1944:[12]

'The hard and costly struggle against Bolshevism during the last two and a half years, which has involved the bulk of our military strength in the East, has demanded extreme exertions. The greatness of the danger and the general situation demanded it. But the situation has since changed. The danger in the East remains, but a greater danger now appears in the West: an Anglo-Saxon landing! In the East, the vast extent of the territory makes it possible for us to lose ground, even on a large scale, without a fatal blow being dealt to the nervous system of Germany.

It is very different in the West! Should the enemy succeed in breaching our defences on a wide front here, the immediate consequences would be unpredictable. Everything indicates that the enemy will launch an offensive against the Western Front of Europe, at the latest in the spring, perhaps even earlier.

I can therefore no longer take responsibility for further weakening the West, in favour of other theatres of war. I have therefore decided to reinforce its defences, *particularly those places from which the long-range bombardment of England will begin. For it is here that the enemy must and will attack, and it is here – unless all indications are misleading – that the decisive battle against the landing forces will be fought.* (emphasis added).

Holding and diversionary attacks are to be expected on other fronts. A large scale attack on Denmark is also not out of the question. From a naval point of view such an attack would be more difficult to deliver, nor could it be as effectively supported by air; but if successful, its political and operational repercussions would be very great.

At the beginning of the battle, the whole offensive strength of the enemy is bound to be thrown against our forces holding the coastline ... The ground weapons which will shortly reach Denmark and the occupied areas in the West ... will be concentrated at strong points in the most threatened areas on the coast. Because of this, we must face the fact that the defence of less threatened sectors cannot be improved in the near future'.

The contents of the directive indicate that the *strategic* deception intended by *Bodyguard* was a lost cause even before the plan was made. Hitler's eyes were now firmly fixed on the Channel coast, and from that theatre they were not now to waver. But the directive also indicated not only that within the threatened theatre it was of the utmost importance to mislead the Germans as to where along the Channel coast the real threat lay, but also that on this level the cause was in a good way to being won. The italicised sentence indicates that Hitler's eyes were fixed in particular on that region where the emplacement of V-weapons had begun – a matter to which we shall return later in this work. This consisted primarily of the stretch of the Pas de Calais which had been the prime target of *Cockade* in summer 1943; a deception which had provided precisely those 'indications' to which the Führer Directive referred. And that was the area which, as we have seen, the deception staffs had already picked as the notional target in their ill-fated 'Appendix Y'.

Although the London Controlling Section had devised Operation *Bodyguard* and remained responsible to the Chiefs of Staff Committee for its implementation, deception measures specifically associated with military operations were the responsibility of the operational commanders and their staffs. When General Eisenhower returned to England in January 1944 as Supreme Allied Commander, he formed a new Supreme Headquarters, Allied Expeditionary Force (SHAEF) to take over the duties of COSSAC, deception plans included. As we have seen, deception on COSSAC's staff had been handled by a section called Ops (B) consisting initially of a single officer, Lieut Col JVB Jervis Reed. This was now expanded. A full colonel, HN Wild, arrived from the Mediterranean theatre to take charge, bringing long experience of service with 'A' Force. Lieut Col Jervis Reed served as his deputy. Within the expanded staff a British officer, Major Roger Fleetwood Hesketh, was responsible for 'intelligence' (which in fact meant 'Special Means'), and worked closely with BıA. Colonel Wild himself became a full member of the Twenty Committee. A formal structure of responsibility was created in January. SHAEF Ops B was made responsible for the supervision of deception operations within General Eisenhower's command, for giving MI5, MI6 and the LCS instructions with regard to the deception material to be passed over their respective channels, and for securing the necessary co-ordination between all these channels. The London Controlling Section was to be 'the authority through which co-ordination of implementation ... of European cover plans should be conducted'. This clumsy bureaucratic formula might have created all sorts of problems, but it did not; largely because responsibility still lay with a handful of men who knew each other intimately and cut corners. Colonel Wild and Major Hesketh at SHAEF, Colonel Bevan and Sir Ronald Wingate of the London Controlling Section, Lieut Col Robertson, Major Masterman and Major Marriott and the case officers from MI5, were in constant touch with one another, and conducted business with a speed and informality which has, unfortunately, left practically no traces for the historian.[13]

Detailed planning of deception operations was, as before, the responsibility of the operational commanders. Under General Eisenhower's immediate command came 21st Army Group under General Sir Bernard Montgomery, who created on his staff a deception section modelled largely on 'A' Force which had served him so well in the Mediterranean. Commanded by Lieut Col David Strangeways, it was named the G(R) Staff, and the specialist troops under its command were called 'R' Force. The organisation adopted by the Americans falls outside the scope of this work; suffice to say that in March General Bradley established a 'Special Plans' section to prepare and implement deception and cover plans for all United States forces in the United Kingdom, and a month later Colonel William A Harris was appointed to take charge of it. The initial scepticism which Colonel Harris had shown the previous autumn towards British deception activities had now completely disappeared, and the co-operation of his section with the British was to be whole-hearted and complete.

These were the men who devised and advised the responsible commanders on the implementation of the cover plan for *Overlord* in the United Kingdom: Operation *Fortitude*.

This plan consisted of two sections: a threat against Scandinavia (*Fortitude North*), and a threat against the Pas de Calais (*Fortitude South*). The 'story', as approved by General Eisenhower on 23 February,[14] fell into two consecutive parts. Before D-day for the real landings, (*Neptune*), which had now been set at 1 June,* the Germans should be led to believe that the cross-Channel attack was being prepared only to take advantage of any German weakening and would take place only after other diversionary attacks had been launched, particularly against northern Europe. Operations would initially be mounted, first against south Norway, with an initial assault at Stavanger as threatened in Operation *Tindall* the previous year, aiming ultimately at Oslo, and then against north Norway, to join hands with the Russians and obtain access to the Swedish ore fields. Only after these had succeeded would an assault be launched across the Channel, in mid-July. Then six assault divisions would land in the Pas de Calais area, building up a force 50 divisions strong to expand the bridgehead to Antwerp and Brussels.

---

* Later to be postponed to 6 June.

Once the real landings had been made in Normandy, however, the story would enter its second phase. The Normandy landings, it would be indicated, were a feint to draw in the German reserves. The main assault force was assembling in south-east England and would attack the Pas de Calais as soon as the right moment came. And once the assaults were complete, the shipping would be available for the notionally delayed operations against Norway.

Once this plan was approved, Eisenhower sent a directive to the commanders concerned, General Montgomery, Admiral Sir Bertram Ramsay and Air Chief Marshal Sir Trafford Leigh-Mallory, respectively commanders of the land, naval and air components of the Allied Expeditionary Force.[15] These officers were made responsible for 'directing towards the Pas de Calais the threat created by the forces under their control and for concealing the state of readiness of these forces so as to indicate *Neptune* D + 45 as the real target date'. *Fortitude North* was the responsibility of GOC Scottish Command, Lieut General Sir Andrew Thorne. By a useful coincidence, General Thorne had been Military Attaché in Berlin in 1934, and was personally known to Hitler, having fought on the same front as the Führer in the first battle of Ypres; a circumstance which would, it was hoped help to focus the Führer's attention on the threat posed to Scandinavia by the forces under his command.*

As soon as the Combined Chiefs of Staff had given their formal approval to *Bodyguard*, on 23 January 1944, Colonel Bevan visited the Soviet Union to arrange for co-operation over the details to which Stalin had agreed in principle at Tehran. Together with Colonel William H Baumer of United States Joint Security Control, Bevan flew to Moscow on 30 January and remained there until 6 March, experiencing all the frustrations common to everyone who tried to negotiate with the Russians on any subject below the very highest level of command.[16] No meetings were arranged for a week: the officials whom Bevan and Baumer contacted expressed complete ignorance of the whole affair. Only after a direct appeal had been made to Stalin and Molotov did the ice thaw, and then between 7 and 14 February a series of meetings were held at which *Bodyguard* was expounded and discussed in a friendly spirit of constructive criticism. Predictably the Russians gave nothing away about their own deception techniques, but they discussed with some expertise the inconvenience of the notional D-day proposed, the technical problems of mounting a notional threat to northern Norway, and their preference for concentrating their amphibious threat in the Black Sea on Romania rather than Bulgaria. A final meeting to confirm

---

* That there is some reason to believe that it did is suggested by the fact that a German translation of an article about the Battle of Gheluvelt in 1914 by General Thorne was found in the Führer's bunker in the Reich Chancellery after the war. (Documents communicated to the author by Lieut Col Peter Thorne).

all arrangements was arranged for 16 February, and then once more, without warning, all communication ceased. The meeting was cancelled at a few hours' notice. Nothing more was heard until 24 February, when the Russians asked for the clarification of certain details. Then at midnight on 5 March Bevan and Baumer were suddenly summoned to a meeting at one hour's notice, at which the Russians accepted *Bodyguard* without further discussion, in its entirety and in its original form. And when the time came, so far as could be established, they completely fulfilled their commitments; mounting menacing operations both in the Arctic and in the Black Sea, bringing diplomatic pressure against Bulgaria and Romania and launching misleading information into the German intelligence network through their own channels.[17]

By the time Bevan got back to London, after five weeks' absence, *Fortitude* had been approved and preparations were well under way. It was now that the full advantage of the previous year's experience became evident. *Cockade* had, as we have seen, failed in its main purpose as strategic deception, but in every respect it had been a valuable rehearsal for the real performance of 1944 – and a rehearsal which had enabled the British, through Sigint, to gauge audience reaction. *Fortitude North* prolonged the threat to Scandinavia already posed by *Tindall*, while *Fortitude South* was playing on an exposed nerve whose sensitivity had been revealed by *Starkey*. But neither these nor any other deception operations would have been feasible but for the slow, patient build-up of the notional Allied Order of Battle, both in the United Kingdom and in the Mediterranean, that had now been in operation since 1942 and on which all else depended.

In projecting this notional Order of Battle to enemy intelligence the United Kingdom and the Mediterranean Theatres, and indeed Allied global deployment in its entirety had to be treated as a single whole. If notional formations were moved from one theatre to another, evidence had to be provided of their transit and arrival. If the movement of real formations had to be concealed, cover had to be devised by the authorities in the theatres both of departure and of arrival. In fact the latter, the movement of real formations, was now the problem rather than that of notional ones. It was part of the object of *Bodyguard* to emphasise the strength of Allied forces in the Mediterranean theatre and to minimise that in the United Kingdom. But an essential part of the Allied redeployment in preparation for *Overlord* was the return of seven seasoned divisions, including such world-famous formations as 7th Armoured Division, from the Mediterranean to Britain; together with some seventy landing-craft, whose passage through the Straits of Gibraltar could hardly be concealed from the agents of the Abwehr. Concealment and cover for this major redeployment was given the codename *Foynes*.[18]

It was the transfer of landing-craft that caused the most anxiety. The Abwehr maintained five observation posts on the European side of the Straits of Gibraltar and seven on the African, equipped with various detection devices. With both coasts blazing with lights all night, the silhouettes of all vessels passing the Straits showed up clearly. The fact that landing-craft in considerable numbers were passing through the Straits from east to west could not be concealed. So the story was devised by 'A' Force and the London Controlling Section that 'Facilities in the Mediterranean for the repair of landing-craft have proved quite inadequate. A number of landing-craft are returning to the United Kingdom for repair; some of these will subsequently return to the Mediterranean. New and improved landing-craft are being despatched direct from the United States to the Mediterranean'.[19]

The Allies need not have worried. German intelligence had picked up the movements as soon as they began in October 1943, but both their naval and military appreciations emphasised that these did not affect the capacity of the Allies to launch further amphibious operations in the Mediterranean on a large scale.[20] Moreover the count of vessels passing the Straits did not in itself give the enemy enough information on which to base any firm conclusions. 'Our defective aerial reconnaissance in the Mediterranean' admitted FHW on 22 October, 'does not provide us with a clear insight into the disposition of enemy landing-craft, which earlier gave us valuable hints about the enemy's intentions. We have no information whatever about their present dispositions'.[21] Six months later, when the Allied redeployment was complete, the Germans were still no better informed. 'We cannot estimate the numbers of the enemy's landing-craft', they confessed on 16th April 1944. 'According to our previous experience, the enemy command has a masterly grasp of the art of camouflaging their landing-craft over a wide area. We must therefore expect these craft to be still in the western Mediterranean.'[22] The 'story' put out by the deception staffs was thus hardly necessary. The Germans deceived themselves quite adequately by taking counsel of their fears.

German intelligence was equally credulous about the movement of the Allied divisions from the Mediterranean. Plans for the concealment of this had been laid as early as October 1943, as part of the original Operation *Jael*, and 'A' Force and the London Controlling Section had been quietly implementing it throughout the autumn. The presence in the United Kingdom of troops withdrawn from the Mediterranean could not be wholly concealed; their return was bound to be a matter of local gossip and family rejoicing. So the story was first put out – notably through the double agents[23] – that individuals from battle-seasoned divisions were coming home on prolonged leave; then, when the presence of the formations themselves became impossible to conceal, it would be said that these formations consisted simply of cadres sent home to train recruits, leaving all their vehicles and heavy equipment behind. The number of formations in the Mediterranean, it was suggested, had actually been *increased*, through the transfer of notional formations from the United Kingdom. In implementing this story a natural conflict of interest arose between 'A' Force, which wished to keep the return of the divisions to Britain secret for as long as possible, and the London Controlling Section, which feared that the credibility of the double agents would be seriously impaired if they did not eventually encounter formations whose presence in the United Kingdom was a matter of common knowledge. By April the LCS assumed that the Abwehr must by now have learned of the transfers, and permitted the names of the majority of the formations concerned to be released to the Press. But it had already arranged for the information to be transmitted by the double agents to the Abwehr in good time ahead of the Press announcement; a leak which further reassured the Abwehr as to the reliability of the sources. But the success of *Foynes* owed in fact a very great deal to the methods employed by the Germans themselves. Their intelligence officers in the Mediterranean theatre might report—as indeed they did—that they could no longer identify specific Allied formations on their front. But unless these formations were firmly identified elsewhere, FHW assumed that they were still in the Mediterranean. Once a formation, whether real or bogus, appeared on the Allied Mediterranean Order of Battle charts maintained in Berlin, it stayed there until a good reason occurred for removing it. By the end of 1943 Allied intelligence was well aware of this element of inertia, and of over-insurance, in all German assessments, and the deception authorities were able quite deliberately to exploit it.

As a result the entire redeployment of Allied forces from the Mediterranean to the United Kingdom took place without the Germans getting wind of it. Even by the end of 1943 all the divisions concerned had either returned home or were well on their way. Nevertheless the situation report issued by FHW on 31 December (and circulated to recipients of Sigint on 2 January) stated: [there is] 'no indication of any kind of considerable forces being transported away from the Mediterranean area. The Allied command obviously intends to concentrate its main efforts in the England area and will not employ any considerable reinforcements in the Mediterranean area. The intended withdrawal of single specialised units to England is not out of the question, though hitherto there have been no signs whatever pointing in this direction. Allies still have at their disposal in the Mediterranean considerable reserves ... '. Having thus firmly made up their minds that no transfers were taking place from the Mediterranean, in spite of the Allies' intention to make their main effort from the United Kingdom, it is not surprising that FHW dismissed an Abwehr report from Vichy of 5 January, that Allied formations were on their way home via Gibraltar, with the comment: 'Conclusions about the disposition of major formations cannot be drawn from this report, whose source rates as "questionable".[24]

The effect on German strategic appreciations of their continuing belief in the presence of major Allied reserves in the Mediterranean theatre will be considered in the next chapter. So far as the United Kingdom was concerned, FHW assessed the forces available for the invasion of the continent, in January 1944, at 55 divisions. In fact there were about 37. By the end of May the German assessment had risen to 79, with landing-craft and assault shipping available for at least 15. In fact there were still only about 52. It was this misconception, carefully cultivated over the years, that made the threats both to Scandinavia and to the Pas de Calais appear perfectly credible to the Germans, even after the Normandy landings had already begun.

The threat to Scandinavia, *Fortitude North*, was mounted, as we have seen, by a notional Fourth Army, based on Scottish Command, under the command of Lieut General Sir Andrew Thorne. The operations were, again notionally, co-ordinated with the Soviet forces, and the Russians co-operated to the extent of putting out a great deal of information through their own channels; including a story that senior Soviet officers had been sent to Scotland to complete the necessary arrangements.[25] The attack on Norway was notionally to be mounted by eight divisions; one Corps – two divisions strong – to attack Narvik and open communications with northern Sweden, two Corps, totalling six divisions, to seize Stavanger and exploit inland to Oslo and beyond. Given the uncertainties of the Scottish climate, little attempt was made to mount visual displays to mislead enemy reconnaissance aircraft. Reliance was placed on bogus radio traffic and reporting by double agents. It was not in fact necessary to create many bogus formations. 52nd (Lowland) Division and 3rd Infantry Division were already stationed, the one near Dundee and the other on the Moray Firth, carrying out actual assault training in preparation for the Normandy landings. There was a large concentration of Polish units in the Lowlands, giving *Brutus* an excuse to pay a prolonged visit to the area. A contingent of Norwegian forces was stationed near Dingwall, and 113 Independent Infantry Brigade garrisoned the Orkneys. In Northern Ireland there were stationed 55 Division and XV US Corps with three divisions (2nd, 5th, 8th) under command. Finally, a notional 55th US Division (not to be confused with 55th British Division in Northern Ireland) was reported to be stationed in Iceland by the two double agents installed there, *Cobweb* and *Beetle*.

The assault on Narvik was to be carried out by a notional VII British Corps, having under its command 52nd Lowland Division, the notional 55th US Division (sailing direct from Iceland) and the Norwegian contingent. The attack on Stavanger was the responsibility of a real II British Corps HQ, commanding 3rd and 55th Divisions and 113 Infantry Brigade, with US XV Corps providing the follow-up force. At a later stage in the plan the need to move 3rd Division to the south coast for real training (where it might be identified) made it necessary to create at very short notice a new notional 58th Division, allegedly built round cadres of Scottish units returned from the Mediterranean, to take its place. Two notional naval forces were created to serve the two Corps, and notional amphibious training was carried out with them, primarily through bogus radio traffic, from mid-April. All available shipping was anchored in the Firth of Forth, where the number of vessels berthed rose from 26 at the beginning of April to 71 by mid-May. The Commander-in-Chief Home Fleet mounted a carrier-borne aerial reconnaissance against the Narvik area on 26 April. The Royal Air Force simulated the transfer of four medium bomber squadrons from Suffolk to east Scotland, and made a discreet display of both real and dummy fighter squadrons at Peterhead. By mid-May, to all visual and audible appearances, all the land and naval forces for both landings were assembled in the area of the Clyde, ready to sail at short notice.

The contribution to the deception of the double agents in Iceland, *Cobweb* and *Beetle*, has already been noted, as have the advantages that the presence of Polish units in Scotland gave *Brutus*. On 12 April *Brutus* reported to his German control after a notional trip to Scotland, during which he had identified the insignia of Fourth Army HQ at Edinburgh, II Corps at Stirling and VII Corps at Dundee. He had also identified the bogus 58th Division, with its distinctive stag's antlers insignia, southeast of Stirling and observed that many of its men were wearing the Africa Star. Shortly afterwards, on 4 May, he reported that a Soviet naval and military mission had established itself in Edinburgh. Other agents reported useful gossip. *Tricycle's* Yugoslav colleague, *Freak*, described on 30 March how he had had a fortunate encounter in London with an indiscreet American officer from XV Corps in Northern Ireland who had recently taken up a post on General Thorne's staff at Fourth Army HQ. 'Congratulations' replied his control 'Please state exact number of divisions etc belonging to Fourth Army under General Thorne. Is anything pointing to intended landings in the German Bight, Denmark, and South Sweden'? Clearly the Abwehr was anxious to corroborate the expectations of a direct attack against Denmark which obsessed the Führer himself.

The Norwegian double agent, *Mutt*, also provided a stream of detailed misinformation about troop movements in Scotland. But the most valuable reports which the Abwehr received about the Allied preparations in Scotland came from an imaginary member of *Garbo's* non-existent network; a British sailor with Communist leanings stationed on the Clyde, who believed that he was supplying information to a Soviet espionage network. *Garbo* had received on 7 March an urgent request for information about military preparations in Scotland and north-east England, and this information he set out prolifically to supply. Hardly a day passed, between March and June, without some item of information about *Fortitude North* being passed to his control in Madrid – information which was still being supplied as late as August, when he reported that the 'enormous activity arrival of US troops and equipment in Clyde and western ports [was] considered by [this] agent to be greater than any time since entry of America into war'.

It was almost entirely due to the work of *Garbo*, *Brutus* and their associates that FHW built up a picture of Fourth Army and its intentions which corresponded very largely to that projected by the deception staffs. There is little evidence that the elaborate measures for radio deception registered with the German radio intercept service (though its absence would have involved running a quite unacceptable risk) and German air reconnaissance was too fleeting and infrequent to contribute much to what the Germans knew – or thought they knew. The need for air reconnaissance to confirm these agents' reports was indeed a matter of continuous concern to FHW.

But although the deception was successful in that the Germans were persuaded to believe in the existence of Fourth Army and its hostile intentions, it failed substantially to affect enemy dispositions. The size of the German garrison in Norway remained at 12 divisions. Although Hitler himself, as we know, was mildly obsessed with the threat to Scandinavia, especially to Denmark, FHW never entirely took the bait. It noted the concentrations in Scotland as early as January 1944, but considered that the problem of providing air cover would restrict any British attacks on Norway to purely localised affairs.[26] On 1 March, when the first detailed reports from agents were beginning to come in, FHW very accurately observed 'that, seeing that what the enemy leadership is up to in the present stage of operations is to do everything to tie down the German forces on subsidiary fronts, and indeed divert them from the decisive Atlantic front; and seeing that they have already tried to do this in Italy, it seems possible that they have decided to do the same in the Scandinavian region'.[27] FHW urged increased defensive preparations on the Norwegian coast and more intensive air reconnaissance, in order to prevent the kind of surprise that the enemy had pulled off so successfully at Sicily and Anzio*; but in general it never wavered from its view that the forces at General Thorne's disposal were not enough to mount more than diversionary operations which the existing garrison of Norway should be able to contain.

Before leaving the subject of the notional threat directed against Scandinavia we must consider another deception being mounted in parallel with *Fortitude North* —Operation *Graffham*. The object of this, in the words of the plan drawn up by the LCS on 3 February 1944, was 'to induce the enemy to believe that we are enlisting the active co-operation of Sweden in connection with British and Russian contemplated operations against northern Norway in the Spring of this year'.[28] This was implemented almost entirely through diplomatic channels, although double agents contributed some useful rumours.

Graffham opened in February with instructions being issued by the

Foreign Office to the British Minister in Stockholm, Sir Victor Mallet, to request the Swedish government to permit the British to obtain meteorological reports from Sweden and to instal British air navigation equipment at certain points in Swedish territory; the rumour being put about that, after the Allied landings in Norway, Swedish airfields would be used to supplement the Combined Bomber Offensive against Germany.[29] On 4 April these requests were supplemented by more pressing demands. The British asked for the right to refuel and repair damaged aircraft which had been compelled to land on Swedish territory; for permission to operate their own reconnaissance flights over Sweden; and for talks between British and Swedish transport experts about the movement of supplies into Scandinavia in the event of German forces withdrawing from the theatre.

The Swedish authorities took these requests seriously. They refused to permit reconnaissance flights to take place, though they hinted broadly that they would not be too upset if they actually occurred. They agreed to receive an exploratory delegation of transport specialists; and discussions on the other issues continued throughout the spring, with Mallet being rather ostentatiously recalled to London for consultations and Air Vice Marshal Thornton, formerly British Air Attacheé to Sweden, equally ostentatiously visiting Stockholm. The effect on the Germans was all that could be desired. On 28 May, FHW reported: that 'credibly-sounding reported overtures by an English Air Force officer in Sweden, which were apparently aimed at obtaining air bases in Sweden for invasion purposes, may be interpreted as a hint of a minor landing operation being planned in south Norway or Denmark. The likelihood of a more powerful group landing in those parts as part of the larger operational strategy is still considered to be slight'.[30]

Meanwhile, the United States and the Soviet Union added their voices to that of the British, and on 9 June, three days after the Normandy landings, the three Allied governments jointly demanded an assurance from the Swedes that, in the event of an Allied landing in Norway, the Swedish government would resist German pressure to permit the movement of German troops from Finland through Swedish territory. The Swedish assurances were apparently 'satisfactory'; but even more satisfactory was the effect on the Swedish Press, where Allied landings were now canvassed as being imminent. It was a belief which, understandably, infected the members of the German embassy in Stockholm, where an MI6 source reported on 12 May that, although it was not expected that Sweden would yield to Allied pressures, Scandinavia was 'considered to be an area of extreme importance in the forthcoming operations', and that action against Denmark was 'considered to be a certainty'. These fears continued long after the Normandy landings, but they were not shared by the hard-headed analysts at FHW. On 25 May they noted 'the extraordinarily small number of ships in the east Scottish harbours is remarkable and confirms that no noticeable movement from these areas to Norway is planned. On the other hand', they observed, 'shipping in the Portland area has risen since 20 January from 80 to 1200, permitting the transport of 10 or more divisions'.[31] They at least had no doubt where the Schwerpunkt of the Allied attack really lay.

☐

We have seen that *Fortitude North*, although achieving all that was expected of it in convincing the German High Command of a credible threat to Scandinavia, did not persuade them to alter the dispositions they had already made to take care of such a threat. Whatever the Allies did in that theatre, the Germans knew that it would be on a comparatively small scale, and that the real danger lay across the Channel. It was the success of *Fortitude South* in misleading every level of the German Command, from Hitler himself through Jodl to von Rundstedt and Rommel, as to the precise nature and location of that danger that remains one of the central triumphs of the deception staffs of the entire war.

The essential features of *Fortitude South*, as outlined in General Eisenhower's directive of 23 February 1944, have already been described. The real landings were to be effected on the coast of Normandy between the Cotentin peninsula and the estuary of the Seine. For these, British forces would be concentrated in the region of Southampton and Portsmouth, United States forces further west between Poole and Plymouth. These preparations could not be concealed, but preparations on a comparable scale would be simulated in south-east England, and once the actual landings had taken place these would be intensified. The Normandy landings, it would be indicated, were simply a feint to draw in German reserves. Once this had been done, the main attack would come in against the Pas de Calais.

This involved a fundamental shift of emphasis from the original tentative proposals of 'Appendix Y'. Those had proposed a notional force of only some six divisions to simulate a threat to the Pas de Calais. Yet the preparations involved in simulating even so limited a threat – the shipping movements, the building of roads, camps and embarkation points, the evacuation of civilians, the arrangements for the treatment of casualties and prisoners of war – proved on examination to make demands on resources of men and material which the authorities concerned, absorbed as they now were with the mounting of *real* operations, would be quite unable to meet. We have already seen how sceptical the Americans had been about the whole proposal. General Montgomery and his staff at 21st Army Group turned it down flat. They simply did not have the troops to spare. How, therefore, would it be possible to simulate the far more extensive threat which was ultimately demanded from *Fortitude South*?

It would probably not have been possible at all, but for two factors. The first was the total command of the air which the RAF had now established over Britain itself and the surrounding waters, and the erosion of the German Air Force to the point where regular aerial reconnaissance over south-east England had become almost impossible. Occasional forays were flown over the Straits and the Thames Estuary, making the display of dummy landing-craft a worthwhile investment of resources, but the elaborate lay-out of dummy camps, depots and communications originally intended in Kent and East Anglia was, rightly as it turned out, considered to be unnecessary as well as impracticable. The Germans would not be able to observe it. And secondly, the security authorities were now convinced that they controlled all sources of enemy intelligence within the country. The occasional leak or indiscretion might slip out through a neutral source, freelance agents might make uncomfortably accurate guesses, but the credibility of the hard core of trusted double agents had been tried and tested over more than a year, and what they reported was likely to be considered a great deal more reliable, not only by the Abwehr but by FHW, than the occasional contradictory report that might slip through. Given the virtually total dependence of enemy intelligence on these sources, and on their radio intercept service, it was decided that it would be possible to project a threat of far greater scope than originally intended by relying almost wholly on the double agents and on radio simulation.

Once that was settled, the way was clear for the creation of a complete notional Army Group, as strong as, if not stronger than, General Montgomery's 21st Army Group which was actually to launch the assault. The framework for this lay to hand. A skeletal First United States Army Group HQ already existed, intended to take command of the United States forces in France once these had been built up to a sufficient size to warrant an independent command. All that was necessary was to flesh this out with real and notional formations, and to transfer its original task to General Omar Bradley's 12th Army Group. A commander also lay ready to hand. Lieut General George S Patton had won a considerable reputation in Sicily, commanding United States Seventh Army in the mobile operation which had overrun the western half of the island and beaten General Montgomery's Eighth Army into Messina by a short head. Who could be a more probable choice as commander of the United States Army Group to compete with his old British rival's 21st Army Group in overrunning France? In fact General Patton in the aftermath of the Sicilian campaign, by publicly losing his temper and striking a shell-shocked soldier in hospital, had rendered himself temporarily unemployable; so this notional command, unsatisfying as it was to him, solved an embarrassing problem for the United States military authorities. Further, Patton was not of a retiring disposition. He could be relied upon to figure, controversially and often, in newspaper headlines, and in consequence in German intelligence reports.

First United States Army Group Headquarters (FUSAG), was

notionally located at Wentworth, near Ascot in Berkshire, and had notionally two real armies under command: the First Canadian Army, actually already stationed in Kent and east Sussex as part of 21st Army Group; and Third United States Army, actually forming in Cheshire as a follow-up force for the Normandy landings but notionally depicted as being located in Essex and Suffolk with its HQ at Chelmsford. Each Army consisted of two Corps commanding a grand total of eleven divisions. The FUSAG radio network was activated on 24 April, and for six months was to carry the busy administrative and operational traffic of this huge and spectral force which, had it existed, would have totalled some 150,000 men.

Meanwhile the double agents, working under the instructions of their case-officers as advised by Ops B, were busy reporting the movement and concentration of these units. *Brutus* had the great good fortune to be posted as a Polish liaison officer to FUSAG HQ. *Tricycle* on his visit to Lisbon in March was able to take a mass of detailed information that was gratefully accepted by his control and marked as 'particularly valuable' by FHW.[32] *Tate*, who had had little to do for a year, was notionally moved to Wye in Kent for agricultural work where he was in the centre of troop movements.* But the most valuable information gatherer was, once more, *Garbo*. *Garbo* was instructed by the Abwehr as early as 5 January to find out all he could about forthcoming operations both in the north and in the south, so he was able to deploy his notional team in good time. One, a waiter from Gibraltar now working for the NAAFI, got work in a canteen in 21st Army Group's concentration area, at Otterbourne in Hampshire – a camp actually occupied by 3rd Canadian Division. Three other agents drawn from the Welsh Nationalist network (known to the Germans as *Donny*, *Dick* and *Derrick*) established themselves in Dover, Brighton and Harwich respectively, before security restrictions made movement in these areas too difficult.† All notionally conveyed their information to *Garbo* in invisible ink, to be transmitted direct to the Abwehr over his clandestine radio – the only channel open after security restrictions on outgoing mail had been imposed. Over 500 such transmissions were made between January 1944 and D-day: a daily average of about four.

The task of *Garbo*, as of all the double agents, was complicated by the need, not only to deceive the Germans as to where the assault was coming, but to sow doubt in their minds as to whether it was coming at all.

Garbo did his best. On 21 January he had transmitted, as the opinion of one of his notional agents working in the Ministry of Information, virtually the whole cover-story of *Bodyguard*, as follows:

---

* Unfortunately by this time *Tate* was not rated very highly by his German employers, and little of the information which he transmitted found its way into the reports of FHW.

† For a full account of the *Garbo* network see Appendix 2.

'He considered that the Anglo-American offensive against the continent, *should this take place*, would not happen for a long time. He shares the predominating opinion expressed in certain official circles who think that the collapse of Germany will certainly be brought about by an increase in the air offensive. He bases his argument on definite information of high value which he states is reaching official circles about the destruction in the enemy's war potential. He continued by saying that if the Russian offensive had been successful it was undoubtedly due in great part to the continuous assistance which the Anglo-American bombers had rendered in constant attacks against Germany and that if in consequence the Germans should decide to withdraw from France to reinforce their eastern defences he had no doubt that the Anglo-American would then set foot in that country immediately. He said that there had been an enormous amount of talk and abuse by irresponsible people here with regard to the opening of a Second Front hastily, that the public had no idea of what this undertaking represented. He ended by saying that if it should not be brought to an end by aerial attacks, that the invasion would not take place until an assault force immeasurably greater in number than that which exists had been assembled in the island, and this would take time to realise'.

Garbo continued to plug away gallantly along these lines. On 21 April he sent a stern warning –

'I am surprised to hear through German radio the news which leaves one unsettled, of the nervousness which exists in official circles with regard to the Allied offensive which has been the subject of so much cackling, and I am very surprised, more so after the continuous reports of my agents which I have for some while past been transmitting, telling you that only preparations but no indicative action of concentration is noted. This does not make me fail to appreciate that the Second Front may become a reality, but what I am able to guarantee you once again is that for the moment our strict vigilance has not noted any fact from which we can stress to you the danger of the supposed action ... I recommend therefore once again calm and confidence in our work. The Allies have used tricks to date, and it is deplorable that those in Germany should give credence to the great majority of them'.

To this message *Garbo* received the cautious reply 'Neither we nor anyone outside the High Command can know whether the tricks employed by the Allies in this war are believed or not'. In fact the attempt to deceive the Germans as to the fact and the timing of Operation *Overlord* was a predictable failure. On 23 February FHW expressed its reservations about all such reports, 'since enemy diplomatic sources seem to be systematically spreading information about the postponement of the invasion'.[33] A month later it was convinced that all such accounts were untrue. 'Numerous messages', it reported on 20 March, 'about a postponement of invasion or even of its being given up altogether in favour of increased air raids and smaller diversionary landings ... are in our opinion to be treated as intentional disguise of enemy intentions ... and are contradicted by troop movements observed in England'.[34]

The monitoring of these appreciations may have done something to discourage the efforts of the deception staffs to prolong the story of a postponement, but in any event by mid-March the introduction in the United Kingdom of strict and widespread security precautions made such a course seem very unlikely indeed.

The problem of security arrangements for the invasion was immensely complex, involving as they did a wide range of authorities with mutually incompatible interests. The military were concerned to prevent all possible leakage of information. The civilian authorities wanted to avoid any unnecessary dislocation of free movement, transport and communication. The Foreign Office wished to minimise interference with normal diplomatic channels; while the deception staffs wanted to enhance the credibility of their cover stories. The difficulties became apparent as early as August 1943, when the Inter-Services Security Board had proposed that there should be a complete severance of communications between the United Kingdom and the outside world, but that this should occur only at the last possible moment before the troops were moved to their concentration areas and briefed for the operation. But such a procedure, Colonel Bevan pointed out, would only result in German forces being put, at the crucial moment, on maximum alert along the entire coast. It would be better, he suggested, to take the risk of leakages, which would in any case be low-level and contradictory. (The capacity of the LCS to smother such leakages with credible misinformation was of course known to very few of those involved in these discussions.) If such a ban were imposed, it would have to come early enough to give no indication of the real date of D-day, and last for long enough to cover *Fortitude South*, the notional attack on the Pas de Calais, as well as *Neptune*, the actual attack on Normandy. It was also seen as necessary to let some at least of the civilian authorities into the secret of *Fortitude South*, to enable them to understand the need for the measures in which their co-operation was required. So a small number of senior civil servants were informed that the assault would not be against the Pas de Calais but 'more to the west'; but that these preparations must be seen to be mounted against the Pas de Calais and continue after the main assault had gone in; and that the appearance of a military build-up would need to be accompanied by civil measures of security, evacuation, civil defence and improvements to roads and railways. As we have seen, the scope of these projected measures was considerably reduced once the decision had been taken to rely so largely on 'Special Means' and radio traffic to project the deception.

At the beginning of February, after long interdepartmental consultation, SHAEF had decided on two comparatively limited measures; suspension of civilian travel between the United Kingdom and the Republic of Ireland, and a ban on visitors entering a coastal area extending from Land's End to The Wash, together with the Firth of Forth. But these were described by Mr Churchill, when he was asked to approve them on 9 February, as 'a pill to stop an earthquake'. Security measures, he insisted, should go 'high, wide and handsome'. They should, as he idiosyncratically put it,

'concentrate on messing about with foreigners and other undesirables rather than making life an even greater burden for our own nationals. He is of the opinion [reported General Morgan] that nothing will ever stop people in this country from chattering and we might as well let them go on chattering but take steps to see that the chatter stays in this country and does not go out of it. His general idea was that for some considerable period we should stop communications of all kinds as between British Isles as a whole and the outside world. He would even go so far as to deprive all foreign embassies ... of diplomatic privileges for quite a period. He would entirely ground civilian airlines and he would do the utmost possible to immobilise all commercial shipping'.[35]*

Churchill's drastic proposals carried the day. Travel to Ireland was suspended immediately, and the coasts declared prohibited areas to a depth of ten miles inland. In addition all service leave was stopped; the airmail service to Lisbon was suspended at the end of March; and the following month not only was all travel to and from the United Kingdom banned, but the mail of all diplomatic missions was declared subject to censorship and the use of cyphers forbidden.[36]

These last measures caused much inconvenience to the LCS and BiA, whose channels for misinforming the enemy were thereby severely restricted. *Garbo* in particular could no longer send his long and verbose letters by the Lisbon mail. But once the ban *was* imposed, it was a matter of the highest importance that it should be maintained for long enough to cover *Fortitude South* as well as *Neptune*: so the LCS asked that it should remain in force until D + 30. But to this the Foreign Office objected strongly. The Foreign Secretary made it clear that 'he would never have agreed to the ban except on the understanding that it would cease once *Overlord* had been launched. The Foreign Office was quite certain that, once it was common knowledge that the Allied forces had landed on the continent, they would be quite unable to hold the position either with the Allies or with the neutrals'.[37]

In the face of this pressure the Chiefs of Staff yielded and agreed to relax the ban, in principle on D + 2, in practice on D + 7. The deception staffs were thus left with the task of explaining to the Germans why security restrictions had been thought necessary before the Normandy landings but not before those imminent at the Pas de Calais. An ingenious story was devised for transmission by *Garbo* as coming from his informant at the Ministry of Information, to the effect that while the military had wanted to maintain the ban, they would have been able to do so only by telling neutral diplomats about the Pas

---

* also dealt with in Hinsley, op cit, Vol 4, Chapter 14.

de Calais landings; which would have been a yet greater security risk. In fact this stratagem proved unnecessary. General Eisenhower insisted on the diplomatic ban remaining in force until D + 15 (21 June) and all other restrictions until 1 July at earliest. They were not in practice lifted until 25 August. As will be seen the security for *Fortitude South* remained intact until the very end.

Fortitude was not the only stratagem employed to confuse the enemy and prevent him from identifying the Normandy landings as the main Allied thrust. It was complemented in the Mediterranean by the no less comprehensive Operation *Zeppelin*, which will be described in due course. But a further feint was mounted against the west coast of France in the region of Bordeaux, with the intention of tying down the German reserves, especially 17th SS Panzer Grenadier Division, which were held between the Loire and the Dordogne and might have been used either on the Normandy front or against the Allied landings in the south of France. The 'story' of this deception, Operation *Ironside*, was that an Allied expeditionary force, largely American, was preparing to embark at west coast ports in the United Kingdom to capture Bordeaux, which would then be used as a port of entry by United States forces sailing directly from America.[38] The deception staffs did their best to implement this rather implausible story, but their hearts were not in it. In default of physical resources they had to rely on rumours picked up by double agents, and they were unwilling to impair the credibility of the agents more than was strictly necessary. *Bronx*, one of their sociable ladies, heard of the forthcoming operation from a drunken American officer in a London night club and on 29 May sent a coded telegram warning the Germans to expect a landing in the Bay of Biscay within the week. At the same time *Tate* learned from his girl friend Mary, who had just returned from Washington, that an expeditionary force was being prepared in the United States. Finally on 5 June *Garbo* relayed, with many expressed reservations, a report from one of his agents that a US assault division was assembling in Liverpool 'destined for an attack on the south Atlantic French coast in co-operation with a large army which will come direct from America'. These and other such reports were a slender foundation on which to convince the Germans of Allied intentions, and there seems no evidence that anyone took them seriously.

More lighthearted, but little more effective, was Operation *Copperhead*, the now famous impersonation of Field Marshal Montgomery by Lieutenant Clifton James of the Royal Army Pay Corps. It was arranged for Montgomery to pay a notional visit to Algiers at the end of May, landing at Gibraltar *en route*, to co-ordinate his operations with those being planned against the south of France. His appearance would, it was hoped, be noted by Abwehr agents and lull the Germans into a state of false security just before the Normandy landings on 6 June.[39] The arrival of 'Montgomery' at Maison Blanche airfield on 28 May, where General Maitland Wilson's car was waiting for him, was duly reported by a controlled agent and FHW took note of it.[40] But it did not draw the appropriate conclusion. FHW informed Kessel-ring in Italy that 'the meeting said to have taken place between Mont-gomery and Wilson in north Africa would, should it be true, indicate southern France [as the objective of Allied forces in French north Africa]; but there is always the possibility that plans will be changed should there be a stalemate in the fighting in Italy'.[41] No evidence has yet come to light to show that von Rundstedt was informed as well, and there is nothing to indicate that this deception contributed to the tactical surprise achieved on the Normandy beaches on 6 June.

Further cover to prolong the deception was provided by Operation *Royal Flush*.[42] This was initially a somewhat grandiose project intended, by bringing open diplomatic pressure to bear on neutral governments, to indicate an imminent Allied assault at almost every point on the German defences. It included those aspects of Operation *Graffham* by which, it will be recalled, the Swedes were alerted to an imminent Allied assault on Norway by a joint Allied demand that they should resist any German violation of their territory and deny German troops transit rights from Finland. *Royal Flush* was also to involve an Anglo-American démarche in Ankara, two days after the Normandy landings, demanding passage for Allied forces through Turkey, while simulta-neously the Russians were to demand from Sofia permission to land forces on the Bulgarian coast. Over this plan, however, second thoughts prevailed; it might, the Foreign Office pointed out, too easily provoke a pre-emptive German occupation of Turkey. Instead, the passage of six small German naval vessels through the Straits at the beginning of June gave the British Ambassador the opportunity to lodge an official protest, in which he particularly stressed the wish of the Allies *not* to see the German garrisons in the Aegean strengthened at this of all moments. The Turkish reaction was all that could have been desired. They apologised for permitting this infringement of the Montreux Con-vention, and declared themselves ready to break off diplomatic relations with Germany whenever the Allies thought it appropriate for them to do so. The Germans themselves, however, do not seem to have taken any additional precautions.

Finally, measures were taken at the other end of the Mediterranean, in Spain. As we shall see later, one of the components of *Zeppelin* was a notional threat against the Mediterranean coast of France in the region of Sète and Narbonne. In order to reinforce this, it had originally been intended that the British and American governments should pres-ent an ultimatum to Spain demanding the right to land forces at Barce-lona and in the Gulf of Rosas in preparation for an attack on France. As in the case of Turkey, it was felt that this was going rather far. Instead, the Allied governments asked for facilities simply to evacuate wounded and to land non-military supplies; a request made by the

American Ambassador on 3 June and the British two days later. The Spaniards replied that they would be prepared to grant such facilities under the supervision of the Red Cross if the need arose. To rub the matter in further, the British and American Consuls in Barcelona called on the Governor with the same request, and were assured 'of the amplitude of port and warehouse facilities and of his desire to assist "in this humanitarian project".'[43]

Then problems arose. The Allies actually were going to land on 9 August in the south of France, in the Bay of Toulon; so 'A' Force naturally wanted to give the impression, once the Normandy beachheads were secure, that Allied intentions in the Mediterranean had changed and that no landings were intended after all. SHAEF on the other hand wanted the threat maintained for as long as possible, to delay any move of German reinforcements from south to north. A reasonable compromise was reached. On 14 July the British Consul General informed the authorities in Barcelona that 'owing to the progress of the campaign it appears unlikely that we shall need the facilities promised, for which we are most grateful'. He added 'that we are pleased to know that these are still available if events at present unforeseen should make it necessary to use them'.[44] This démarche naturally reached the ears of the Abwehr and was duly transmitted to OKW. Unfortunately, as we shall see later, the German High Command did not take the bait.*

The German intelligence services were not in general very impressed by information emanating from Allied embassies in neutral countries. 'It must be strongly emphasised' stated a FHW report of 21 July 1943 'that the numerous reports of the enemy's strategic plans which we are receiving at present from enemy embassies in neutral countries are valueless. For quite a long time the Anglo-Saxon embassies have been recognised as outspoken deception centres, from which not a single piece of reliable news, but many false reports, have been coming'.[45] Nor were the rumours planted on neutral diplomats in London, carefully orchestrated as they were by a special section of MI5 under the general direction of the LCS, considered to be of much significance. Even if they penetrated to the Germans and commanded credibility they were likely to be unpredictably distorted on the way. This was appreciated early in 1944, and by March the practice had been abandoned. Such rumours could be conveyed much more accurately and more rapidly by the double agents; and in spite of the elaborate and ingenious arrangements for visual and aural deception, in spite of the dummy landing-craft† and embarkation points and aircraft, in spite of the now highly sophisticated radio traffic transmitted for the benefit

---

* See p 152 below.
† By 12 June 255 dummy craft were displayed at Great Yarmouth, at Lowestoft, in the rivers Deben and Orwell, and at Dover and Folkestone.

of the German radio intercept service, it was almost wholly on the double agents that both the British deception staffs and FHW had now come to rely.

The arrangements for the last weeks before D-day were very carefully orchestrated indeed. The double agents, especially *Garbo*, mixed with their misinformation about the bogus structure of FUSAG some true information about units serving with 21st Army Group, whose recognition, once they arrived in Normandy, would enhance the credibility of their reports. *Garbo* continued to relay reports that the attack would not come until more American troops were available and after several diversionary attacks had been launched elsewhere. It was necessary however that *somehow* he should give warning of the attack when it came – so long as he did so too late for anything to be done about it. General Eisenhower authorised the despatch of such a message 3½ hours before the expected moment of disembarkation at 0630 – that is, at 0300 on 6 June. So *Garbo* devised a story to persuade his control in Madrid to be listening for a radio message at that time. His agent on the Clyde explained *Garbo*, was expected to come through with important information about the forces notionally assembling there. But, unexpectedly, the agent he had notionally established in the assembly camp near Southampton, from whom he had heard nothing since the area had been sealed off from communication, had broken camp and rung up with the news that the whole place was on the move: the Canadian troops with whom he was serving had been issued with iron rations and vomit bags. *Garbo* was thus all ready to pass over his vital piece of news as well as the latest reports from the Clyde. Unfortunately when he went on the air at the crucial moment, nobody was listening at the other end.

The strictly operational measures of deception which were used to mask the landings have been described elsewhere.[46] Great precautions were taken, in particular, to ensure that nothing was given away by the pattern of air bombardment. Of the 49 airfields within 150 miles of Caen attacked before D-day, 11 were in the Pas de Calais and only 4 in the area of the actual landing. 19 rail junctions supplying the Pas de Calais were attacked. The bridges over the Seine were bombed, but this impeded lateral communication equally between both areas; and attacks on bridges over the Meuse, the Oise and the Albert Canal all pointed to the northern sector. Direct attacks on coastal defences and radar installations on the cover area were twice as heavy as those on the actual target region. The display of dummies could not conceal the fact from a possible German Air Force reconnaissance that fighters and fighter-bombers were more thickly concentrated on airfields in Hampshire than on those in Kent, but on 29 May the Kent airfields were used as advance bases by squadrons of British Second Tactical Air Force for a massive attack against the Pas de Calais. The difficulties which the deception staffs had experienced in earlier years of persuading the air forces to divert their scarce resources to cover targets had at last been solved.

The Royal Navy collaborated with simulated operations, using sonic and other devices, against radar stations on the north coast of the Cotentin peninsula, and with feint landings north of the Seine estuary and against the Pas de Calais itself.[47] 21st Army Group, finally, used operational deception on a major scale in a series of airdrops with dummies and sonic deception. One airborne landing in divisional strength was simulated north of the Seine, and another west of St Lo, while smaller airborne landings were simulated to the east and to the south-west of Caen. Their success is indicated by a statement by Jodl as late as 3 July that 'The British Second Army planned to land between the mouth of the Orne river and Le Havre and capture Le Havre immediately; but their landings in the Le Havre area were frustrated'. The confusion caused to the German command in the first vital hours of the attack was a major factor in the Allied success in getting and remaining ashore when the main invasion forces disembarked on the Normandy beaches at 0630 hours on 6 June.

Less than twenty-four hours before the landing, FHW had complained how 'the enemy command continues to attempt, by every method of nerve warfare, to obscure its invasion plans. Rumours of political differences, which compel a postponement of the invasion alternate with announcements of imminent attack. The object of these machinations is the gradual blunting of German watchfulness designed to bring about the conditions necessary for successful surprise.'[48] It was indeed, and the object was most successfully achieved.

At the beginning of June the Germans had no greater insight into Allied intentions than they had possessed six months earlier. They had never altered their perfectly correct belief that the main Allied concentrations were in south and south-east England and that the main attack would be launched across the Channel, with or without diversionary attacks elsewhere first. But as to exact date and place they remained completely uncertain.* On 10 April a FHW situation report stated that the combined statements of captured saboteurs and British officers had pointed to the end of May and the beginning of June, but 'precisely the agreement in these statements causes us to conclude that they speak under instruction and hence to doubt their truth'.[49] A subsequent report only five days later, however, stated that 'the numerous dates for a landing mostly speak of the last third of April as the weather should be favourable then ... but so far no concrete documents and so the possibility of deception'.[50]

As to place, a FHW report of 20 April suggested a little vaguely

---

* On 25 May the Japanese Minister in Madrid had reported "from British sources" the likelihood of further postponement owing to failure to agree with the Russians on spheres of responsibility'.

that troop concentrations in southern England 'points to the main effort being in the eastern end of the Channel';[51] while a situation report from von Rundstedt's HQ of 24 April suggested equally unhelpfully that the pattern of interdiction attacks on railways showed that 'the focal point is still the Channel coast from the Scheldt (inclusive) to Normandy or even to Brest (inclusive)'.[52] But at the end of April the discovery by air reconnaissance of substantial concentrations of invasion shipping along the coasts of south-west England drew the attention of von Rundstedt's staff to the particular possibilities of Normandy and Brittany, and on 29 April von Rundstedt warned Rommel, as Commander of the Army Group responsible for that area, that 'the focal point remains the Channel front. The two peninsulas of Normandy and Brittany which are especially open to encirclement and the formation of bridgeheads, and which possess ports, constitute as before a special attraction for the enemy'.[53]

Three days later Hitler himself examined the situation and reached the same conclusion as von Rundstedt. On 2 May Warlimont telephoned von Rundstedt's HQ from OKW. 'On his own initiative' he reported 'the Führer has today given an estimate of the situation in the west. Besides the Channel front, he regards the two peninsulas of Normandy and Brittany as primarily threatened. A partial success by the enemy in the two peninsulas would inevitably at once tie down very strong forces of C-in-C West. The Army will therefore do everything they can to reinforce the coastal defence with weapons, especially anti-tank weapons'. Four days later Jodl himself reiterated the order in a call to von Rundstedt's Chief of Staff, General Blumentritt. 'The Führer attaches exceptional importance to Normandy and its defence. Measures to be improvised to strengthen Normandy against attack, especially by air landing troops'. OKW would release units of 2nd Parachute Division to be deployed in the defence of Normandy.[54]

Rommel himself suggested on 4 May that the best way to strengthen the defences of Normandy and Brittany would be to move up the entire OKW strategic reserve, I SS Panzer Corps with Panzer Lehr Division and 12th SS Panzer Division. But von Rundstedt cautiously refused to commit his last resources on the assumption that Normandy was the only area under threat.[55] His situation report of 8 May admitted that Allied landing-craft concentrations in 'the area north of the Isle of Wight' suggested that the Allied Schwerpunkt seemed to be directed 'at an area roughly between Boulogne and Normandy (inclusive)';[56] but a week later he was not prepared to be even so definite as that.

'Judging from air attacks on railways and rail installations and on coastal defences, [ran his situation appreciation of 15 May], the point of main effort is still to be *between the Scheldt and Normandy*, (emphasis added) while the possibility of operations against parts of Brittany (Brest) remains open ... As before, the first operational aim of the enemy must be to win large and capacious harbours. Le Havre and Cherbourg are primarily to be considered for this purpose. Boulogne and Brest secondarily. The attempt to form a bridgehead rapidly on the Cotentin peninsula in the first phase would therefore seem very natural ... This action will perhaps be the enemy's prerequisite condition for a subsequent descent on the Channel coast between Calais and Cherbourg. Deception and diversionary operations in other coastal sectors—including the Biscay front – are very possible at the same time, or shortly before'.[57]

The 'story' for *Fortitude South* had thus become firmly lodged in von Rundstedt's mind; the forthcoming attack on Normandy (preparations for which it was now impossible to conceal) would be preliminary to a 'subsequent descent' further east. More to the point, the inflated figures of forces available for the invasion had become no less firmly lodged in the files both of his own and of OKW's intelligence staffs. A FHW map of 15 May shows 77 divisions and 19 independent brigades available in the United Kingdom, a figure inflated over reality by some 50%. But the full extent to which this figure had been accepted by the Germans and made the basis of their planning was only revealed to the deception staffs when, on 28 May, a telegram was intercepted from the Japanese Ambassador in Berlin to Tokyo, reporting an interview he had had with Hitler the previous day. The Führer had apparently told him that about eighty divisions had been assembled in England. After diversionary operations directed against Norway, Denmark, the south-west and the south coasts of France, these would establish a bridgehead in Normandy or Brittany and then, after seeing how things went, would embark on 'the real second front' across the Channel. When they received this decrypt within a week of D-day, Colonel Bevan and his associates could breathe a quiet *Nunc Dimittis*.

These figures used by Hitler were presumably based on those provided by FHW whose 'survey of the British Empire' of 31 May set the total number of divisions in the United Kingdom at 79, with sea-lift sufficient for at least 15 ¾. The order of battle of these divisions appeared in outline in FHW's situation report of 6 June, based on information thoughtfully provided by *Brutus* and *Garbo*.[58]

'According to reliable Abwehr message of 2 June, the forces at present in the south of England are organised in two Army Groups (21st English and First American). It seems from this report that the American First Army Group contains the First Canadian Army (approximately 13 divisions), known to be in Southern Command, as well as Third American Army between the Thames and the Wash (approximately 12 divisions). It is not yet clear whether they are under the command of General Bradley or General Patton. 21st Army Group commanded by General Montgomery seems to contain the formations at present in the south and south-west of England, which are probably organised in three armies.'

On 2 June OKW asked why von Rundstedt had not yet ordered a full alert in view of the completion of Allied preparations 'which is assumed as certain'.[59] But von Rundstedt clearly did not appreciate how soon he was going to be hit, nor precisely where. In a situation report issued at 2150 on 5 June, little more than eight hours before the invasion begun, his staff recognised that enemy preparations were 'well advanced'.

'As before, front-line point of main attack between Scheldt and Normandy still remaining the probable offensive line, extension to the north coast of Brittany inclusive of Brest not impossible .. [But] where within this area the enemy will attempt a landing is still problematic. Concentration of enemy air action on the coastal defence between Dunkirk and Dieppe on the Seine-Oise bridges might seem to indicate the strong point of projected landings on a large scale, linked up with a paralysing of the south flank between Rouen and so far as (and including) Paris, and the interdiction of supplies. The elimination of the Seine crossings would however have the same effect on troop movements in the event of a possible enemy attack on the area west of the Seine Estuary, Normandy and the north coast of Brittany. That the "invasion" is actually imminent does not seem to be indicated as yet'.[60]

When this report was circulated, presumably during the course of 6 June, there could have been few of its recipients unaware that the landings had already begun.

REFERENCES

1. Helmuth Greiner and Percy F Schramm, *Kriegstagebuch des Oberkommandos der Wehrmacht* (Frankfurt am Main 1965), Vol III, p 1404.
2. CAB 154/101, Historical Record of Deception in the War against Germany and Italy (Sir Ronald Wingate's Narrative), Vol II, p 196.
3. CAB 81/83, LCS(43) (P) 5 of 23 October; CAB 154/60, LCS(43) I/G2 (8 September to 27 October)
4. CAB 154/101, pp 198–199.
5. Interviews with Col Bevan and others concerned.
6. Gordon A Harrison, *Cross Channel Attack* (Washington DC 1951, in the series US Army in World War II), pp 70–78.
7. WO 205/3, Appendix Y to COSSAC(43) 28 of 20 November. (Para 5 contains the Directive.)
8. ibid.
9. Winston S Churchill, *The Second World War*, Vol V (1952), p 338.
10. CAB 80/77, COS(43) 779 (o) of 24 December.
11. CAB 154/45–47, LCS(44) IF5.
12. H R Trevor-Roper, *Hitler's War Directives 1939–45* (1964), p 149.
13. Interviews with those principally concerned.
14. WO 208/4373, SHAEF(44) 13 of 23 February, Appendix II (also SHAEF(44) 21, Appendix A).
15. ibid, SHAEF(44) 21 of 26 February, Appendix III.
16. CAB 154/101, p 232 et seq.
17. CAB 81/78, LCS(44) 5 and 6 of 14–15 February for Bevan's telegrams from Moscow, LCS(44) 10 of 2 April for Bevan's report. For Russian co-operation see Report of US Military Mission, Moscow, of 19 May in CCS 385 (6–25–43) Section 1 Decimal File 1942–45 (Record Group 218, National Archives of the United States).
18. CAB 81/77. LCS(43) 16 of 8 November.

19. CAB 154/4, 'A' Force War Diary, Vol IV, p 4.
20. Imperial War Museum, MI 14/522/2, Kurze Feind Beurteilung West (KFW) 1060 of 22 October 1943; MI 14/499, KFW 1170 of 9 February 1944.
21. Imperial War Museum, MI 14/522/2, KFW 1060 of 22 October 1943.
22. ibid, KFW 1108 of 9 December 1943.
23. CAB 154/101, pp 203–205.
24. Imperial War Museum, AL 1828/2, OKW/WFSt, 1C file on Allied invasion plans in the Mediterranean, September 1943–July 1944.
25. CAB 154/53. LCS(44)I/F 20, Serials 17A and 18A.
26. Greiner and Schramm, Vol IV, p 83.
27. Imperial War Museum, AL 1828/1.
28. CAB 121/373, SIC file D/France/6/2, COS(44) 126(o) of 3 February (LCS(44)1).
29. CAB 154/101, p 249 et seq.
30. Imperial War Museum, MI 14/499, KFW 1279 of 28 May 1944.
31. ibid, KFW 1276 of 25 May 1944.
32. ibid, Lagebeurteilung West (LBW) 1199 of 9 March 1944.
33. ibid, KFW 1185 of 24 February 1944.
34. ibid, KFW 1210 of 20 March 1944.
35. WO 219/250, Gen F E Morgan memo to G2(int) Division SHAEF, 9 February 1944; SHAEF SGS Security for Operations 380.01/4 (Records of Allied Operational and Occupational HQ in World War II, Record Group 331 in National Archives of the United States); CAB 121/381, SIC file D/France/6/7. OP(44) 2nd Meeting, 9 February.
36. CAB 154/101, pp 236–238.
37. WO 219/2238, Serial 7A.
38. WO 219/317, SHAEF SGS 381 Operation *Ironside* series (also SHAEF SGS 381 Operation *Ironside*, Record Group 331 in National Archives of the United States).
39. The plan is in WO 219/1847; a full account is in CAB 154/4, pp 85–90.
40. Imperial War Museum, AL 1828/2, Report of 30 May 1944.
41. Imperial War Museum, MI 14/499, LBW 1283 of 1 June 1944.
42. CAB 81/78, LCS(44) 11 and 21 of 17 May and 22 July respectively; for full accounts see CAB 154/101, p 239 and CAB 154/4, p 69.
43. CCS 385 (5–19–44) Plan *Royal Flush* (CCS Decimal File 1942–45, Record Group 218, National Archives of the United States).
44. loc cit.
45. Imperial War Museum, MI 14–522–2, KFW 978 of 21 July 1943.
46. L F Ellis, *Victory in the West*, Vol I (1962), pp 159–160.
47. CAB 154/101, p 260.
48. Imperial War Museum, MI 14–499, LBW 1287 of 5 June 1944.
49. ibid, KFW 1231 of 10 April 1944.
50. ibid, KFW 1237 of 16 April 1944.
51. ibid, KFW 1241 of 20 April 1944.
52. CAB 146–332, Enemy Documents Section (EDS) file II/4/iii, item 6.
53. CAB 1466–333, EDS file II/4/iii, item 46.
54. ibid.
55. Imperial War Museum, AL 1634/1, OB West War Diary, 4 May 1944.
56. Imperial War Museum, AL 1634/2, Appendices to Lagebeurteilung West, 8 May 1944; CAB 146/332, item 6.
57. CAB 146/332, item 6.
58. Imperial War Museum, MI 14/499, LBW 1288 of 6 June 1944.
59. Imperial War Museum, AL 1635/1, OB West War Diary, 2 June 1944.
60. Ellis, op cit, Vol I, p 129, quoting Lagebeurteilung West, 5 June 1944; Imperial War Museum, AL 1635–2, Appendices to OB West War Diary.

CHAPTER 7

Zeppelin: The Mediterranean, January–December 1944

IN JANUARY 1944, when the centre of gravity of the Allied Force in the European theatre shifted decisively from the Mediterranean to north-west Europe, the most experienced Allied commanders and their staffs were transferred from the former theatre to the latter to take charge of the forthcoming cross-Channel attack. General Eisenhower and his principal lieutenants, General Bradley of the United States Army, General Montgomery of the British Army and Air Chief Marshal Tedder of the Royal Air Force, all returned to London with the staffs which they had trained and on which they had learned to depend in the Mediterranean theatre; and these naturally included many of the leading figures in 'A' Force.

It will be recalled that throughout 1943 Main HQ of 'A' Force had remained in Cairo under (as he now was) Brigadier Dudley Clarke, with Lieut Col H N Wild acting as his deputy. An Advanced HQ had been established with Allied Force HQ in Algiers under Lieut Col M H Crichton and Col E H Goldbranson (US Army); while a Tactical HQ was established under Lieut Col DI Strangeways with General Alexander's 18th Army Group, moving eventually from north Africa into Italy. At the end of the year Lieut Col Wild returned to London and assumed control, as we have seen, of Ops B at Supreme HQ Allied Expeditionary Force. Lieut Col Strangeways also left to take charge of deception operations at General Montgomery's 21st Army Group. Lieut Col Wild was succeeded in Cairo by Lieut Col Crichton, and Lieut Col Strangeways by Lieut Col S B D Hood, working in close liaison with the operational staff of Alexander's 15th Army Group at Caserta. At the same time a general rationalisation of responsibilities took place in the Mediterranean. With the focussing of the war against Germany on western and central Europe, the Middle East and the Indian Ocean were gradually becoming of less direct importance to the conduct of operations in the European theatre. During the course of 1944, therefore, responsibility for the channels which 'A' Force had established in Persia and Iraq, east Africa and southern Africa was taken over by 'D' Division at South-East Asia Command in Delhi. Within 'A' Force two 'Advanced HQ' were established, that in Algiers and a new one in Cairo; which left Main HQ under Brigadier Clarke free to supervise the entire Mediterranean.[1]

Cairo indeed was no longer the focus of intelligence operations that it had been at the beginning of 1943. We have seen how contact with the *Deuxième Bureau* in Algiers had provided 'A' Force with a new range of channels to the Abwehr through Spain and Vichy France. The occupation of Sicily and southern Italy had increased these yet further. Perhaps the best was a senior officer in the Italian Air Force codenamed *Armour,* who made contact with the Allied intelligence authorities immediately after the fall of Rome. *Armour* moved in the highest social and political circles in Italy and was reported to be a personal friend of Marshal Badoglio himself. The Germans regarded him as their man, and he did indeed provide them with a continuous flow of high-level information. In fact he had been planted on the Abwehr by the Italian intelligence services during the heyday of the Axis, and his cover was never to be blown. Then there was *Apprentice,* a White Russian naturalised Yugoslav. His quite genuine hatred of the Communist Partisans in his own country had gained him the confidence of the German intelligence services, who parachuted him behind the Allied lines in 1944. He promptly surrendered, hoping to join the Royal Yugoslav Air Force for active duties. Instead he was persuaded to accept (notionally) the more humdrum task of teaching Serb to Allied officers, whose indiscreet conversation he duly reported back to his Abwehr control. There were also three employees of the Italian airlines known as *Primo,* who having been recruited and trained by the Abwehr as radio agents, landed behind the Allied lines on the Garigliano in January 1944 and promptly gave themselves up. Altogether about half a dozen good channels were eventually opened up in Italy, although, as we shall see, they took some time to get going. When these were added to such star performers in Algiers as *Gilbert* and *Whiskers* and to the oldest and most successful of them all, *Cheese,* who was still transmitting regularly from Cairo, they provided a highly effective instrument at the disposal of Brigadier Clarke and his colleagues.[2]

The picture of Allied intentions for 1944 which these channels were required to convey we shall consider in a moment. But by far the most important task of 'A' Force, as of all other Allied deception organisations, consisted in their contribution to fixing in the heads and in the files of enemy intelligence the false Order of Battle on which all other deception operations depended for their success. An intrinsic part of this was Operation *Foynes,* which has already been described – the concealment of the return of the seven divisions and their associated landing-craft from the Mediterranean to the United Kingdom. This, as we have seen, was completely successful. Although the Germans knew from their operational intelligence that the units in question had been withdrawn from contact, they assumed, on the basis of agents' reports, that they had not left the Mediterranean theatre, and it was only after some five months, in March 1944, that Fremde Heere West (FHW) was finally satisfied that they had in fact returned to England. At the same time, however, three bogus British divisions, 40th, 42nd and 57th, constituting a bogus XIV Corps, were notionally transferred from the United Kingdom to the Mediterranean and further swelled the already inflated Order of Battle there.[3]

This inflation dated back to the initiation of Operation *Cascade* nearly two years earlier, in March 1942. By January 1944 there already existed, (or, rather, did not exist) in the Mediterranean theatre 18 divisions, two independent brigades, three Corps HQs and one Army HQ; all entirely notional, all accepted by German intelligence as real.[4] In fact there were in the Mediterranean some 44 Allied divisions, including 10 US and 11 French. If all other available units were added in, it could be said that real forces available to the Allies throughout the theatre totalled 52 divisions. The notional Allied strength in the Mediterranean theatre thus totalled some 70 divisions of which about one in four was bogus.

The task given to 'A' Force in February 1944, codenamed *Wantage*, was to increase the proportion of bogus formations from a quarter to a third, in order 'to induce the enemy to believe that sufficient reserves exist both in the eastern and western Mediterranean to undertake large scale invasions of southern Europe'.[5] There were already 23 real divisions in Italy in the British Eighth and US Fifth Armies; to create any bogus units there, given the dubious security of the area, was considered unwise. It was proposed therefore to build up the units outside Italy, which in fact totalled 18 divisions, to a total of 39, of which 24 were notionally available for offensive operations. Twelve of them notionally constituted the British Twelfth Army based on Egypt (5 real and 7 bogus divisions) and twelve an American Seventh Army in Algeria (9 real and 3 bogus divisions, including the French). The strength of the Twelfth Army was faithfully reported by *Cheese* in Cairo, that of the Seventh Army by *Gilbert* and others in Algiers.[6]

All but a very few of these formations were accepted by FHW. Able only intermittently to carry out aerial reconnaissance, the Germans were increasingly independent on agents' reports for all their information about Allied units outside the immediate operational area. And more important even than their miscalculation of available Allied strength was their miscalculation of available shipping. By 1944 the shrewd appraisals which had made their strategic appreciations so realistic the previous year were no longer possible. German naval intelligence had fallen back very largely on guesswork. An appreciation by Seekriegsleitung of 2 March 1944 stated that the Allies should have no difficulty in finding the 7 million tons of shipping needed to mount another invasion in the Mediterranean area.[7] As for the availability of landing-craft, the Germans were, as we have seen already, no longer prepared even to guess.*

---

* See p. 113 above.

It was the notional forces created by the *Wantage* operation that enabled 'A' Force to play its part within the general framework of *Bodyguard*, the overall deception plan for 1944 approved by the three major Allies at Tehran. The 'story' of *Bodyguard*, it will be recalled, was that the western Allies would not be ready to launch an invasion of north-west Europe, if indeed they were able to launch one at all, until the late summer of 1944; and that in consequence the main Allied effort for the year would be directed against the Balkan peninsula. The mounting of this notional threat to the Balkans was primarily the responsibility of 'A' Force, and received the codename *Zeppelin*.

Zeppelin comprised a threat to Crete and the Peloponnese mounted by the notional Twelfth Army in the Middle East, combined with a notional attack across the Adriatic against the Istrian peninsula and the coasts of northern Dalmatia by the (real) US Seventh Army with a Polish Corps under command, operating out of Italy. This had been notionally agreed by the Combined Chiefs of Staff at the conference the previous December; and it had been to control this complex operation, mounted, like the invasion of Sicily, from two widely separated bases, that General Sir Henry Maitland Wilson had been transferred from his appointment as GOC Middle East to succeed General Eisenhower as Supreme Allied Commander, Mediterranean Theatre. The Allied offensives from south-east and west were, finally, to be complimented by an amphibious assault by Soviet forces against the coast of Bulgaria.[8]

Subsidiary to this Balkan threat, but of increasing importance as the year went on, was a notional invasion of the south of France being prepared by French and American forces from Morocco and Algeria. But before going into any further details about this we must consider the deception operations which had actually been in progress in the Mediterranean theatre since those already described in Chapter 5 which took the story up to November 1943.

□

Even before the drafting of *Zeppelin*, 'A' Force had been engaged in a major strategic deception, *Fairlands*, intended to keep as many German forces as possible in the Mediterranean theatre, especially in south-east Europe; and within this overall framework a second plan had been mounted, *Oakfield*, to pin down German forces in north Italy by posing the threat of simultaneous landings on the Ligurian coast in the region of Genoa and the Adriatic coast around Rimini.* At the beginning of 1944 this latter plan was modified to take account, first of the passage of a strong naval task force through the Mediterranean whose ultimate

---

* The tactical dispositions for this deception managed by Lieut Col Hood's Tactical HQ received the codename *Chettyford*.

destination in the Far East it was intended to conceal; and second, of the plans for real landings behind the German lines at Anzio, (Operation *Shingle)* which was being prepared during December 1943 and carried out on 22 January 1944. To cover the all-too-evident preparations for this expedition in the neighbourhood of Naples, the story was put over that an attack was being mounted by General Patton's US Seventh Army which would carry out a pincer movement against north Italy with two forces, one landing at Pisa on the west coast and one at Rimini in the east, to join forces at Bologna and seal off the German forces to the south.[9]

The US Seventh Army was notionally able to field eleven divisions for the attack. Two of the real formations, notionally intended for the Pisa landings, were in fact training near Naples for the Anzio operation. A further two were Polish divisions training in the Middle East who were in fact about to sail to join General Alexander's forces in Italy. The Rimini assault would notionally be covered by the naval task force, consisting of the battleships *Renown, Valiant, Queen Elizabeth* and the fleet carrier *Illustrious,* which passed the Straits of Gibraltar on 5 January and were inspected by German aircraft the following day. The notional target areas of the assault near Pisa and Rimini were reconnoitred by air and from the sea and bombed. Maps and pamphlets were distributed to the assault forces, with details of the local artistic treasures which were if possible to be preserved. In Corsica, which was the notional jumping-off point for the Pisa assault, visual displays were mounted of camps, roads, aircraft, hospital accommodation and assault-craft assembly points. Prolific radio traffic was put out by the skeletal US Seventh Army HQ in Sicily. General Patton himself visited Cairo and indiscreetly allowed himself to be photographed with senior Polish commanders. From *Cheese* and others in Cairo the Abwehr was kept informed of the progress of the operation. Originally intended for 17 January, it was postponed for ten days because of notional repairs to HMS *Illustrious* in Alexandria. On 20 January the Abwehr was told that the *Illustrious* was now ready but that bad weather meant further delays. On 22 January (by which date the Polish formations had docked at Bari and the naval task force had passed through the Canal and was safe in the Gulf of Suez) the firm date for the assault was transmitted: 31 January. The same day the Allies actually landed at Anzio, achieving total surprise.[10]

It would be satisfying to be able to record that this surprise was due to the activities of the deception staffs and the double agents which we have described. Unfortunately there is no evidence from the German side to suggest that these had anything to do with it at all. Thanks to the complete command of the air which the Allies now enjoyed throughout the Mediterranean theatre, German aerial reconnaissance had failed to report either the bogus preparations in Corsica or the genuine ones in the Bay of Naples.[11] The passage through the Mediterranean of the *Illustrious* and its companion vessels was observed and certainly aroused momentary concern at German naval and military headquarters. By 12 January the German Admiralty complained that, for the lack of adequate air reconnaissance, information about the Allied naval force was 'insufficient and confused'. Hitler himself was afraid that the movement might presage increasing pressure on Turkey to enter the war, and ordered a maximum alert throughout the Aegean.[12] By 15 January, however, the German Naval Staff had come to the correct conclusion that the force had passed through the Suez Canal and was now on its way to the Far East.[13] Although the Abwehr Stelle in Paris warned, on 3 January, that General Wilson was contemplating landings on both sides of the Italian peninsula, probably on 15 January, none of the carefully timed and orchestrated messages passed by 'A' Force about the progress and intentions of the naval force appear to have reached German naval or military authorities, and certainly they were not taken seriously if they did. In its situation report of 21 January FHW did indeed note the increase in indications that Polish troops assembling in the Alexandria area would soon move to Italy, but even so it emphasised that reliable evidence for this was still lacking.[14]

Indeed, so far from expecting a pincer operation of the ambitious scope projected by 'A' Force, the Germans did not believe the Allies to have the resources available in Italy even for the limited attack, four divisions strong, which they actually delivered at Anzio. On 6 January Kesselring had informed Jodl when the latter visited his HQ that there were no signs that the Allies intended any landings on 'an operational scale' in the near future, all their available resources being employed in frontal attacks.[15] On 15 January his Chief of Staff, General Westphal, authorised the movement of 3rd Panzer Division from the area of Rome to reinforce the German defences on the Cassino front since 'it is out of the question that we should have to expect large-scale landing operations within the next four to six weeks'.[16] On the eve of the Anzio landings, 21 January, FHW stated firmly that all available Allied formations had been drawn in to the Fifth Army's offensive along the Garigliano, and that though the enemy must realise that central Italy had been denuded of German forces and that deep flank attacks would thus pay him considerable dividends, there were no 'credible indications' that he was planning anything of the kind. A report of 19 January from a 'reliable' Abwehr agent in Rome about a major Allied landing planned for between 20 and 30 January on the Ligurian coast was dismissed at XIV Army HQ as being based purely on local rumours.[17] And at OKW the Intelligence Branch confirmed that German Air Force and naval intelligence also indicated that no large-scale operations were imminent.[18]

The surprise which the Allies achieved at Anzio, and which they so signally failed to exploit, thus owed little to the activities of 'A' Force. It was due primarily to the inability of the Germans to carry out air reconnaissance and to the excellent security, especially radio security, of the Allied forces concerned. The absence of air reconnaissance meant that the visual displays mounted in Corsica and elsewhere were not picked up by enemy intelligence, any more than were those mounted in the United Kingdom for *Fortitude South*. As for the double agents, the signals sent from those in Cairo were lost in the general hubbub of rumour and counter-rumour proliferating in the Near East; while those in Italy were not yet sufficiently established to give much service. *Primo* had arrived only on the eve of the Anzio attack, and neither *Armour* nor *Apprentice* appeared for another four months. The Abwehr indeed, defending its failure to give warning of the attack, had to confess that it had no effective network of agents in south Italy, and was entirely dependent for information on short-range 'line-crossers'.[19] Its incompetence over this issue was to provide additional ammunition for its rivals in the SS and may have contributed to the fall of Canaris a few weeks later.

Nevertheless it cannot be said that the work of 'A' Force was wasted, any more than any form of insurance is wasted. The Allies were very lucky indeed. It would have been highly irresponsible for their planners to assume that the great concourse of shipping marshalled in the Bay of Naples would not be observed even by one German reconnaissance aircraft; and even in retrospect it seems almost incredible that the Abwehr had not succeeded in leaving behind a single reliable agent in Naples capable of giving some indication of what was going on. Had any intelligence of the impending operation reached the Germans, they might had been more alert to the clues which 'A' Force were planting on them. As it turned out, security was so good that deception proved unnecessary.

□

If the Germans were unreceptive to the signals which the Allies were trying to convey to them about their intentions in Italy itself, they were much more credulous about Allied plans for the Mediterranean as a whole. They were under no illusions at any level, from Hitler downwards, about the inevitability of a major assault in North West Europe some time in 1944, but they were prepared to believe that a great deal might happen elsewhere first.

A summary of the War Diary kept at OKW[20] shows that at the beginning of 1944 the German High Command was already uneasy about the number of Allied forces still in north Africa, which were not only available as reinforcements for Italy but might also be used, given the availability of landing craft, for operations against the Ligurian coast of Italy or the Mediterranean coast of France. The south-east theatre was also, in their view, one of increased sensitivity:

'for in the Egyptian-Syrian-Palestinian area the adversary had available a quantity of formations, if as yet little landing capability. A limited landing operation, such as one against Rhodes or the Aegean islands, was always possible for him. The strong enemy air and naval activity in the Aegean had to be taken into consideration. Beyond this, at a later stage an Anglo-Saxon offensive from Italy against the Dalmatian Coast had to be reckoned with, but it was accepted that the enemy would not start on this before a further broadening and strengthening of his base in Italy'.

In addition, the question of Turkey had to be considered in the light of Allied supremacy in the eastern Mediterranean. If Turkey joined the Allies there would be few German forces available to defend Bulgaria. And finally there were Partisans in Yugoslavia, to be reckoned at 100,000 well-organised and equipped men, holding down a 'disproportionately high commitment' of German forces.

The German High Command was thus well prepared at the beginning of 1944 to accept the picture of Allied intentions projected by *Zeppelin*, and its fears were well known to the Allied deception authorities thanks to their Sigint. The German apprehensions were indeed even more widespread than the Allies expected, for early in January OKW suddenly took alarm at the possibility that the Allies might be about to land in Portugal and south-west France;[21] which were in fact almost the only stretches in the coast of western Europe about which the deception authorities were *not* at that time attempting to arouse Germans fears. But the main continuing concern of OKW was the Balkans and the Aegean, as the Allies intended that it should be. The Wehrmachtführungsstab could never quite bring themselves to believe that the Allies did not intend an operation in that theatre. Throughout January the German naval forces in the eastern Mediterranean were reinforced at the expense of those in the west. A directive of 1 January from OKW to Field Marshal von Weichs, Commander-in-Chief South-East, went so far as to warn him that Allied preparations for an attack on north-west Europe were being stressed so heavily that they might be a cover, and 'the impression has now arisen' that the main blow might fall elsewhere; in which case both for political and economic reasons the Balkans was the most likely target. A long assessment by FHW on 5 January came to the conclusion that, on balance, an assault in the west was still the most likely course for the Allies to take; but nevertheless far-reaching arrangements should be made to reinforce the south-east theatre in the event of its coming under attack.[22] A further appreciation, of 19 January, emphasised the need to reinforce the garrisons in the Aegean in the light of 'reliable information' about Allied intentions allegedly communicated to the Turkish government. In any case, FHW stressed, the main Allied attack was likely to be preceded by assaults at several points with all forces available.

The landings at Anzio three days later thus did nothing to reduce apprehensions about the south-east Theatre.[23] Indeed, an FHW situation report on 21 January (the day before the landings took place) warned that a major objective of the Fifth Army's attack might be 'to pin down German forces in Italy and to create favourable conditions for a possible later Balkans operation of limited scope, the first stage of which would be an attack in the Fiume area'.[24] On 27 January the German military command in Greece ordered particular vigilance in the light of the failure of reliable sources to provide warning about either the Sicily or the Salerno or the Anzio landings; while the naval commander in the Aegean, on 8 February, transmitted an order, which was read at Bletchley Park, for all defences to be re-organised in accordance with 'present urgency and in order that as strong forces as possible could be thrown against an Allied landing, whenever it should be made'.

It was no doubt the inherent military probability of an Allied attack in the south-east theatre that led the Germans to devote so much attention to it, rather than the multitude of conflicting messages which reached them through Abwehr and other sources, some of which may have originated with 'A' Force but many of which quite certainly did not. One from Ankara of 19 January, which quoted the Swiss Military Attaché as saying that a Balkan landing was probable in March, the Allies having abandoned an attack on the west as being too dangerous, almost certainly did,[25] as did that from an Abwehr agent in Rome of 31 January reporting from sources in London and Istanbul that the invasion would come not in the west, but through Dalmatia.[26] So, probably, did a diplomatic report from Berne of 18 April, reporting American gossip to the effect that Anglo-American forces were about to land on the Dalmatian coast and that when the Allies finally *did* land in the west, they would probably do so in the south of France. But what is one to think of an Abwehr report of 21 April stating that influential French sources with close connections with Madrid believed that a Russian expeditionary force, escorted by the Italian fleet, would launch an attack early in May against the Dalmatian coast from bases in Egypt and Asia Minor, while simultaneously the western Allies would land on the west coast of France, the Dutch coast and the German shores of the North Sea?[27] Or one from the German Consul in Barcelona of 5 April, who had heard from a Spanish general via a Soviet agent that 150,000 fully armed Allied troops were about to be parachuted into France, from Amiens in the north to Toulouse in the south?[28] At least 'A' Force took care to see that its notional operations were logistically feasible. But all these rumours made enough noise to drown out a bleakly accurate message from Stockholm on 9 May, that no one in London expected any serious operations against the Balkans nor any but the most limited attacks in the Aegean.[29]

Meanwhile 'A' Force HQ in Cairo under Colonel Crichton laboured to sustain the illusion of a British Twelfth Army in the Middle East posied to attack. This force consisted notionally of twelve divisions, and initially its core was constituted by five real divisions and three real, but inflated, brigades. But during the months of February and

March the requirements of the Italian campaign siphoned off three of these divisions, which had to be replaced by bogus ones; so by April the real core of the 'Army' consisted only of two divisions and three brigades, none of them in any condition to take the field. Moreover within these units the operational staffs were, in the eyes of 'A' Force at least, beginning to show a marked lack of enthusiasm for deception activities from which they were not going to benefit, and a consequent reluctance to put themselves out in implementing 'A' Force's plans. The Supreme Allied Commander in the Mediterranean, General Sir Henry Maitland Wilson, therefore found it necessary to issue, on 3 April 1944, a stern directive to his old command at GHQ Middle East laying down 'the main role of Middle East – second only to preserving security in the area – as being to simulate greatest possible threat to Balkans from now until the end of June ... considerations of economy and administrative convenience should give way to this overriding need'.[30]

Colonel Crichton and his colleagues implemented their deception by means at which they had become very adept over the past two years. They filled their 'channels' with comprehensive misinformation. They arranged for manoeuvres by real armoured forces within a convenient distance of the Turko-Syrian frontier, and for combined operations training in Egyptian ports, largely by Greek forces. Near Tobruk and other Libyan ports they mounted large visual displays of camps and airfields (crowded with dummy aircraft and gliders and defended by real AA units) while in the harbours dummy landing-craft were discreetly displayed; and they filled the ether with the appropriate radio traffic.[31]

Thanks, once more, to the weakness of the German Air Force and the vigilance of the RAF, these displays were of limited effectiveness.* During the early months of 1944 the German High Command was guided in its appreciation of Allied intentions in the Middle East by considerations largely outside 'A' Force's control. Not least among them was the cooling of Allied relations with Turkey, who was making increasingly clear her reluctance to enter the war on the side of the Allies as had been the hope, if not the expectation, of the British High Command throughout 1943. As the threat of German invasion dwindled, so did Turkish need for Allied support and her consequent willingness to hold out hopes of actively participating in the war. Unfortunately

---

* Though when a German reconnaissance aircraft did penetrate to the eastern Mediterranean the result was not always that expected. On 11 February 1944 Bletchley read a report from Kesselring's HQ that an air reconnaissance of Alexandria harbour on 23 January had revealed *no* landing craft, and there was unlikely to be sufficient in the Mediterranean to mount another attack on the scale of the Anzio landings for some time to come. On the other hand the German Admiralty concluded after a reconnaissance of Anzio harbour, on 30 January, that the Allies were not employing all the special craft available to them, and there might be others withheld for some special purpose, possibly landings in the Aegean.

during this period the Germans were particularly well informed about Anglo-Turkish relations thanks to the free access which their agent CICERO* briefly enjoyed to the confidential papers of the British Ambassador in Ankara – a source which also confirmed German expectations that the main Allied blow in 1944 would be struck, not in the Balkans, but in the west.[32] On 28 February a FHW appreciation concluded that the withdrawal of Turkish support would lead the Allies to abandon their intentions in the eastern Mediterranean 'at least for the time being'; while in early March Field Marshal von Weichs informed OKW that the failure of the British to persuade Turkey to enter the war had brought about a considerable decrease of tension in the Balkans. Without Turkish support he thought it unlikely that the Allies would mount an offensive against Thrace or northern Greece via the Aegean. Rather, he considered, they would leave it to the Partisans to pin down German forces in the Balkans, and would otherwise leave the area to itself.[33]

On this assumption OKW had already, on 13 February, ordered von Weichs to select two divisions from the south-east theatre for transfer to Italy or France,[34] when another event occurred, also beyond the control of 'A' Force, to focus attention on south-east Europe; something considerably more serious than anything the British could either really or notionally threaten. This was the opening of the major Soviet offensive on the southern part of the eastern front on 4 March, which, before it was brought to a standstill by the spring thaws in mid-April, was to steam-roller its way through the two German Army Groups defending the Ukraine and bring the war to the frontiers of Hungary and Romania. So seriously was this taken at OKW that not only was von Weichs ordered to transfer five divisions to the eastern front, but von Rundstedt himself was stripped of three divisions, two of them armoured, just at the moment when *Overlord* was becoming operationally feasible. To safeguard their lines of communication, the Germans occupied Hungary on 19 March, much as they had occupied Italy six months earlier; a move which forced von Weichs to thin out his forces in Yugoslavia, thus enabling Tito to launch, on 21 March, a particularly well-timed offensive from Visegrad into Serbia. If the British had really been capable of mounting an attack on the Balkan peninsula, now would have been the moment to do it. But they did not, and the Germans did not expect that they would. On 11 March FHW expressed the absolutely accurate view that, although minor forays must be expected on the Dalmatian coast and elsewhere, the eastern Mediterranean was now simply a reservoir from which the Allies would draw forces for operations elsewhere in the theatre.[35]

---

* CICERO is also dealt with in F. H. Hinsley and C. A. G. Simkins, *British Intelligence in the Second World War: Volume 4: Security and Counter-Intelligence* (1990), Chapter XII.

By the end of March 'A' Force was well aware of its lack of impact on the German south-east theatre; hence the directive from the Supreme Allied Commander, quoted above, insisting on the high priority which must be given to deception in the Middle East. In April the situation improved, though how far this was the result of 'A' Force's activities it is impossible to say. In a major appreciation of the overall German position issued on 7 April, Jodl did not discount the possibility of an Allied attack on Greece, and considered the strategic problems which the Germans would face if the Allies did succeed in establishing themselves along a line from Corfu to Olympia. In appreciations dated 12 and 27 April FHW stated that limited Allied operations against Albania, western Greece and the Aegean islands were quite probable; the more so when on 21 April Turkey, in a major shift of her position, prohibited all further exports of chrome to Germany.[36]

By the beginning of May, indeed, OKW was becoming seriously alarmed. On 5 May General Warlimont of the Wehrmachtführungsstab drew up an appreciation which stated that reports from 'unquestionable' (*einwandfrei*) sources confirmed that the Allies were preparing an assault on the Balkan peninsula from Egypt and Libya.[37] He made the interesting point, which was now occurring increasingly in German intelligence appreciations, that sensitivity about Soviet interests in the Balkans was likely to limit the scope of these landings to the southern part of the peninsula; Greece, Albania and the Ionian islands. But even within these limits, he warned, Allied successes could have grave implications. They would encourage the Partisans; they might bring about Turkey's entry into the war and Bulgaria's exit from it, they would threaten German communications with their garrisons in the Aegean islands and Crete; and they would provide additional bases from which the Allied Air Forces could attack the economic resources in the region – chrome, bauxite, above all oil – on which the German war economy depended. For these operations, he reckoned, the Allies had available in Egypt and Libya six infantry and three armoured divisions, with further miscellaneous units amounting to some five further divisions; five of which formations (three infantry and two armoured) were ready for immediate action.

These latter figures were derived from FHW appreciations, which on 8 May had referred to the 'build-up' of British forces in Egypt as being of 'mounting significance'.[38] Hitler himself, in the course of a conference with his naval chiefs between 4 and 6 May, referred to 'the proven presence of battle-strength enemy divisions in Egypt'.[38] The Führer considered that this might presage an operation against the Rhodes-Crete-Peloponnese area, and this view seems to have been widely held in the German High Command. Warlimont expressed the view, in the document referred to above, that so long as sufficient air support could be found, von Weichs had sufficient resources to deal with such an attack. He disposed of three mobile divisions in addition to his garrison forces, and OKW could if necessary find for him another two and a half. Von Weichs himself was still more confident. Even with their available forces, he believed, the Allies would regard any attack on the mainland as too dangerous. At most they might try to capture single islands in the Ionians. But he did not question, any more than had Hitler himself, the official OKW assessment of Allied forces in Egypt and Libya: about fourteen divisions, five of them ready for action.

Considering that by now the real Allied forces in this theatre were reduced to three divisions, none of them in any condition to take the field, 'A' Force thus had every cause to congratulate itself. Not only was the Allied order of battle which it had been projecting for so many months now firmly lodged in the German files; the threat to the south part of the Balkan peninsula which *Zeppelin* had required it to mount was no less firmly, on the eve of *Overlord*, lodged in the German mind. It was a most useful addition to the real threats from the Russians in the north and from Tito's increasingly confident Partisans whose activities were proliferating like a terminal cancer through Yugoslavia, and which now compelled OKW to lock up some 22 divisions in their south-east theatre.

By this time however the focus of attention, both Allied and enemy, had shifted from the eastern end of the Mediterranean to the west.

□

It had always been an intrinsic element of Allied planning for the invasion of north-west France, and indeed in German expectations of Allied plans,[40] that the German forces in the south of France should be pinned down by the threat or the reality of an attack on the French Mediterranean coast. It had indeed been only on this condition that the Americans had consented, at the meetings of the Combined Chiefs of Staffs in 1943, at Quebec in August and Tehran-Cairo in November-December, to the continuation of the operations in the Mediterranean for which they had always felt an instinctive aversion. It had been agreed at Tehran that an attack on the French Mediterranean shores, codenamed (appropriately but with appalling lack of security) *Anvil* should be mounted on 1 May 1944, simultaneously with the *Overlord* landings in Normandy. But the stubbornness of German resistance in Italy, the decision to mount the Anzio landings and the shortage of landing-craft that bedevilled all Allied strategic planning destroyed the original simplicity of these plans. The *Overlord* landings had to be postponed for a month, the *Anvil* landings still longer – until August, in fact, by which time the original codename had lost all point and the operation was renamed *Dragoon*.

The creation of a threat in the south sufficient to pin down the German forces in that region (Army Group G, commanded by General von Blaskowitz under the supreme command of von Rundstedt as Commander-in-Chief West) thus became the sole responsibility of 'A' Force. There was a striking parallel with the course of events in 1943, when the inability of the Allies to mount the limited cross-Channel attack prescribed at the Casablanca conference left the responsibility for mounting such a threat entirely in the hands of Ops B at COSSAC and the London Controlling Section. But whereas Colonel Bevan and his colleagues had had to do this with minimal experience and resources, Colonel Clarke and 'A' Force had an entire Army staff at their disposal, and the full support of General Maitland Wilson's Allied Force HQ in Algiers.

They also enjoyed good fortune in another direction. In February and March 1944 the Spanish government, under increasing pressure from the Allies and now convinced that Germany could not win the war, was moving against the German intelligence network both in Spain and Spanish Morocco. Carefully trained and experienced German agents were sent home, their place being filled by hurriedly recruited and inexperienced nationals. On 4 April, for example, Bletchley Park circulated a report by agents in Spanish Morocco, to the effect that 'a large east-bound convoy escorted by 2 aircraft carriers, 3 battleships, 7 cruisers, 25 destroyers and 2 submarines, which had been ascertained beyond doubt', had entered the Mediterranean. The German Air Force could find no trace of this vast and mythical force. With reporting of this quality, the Germans were in no position to scrutinise very carefully the stories which were planted on them. On the other hand it must have done much to erode such credibility as the Abwehr still enjoyed with the German military staffs.

The strategic task laid down for 'A' Force under the overall plan, *Zeppelin*, was to keep German reserves away from the Normandy battlefields until D + 25; that is, until the beginning of July.[41] Specifically 'A' Force was required to ensure that the threat to the south of France should 'reach its peak on D − 5 and be held to the maximum pitch for as long as possible'. It was therefore decided that the mounting of the notional attack should start on 10 May, for its D-Day on 19 June. The background 'story' put across by 'Special Means' was that operations against Crete and the Peloponnese had now been abandoned. The political disturbances which had broken out among the Greek forces in Egypt in April and which, it was assumed, could not be kept secret, provided a useful reason for doing so. General Maitland Wilson, it was asserted, had therefore decided to concentrate his resources on the western Mediterranean, and during a (factual) visit which he had paid to London at the end of April he had received the approval of the Chiefs of Staff for his new plans. The build-up began immediately on his return. The implementation of this deception received the codename *Vendetta*.

The operation notionally consisted of an assault by Seventh US

Army (now based on Algiers and commanded, in succession to Lieut General Patton, by Lieut General A M Patch) against the French coast in the region of Narbonne, with the object of exploiting inland as far as Toulouse.[42] It was an area conveniently distant from the area between Toulon and Nice which was actually due to be attacked in August, and conveniently close to the frontiers of Spain where deceptive rumours could so easily be floated. Notionally Seventh Army had twelve divisions at its disposal – three American, three British and six French, allocated between three Army Corps. Factually, it had only three French divisions, one of them based on Corsica, and one American, the 91st, a brigade of which had in fact to be sent to Italy in the middle of the deception. The French provided two Army Corps HQ, only one of which was real. The US Corps HQ was bogus. All preparations were made on the assumption that the operation would really take place, and only General Patch and the Commander-in-Chief of the French forces, General de Lattre de Tassigny, together with their immediate staffs, knew that it would not.

Of the forces involved, two out of the three Corps HQ and nine of the twelve divisions were thus wholly or entirely notional. The gap between the appearance and the reality of naval forces and landing-craft being even greater, huge activity had to be simulated at the three ports designated for assembly; Oran, Ferryville and Bone. In north Africa, 10,000 tons of stores for the assault forces were packaged, labelled, waterproofed and stored. Vehicles were waterproofed and prominently displayed. Dummy craft were floated at Bone and Ferryville. Landing exercises were carried out at Oran. Smoke screens were laid over all three ports, and between 9 and 11 June, a massive amphibious exercise was held. 13,000 men and 2,000 vehicles were actually embarked from Oran and taken to sea for three days. Sixty naval vessels participated, including 25 destroyers, 30 cargo vessels, 14 large transports with appropriate escorts and two aircraft carriers, *Victorious* and *Indomitable,* which were passing through the theatre on the way to the Far East. Radio traffic was intense. Meanwhile fighter aircraft attacked targets around Sète, and heavy bombers raided deep into the Rhone Valley. The Spanish government, as described in Chapter 6 above* was approached and asked for Red Cross facilities to enable casualties from the operation to be evacuated. Aerial photographs and maps of the threatened region were distributed to the real units involved, and directives were prepared for occupation authorities covering such matters as public health, education, political surveillance and the protection of monuments and works of art.† Finally, the frontiers with Spanish Morocco and Tangier were

---

* See p 127.

† Although these were set up in type, they were not printed or distributed. It was felt that the issues they dealt with were too sensitive for them to become generally known in the heated political atmosphere of Algiers.

closed from 11 June until 6 July, and cypher and diplomatic bag facilities were withdrawn from neutral diplomats, as they had been in the United Kingdom during the weeks preceding the *Overlord* landings; which it will be recalled, had by now taken place, on 6 June.[43]

Although *Vendetta* was intended to maintain its threat into July, circumstances made this impossible. Not only did the two aircraft carriers have to continue their voyage to the Far East, but one of the real formations involved, 9th French Colonial Division, had to be used on 18 June for the invasion of Elba. So on 24 June 'A' Force began to put across the message via 'Special Means' that the attack had been postponed. The Allies, it said, had decided that surprise had been lost. Reconnaissance had revealed German formations to be still in position in southern France, instead of moving north to deal with the Normandy landings. General Maitland Wilson had decided therefore to hold his hand until there was evidence that the defences *were* being substantially thinned out. Factually, General Patch with the rest of 91st US division (still combat loaded) sailed to Italy, where they came under command of the US Fifth Army.

German sources reveal that Operation *Vendetta* itself was only a partial success. Expectations of an attack on the Riviera coast had waxed and waned since the beginning of the year – hardly a day, and certainly not a week, passed without the Abwehr receiving some report of its imminence – and the success first of *Cascade* and then of *Wantage* in misleading the German staffs as to the strength of Allied forces available made it impossible for them to discount it altogether. Any such operation was seen by OKW, quite rightly, as being subsidiary to *Overlord* and intended to distract German forces and attention from the primary front in north west Europe.[44] But the strength of Allied forces in French north Africa was estimated in a FHW memorandum on 16 February at 9–10 infantry divisions (2 British, 4 American, 3–4 French, of which one might be in Corsica), and 5–6 armoured divisions (1 American, 4 French, 1–2 British) in various stages of combat readiness. This assessment[45] went on to suggest that the absence of shipping in such east Mediterranean ports as it had been possible to reconnoitre indicated that the bulk of it must be concentrated in the western basin; while Allied air attacks on communications between the south of France and north Italy, it suggested, also presaged an offensive in the former area. It was assumed, mistakenly, that forces in Algeria and north Africa were still under the command of General Eisenhower, and would therefore be used for operations in connection with *Overlord*, rather than with the Italian campaign. Allied threats against the Balkans, this appreciation concluded, were deception measures designed to hold back German forces from the west, where the true decision lay. This judgement was sufficiently convincing to persuade OKW to reinforce Nineteenth Army which defended the south of France with two further infantry divisions and to order 9th SS Panzer Division to move south from

Amiens to Avignon as a mobile reserve.[46]

Although reports continued to flow into the Abwehr of Allied military preparations in French north Africa, German air reconnaissance in early March revealed the agents' and other reports of major shipping concentrations in Oran and Algiers harbours to be without foundation, and an Abwehr report of 14 March, after a very full analysis of the whole Allied shipping and air dispositions in the Mediterranean, drew the conclusion that a major landing in the south of France was neither being prepared nor was at all likely; not at least until the attack had been launched across the Channel or there had been a major success in Italy.[47] This was accepted at FHW where it was noted on 28 March that the shipping available for landing purposes in the Mediterranean had dropped by up to 50 per cent since its peak in 1943, and finally accepted that the *Foynes* divisions had left the theatre and were now in the United Kingdom.[48] In a message dated 9 March distributed by Bletchley Park the Japanese Military Attaché informed Tokyo that the German command in Italy now expected further landings behind its own front, but none in the south of France.

Nonetheless this lull was temporary. When an Abwehr agent reported on 18 March that British and American air units were being deployed with a view to ultimate operations against the south of France, this deployment to be completed by mid-April, the message was annotated by Krummacher: 'Message confirms our view. Knowledge of the *terminus* of the preparations is stated for the first time!'. In April FHW continued to warn of the Allied build up in Algeria. On 2 April the German Naval Attaché in Madrid reported that the American Attaché had told his Finnish colleagues there, *nach reichlichem Alcoholgenuss*, that strong French and American units would shortly be mounting a major operation from Corsica and Sardinia. FHW however dismissed this as 'inherently inaccurate' as there were not adequate shipping and port facilities in the islands; but an operation from north Africa it considered quite likely. The Sète-Narbonne area does not seem to have been registered as the area particularly under threat: Genoa, Nice, Cannes and Marseilles all figure much more prominently in German intelligence reports of this period.[49]

At the end of May FHW drew attention to the signs of increasing activity in north Africa ports and, ironically enough, suggested that the notional visit of Field Marshal Montgomery to north Africa, intended to distract attention from the imminent landings in Normandy, (Operation *Copperhead*)* might foreshadow operations against the south of France. Then in the first week in June reports started streaming in, from the agents and from neutral capitals, about the build-up of the US Seventh Army in its embarkation ports. On 10 June the German

---

* See p 125 above.

embassy in Madrid reported the Allied request to the Spanish government for Red Cross facilities, adding cautiously 'this may be only a deception manoeuvre'. Jodl minuted the report 'I hold this to be a subtle deception which still leaves a landing in Italy possible'; and another hand, possibly Warlimont's, had underlined the words 'deception manoeuvre' (*Täuschungsmanöver*) and added 'Yes, I think so too' (*Ja, glaube ich auch*).[50] So much for Operation *Royal Flush*! Indeed it can almost be said that 'A' Force had overreached itself. On 19 June FHW warned that 'the present wealth of alarming reports' was undoubtedly fostered by the enemy 'with intent to deceive'. German naval intelligence, in spite of all the Allies could do in the way of display and deception, had expressed the view on 9 June that seaborne operations on a strategic scale were not imminent.[51] While taking note of the Allied activity between 9 and 11 June, FHW advised that, although the enemy had between 14 and 16 divisions available for operations from French north Africa, he had only enough landing craft to lift a third of that number.[52]

It cannot be said, therefore, that Operation *Vendetta* itself made as much impact on German expectations as had been intended. During the first critical weeks after the Normandy landings an Allied attack on the south of France was *not* regarded as imminent. But that was not important. What mattered was that von Rundstedt had made all necessary preparations to receive it if it came. On 6 June, D-day for the Normandy landings, Army Group G was deploying ten divisions, including two panzer divisions, to protect the southern coasts of France. Not until mid-June was one panzer division, 2nd SS, moved north to take part in the operations in Normandy, and no other units were moved until July. German forces in the south of France were thus very effectively contained.

☐

Vendetta was complemented at the other end of the Mediterranean by Operation *Turpitude*. This was intended to maintain German anxiety about the mainland of Greece and the Balkan peninsula. The 'story' was that General Maitland Wilson, during his visit to London during the first week in May, had made final arrangements for an amphibious assault against Salonica, to be followed by a thrust up the Struma valley to link up with Russian forces which would simultaneously be landing at Varna. In preparation for the attack on Salonica, facilities were to be established in Turkey and a preliminary assault would be launched against Rhodes. For all this a considerable force was being built up in the north of Syria. The Royal Air Force mounted a major effort with signals deception, dummy aircraft on airfields and reconnaissance flights. The Navy simulated activity in the harbours of Lattakia and Tripoli, while in both of these harbours and that of Aleppo an elaborate apparatus of searchlights, A A batteries and smoke screens was built up. The Ninth Army, a skeletal formation administering the scattered British units stationed in Syria, mounted displays of force near the Turkish frontier with the (real) 31st Indian Armoured Division and two regiments of Yeomanry, backed up by such bogus formations as the '20th Armoured Division'. The nucleus of this 'division' was provided by 24th Armoured Brigade; the collection of dummy tanks which had been in almost continuous action since Colonel Vivian Jones had first deployed them, or their predecessors, in the Western Desert in 1941. And the appropriate rumours were floated in every port and city in the Levant, from Ankara to Cairo.[53]

All this activity built up gradually at the end of May and continued almost till the end of June. There can be no doubt about its local impact. The British Military Attaché in Ankara reported on 15 June that 'The Turkish consuls at Damascus and Aleppo have sent in the most panicky reports and the excitement had communicated itself to the Turkish 17th Corps at Maras. Iskenderun (Alexandretta) this week had been full of the wildest rumours'. The Turkish General Staff made polite enquiries about the troop movements – on which it showed itself gratifyingly well-informed – to be told that these were simply 'special exercises'.[54] On 10 June von Papen, the German Ambassador in Ankara, reported that the Turkish government was very alarmed in case the imminent Allied operations against the Dodecanese failed to respect Turkish neutrality; and the following day he transmitted a bundle of reports of enemy preparations for attack: air and naval concentrations in Cyprus, concentrations of assault craft in Middle East harbours, Indian and Canadian units moving up from Egypt, Italian warships working up in Haifa, and an English hospital ship at Beirut.[55]

Papen's report was received at OKW with professional scepticism. The intelligence staff minuted that they had received no reports of concentrations of aircraft on Cyprus; that Turkish shipping circles had informed them about the naval concentrations but that lack of air reconnaissance made it impossible to verify them and that they did not in any case exceed what was naturally expected; that the movement of Indian troops was confined to the reinforcement of existing units; and that they knew all about the Canadians. Nevertheless on 8 June OKW had already issued the warning that 'clear indications of imminent operations in the eastern Mediterranean demand quite exceptional vigilance';[56] and other branches of the German intelligence organisation were equally credulous. On 26 May the situation report of the Seekriegsleitung stated that all indications from Egypt suggested a forthcoming major operation against the Aegean and Turkey. Two days later, a little naively, FHW reported that 'The enquiries by the English Command in Cairo for Bulgarian and Russian interpreters point to the enemy's intentions in the Aegean'.[57] A week later, on 1 June, FHW swallowed some further bait. 'The seconding of Yugoslav officers to the English Corps likely to be involved, III and XVI', it reported 'together with underground preparations in Greece for the taking of control by Englishmen confirms the expected strategy in the Balkans'.[58] The attack continued to be expected throughout June. Even when, on 13 July, FHW reported that the British forces on the Turko-Syrian frontier were being withdrawn, 'after carrying out exercises, including landings', it merely noted that 'this underlines our previous viewpoint, that these forces are intended for committal in the Aegean and Grecian areas and not with reference to Turkey ... Russia will on no account be willing that Anglo-American forces should gain a firm foothold on Turkish territory'.[59] Not until the end of July did FHW venture the opinion that 'a large-scale operation against the Balkans is only now probable after developments in the west Mediterranean'.[60]

Field Marshal von Weichs himself, Commander-in-Chief South-East, was less impressed. On 21 June, when *Turpitude* was at its height, he reported to OKW that he did not expect any immediate operations in the Aegean region, while any frontal attack against the defensive ring of Crete and Rhodes was even less likely. At worst he expected strictly limited attacks in the region of Albania and north-west Greece. His main concern thus remained the activities of the Partisans in Yugo-slavia, and he was prepared to deal with the unlikely eventuality of an Allied assault with such limited forces as he had available.[61] To that extent the result of 'A' Force's efforts were disappointing. They did not affect the disposition of enemy troops in the south-east theatre. At best it can be said that they discouraged any inclination OKW may have had to thin out von Weichs' defences and use his forces elsewhere.

But this had, after all, been the object of the deception operations in the Mediterranean both west and east: to pin down German forces in the area until the objectives of *Overlord* were accomplished and Allied forces were securely established in north-west France. On 26 June there-fore General Maitland Wilson was able to despatch to London the following message:[62]

'As a result of the campaign in Italy and other Mediterranean operations in support of *Overlord* of which plan *Zeppelin* forms part, it can be said that:
a. The number of German divisions in the Mediterranean theatre today is the same as in early February.
b. No divisions moved from the Mediterranean theatre to north-west Europe during the preparation period of *Overlord*.
c. So far as is known to date, only one division has moved from the Mediterra-nean theatre towards the *Overlord* area; and none arrived in time to influence the battle during the 'critical' period defined by SHAEF.
d. Finally, captured documents prove that immediately before *Overlord* the German High Command estimated some thirty offensive divisions to be still uncommitted in the Mediterranean theatre'.

'A' Force in fact may have fallen short of the ambitious goals it had set itself, but it had done all that had been expected of it by the Combined Chiefs of Staff.

□

Zeppelin came to a formal end on 6 July and the planners at AFHQ, both of the operational and of the deception staffs, hoped now to turn their attention to preparations for the real landings of the US Seventh Army in the south of France; Operation *Anvil*, or rather *Dragoon*, which was now due to take place on 15 August. For this it was necessary that the German fears of such a landing which had been aroused by Operation *Vendetta* should be appeased. At the same time General Alexander, whose forces had by now taken Rome and were fighting their way north towards the Gothic line between Pisa and Rimini, asked 'A' Force to include in their plans a notional landing in the Gulf of Genoa, to draw German forces away from the centre of Italy where he was planning his main thrust to break through the German defences. To complicate matters further General Eisenhower, while appreciating the need to lull the German garrisons on the French Riviera into a state of false security, was anxious that they should not feel so secure that von Rundstedt could use them to reinforce the defence of Normandy.[63]

These largely conflicting requirements made the planning of Operation *Ferdinand*, the cover plan for *Dragoon*, an exceptionally complex affair. The real operation was to consist of a landing by the Franco-American Seventh Army between Toulon and Nice on 15 August. The story for the cover operation was that the Allies having failed to make the Germans weaken their forces in the south of France, had now abandoned all their intentions in that area. Instead they had decided to concentrate their resources on the Italian theatre – a course of action which was in fact being powerfully urged both by Churchill and by Alexander and combatted with great difficulty by the Combined Chiefs of Staff. On 2 July General Maitland Wilson, as Supreme Allied Commander in the Mediterranean, notionally received a new directive, instructing him to concentrate all his forces on Italy. Instead of landing in the south of France, there was now to be an Allied attack, under Eisenhower's direction, on the Biscay coast of western France. An amphibious landing at Genoa, together with another from the Adriatic at Rimini, would enable Alexander to out-flank the Gothic line. The Seventh Army was notionally allocated to Alexander as a reserve. Finally in the Middle East the British Twelve and Ninth Armies (the first wholly notional, the second consisting mainly of administrative units) were 'to be held in reserve to take advantage of any German weakening in the Balkans, and to exploit through Turkey any favourable situation created by a Russian entry into Bulgaria from the Black Sea'.[64]

Such was Operation *Ferdinand* in outline. In detail, VI Corps of US

Seventh Army, now factually based in the region of Naples, was notionally earmarked for the assault on Genoa, while French II Corps of the same Army, together with a notional US XXXI Corps, was notionally assigned to Alexander as a *masse de manoeuvre* to exploit any breach in the Gothic line. All this was geared in to Alexander's own tactical deception plan, *Ottrington*, of which more will be said below. It was hoped that this would focus German attention on Italy in general, and the Genoa area in particular; but neither Wilson nor Eisenhower felt that it would do enough to contain the reserves in the German Army Group G in central France, which would still be available to move either south against the *Anvil* landings, when they came in August, or north to take part in the Normandy battles. Hence the idea of a threat to the Biscay coast, codenamed *Ironside II*.[65]

This suggestion was examined by the London Controlling Section in early July. Its report was highly critical. The French Biscay coast was already so lightly held, it pointed out, that no forces of any consequence would be pinned down by a threat to it. The German forces on the Mediterranean were already so tightly stretched that none were likely to be disengaged from there to deal with any such threat; and there was no longer any serious uncommitted reserve to be mopped up. It would also be difficult to mount any operationally plausible threat to an area whose marshy coasts were so unsuitable for largescale landing.[66]

All this was conveyed to Wilson, who nevertheless urged, on 19 July, that 'it is felt that the assistance this threat might give will more than justify the effort involved'.[67] With some reluctance therefore Colonel Wild's staff at SHAEF devised a story. Sufficient aid, according to this scenario, was to be sent by sea and air to the Resistance forces in south-west France to enable them to take control of the region for long enough to enable a seaborne force mounted in the United States to sail into the ports of Bayonne and Bordeaux. The story was implemented only by 'Special Means' and diplomatic rumours – the British embassy in Madrid raised with the Spanish government the hypothetical question of what would happen if German forces crossed the frontiers to seek sanctuary – together with some intensification of naval activity in the area and an increase in the quantity of aid delivered to Resistance units. No one in London thought that this would have much effect, and no evidence has become available that it did. Early in July, in fact, two German divisions were transferred from the Biscay coast to the region around Sète and Narbonne which had previously been threatened by the *Vendetta* deception. The largely static divisions in the *Dragoon* area east of Toulon remained where they were; while the single mobile reserve at the disposition of Army Group G, 9th Panzer Division (replaced early in August by the 11th Panzer Division) remained in Avignon, available to repel a Mediterranean rather than a Biscayan attack.[68]

The German reaction to *Ferdinand* itself, however, was highly satisfactory. The Genoa-Leghorn area was, as the British knew from Sigint, a sensitive spot with Hitler himself. As a result of orders which he gave on 11 June, additional formations were already being drafted into the region and Kesselring had thickened up its defences – employing there, together with reliable German divisions, four divisions of Mussolini's Italian forces, commanded by Marshal Graziani and dignified with the title 'the Army of Liguria'.[69] But until mid-July FHW did not itself register any special concern. On 8 July it reported that 'the possibility of several landing operations both in Genoa and in the Marseilles area as well as in the Albanian area is confirmed as regards *strength in manpower*, but there is nowhere any sign that he has the necessary landing-craft shipping space'.[70] And as late as 17 July FHW commented, on a report of Allied reconnaissance of the Toulon area, 'this agreed with the supposition of this branch, that looks upon the coastal region between St Raphael and Hyères as the most endangered sector';[71] which, regrettably, it actually was.

But within a few days this shrewd assessment was to be badly shaken by a message from a double agent. Which agent it has not been possible, at present, to discover; it may have been *Gilbert* from Algiers, or it may have been *Armour* from Italy. FHW referred to him as 'a source which up till now has proved particularly reliable' and summarised his message, briefly on 21 July and at greater length two days later.[72]

'In conversation held a short while ago between the US Secretary for War Mr Stimson, the Commander-in-Chief Middle East General Wilson,* the GOC of Seventh Army, General Patton,* and General Alexander, the decision was made to take advantage of the successes on the Italian front and make Italy the Schwerpunkt of operations while postponing operations against the south of France.'

FHW noted the evidence in favour of this view: the transference of the remaining British forces from north Africa to Italy, and the reinforcement of French troops in Italy from the same source. On the other hand it noted the increasing number of freighters in the western Mediterranean; the presence of strong naval forces, including four escort carriers, in the Algiers-Oran area;[73] and the fact that all French forces were apparently being withdrawn from the Italian front. It was open to question, therefore, 'whether the reports from the said source are not to be looked on as deception propaganda intended to direct the German attention exclusively to the Italian front area. Consequently in order to avoid surprises a special intensification of our reconnaissance activity in the north Africa region seems to be required'.

In spite of these doubts, OKW was sufficiently convinced by the

---

* sic. Wilson was now Supreme Allied Commander in the Mediterranean and the GOC Seventh Army was General Patch. In view of the importance which the Germans attached to Patton's role in north-west Europe, this could be a transcription error.

information coming in to issue, on 24 July, a new directive to Kesselring and to von Weichs.[74] This raised the possibility that the Allies had now given up the idea of attacking the south of France and would instead seek a major victory in Italy. Once they had occupied Leghorn and Ancona, the possibility of further landings in rear of the Appenine positions, in order to break into the Po basin, would have to be taken into account. In the Balkans, strong Partisan activities might tie down German forces and make it possible for Polish and other Slav units to effect landings. So Istria, at the head of the Adriatic, must be strongly held, and von Weichs must take precautions against landings in Albania and north-west Greece. Kesselring was to watch out for a landing in his rear either in the Gulf of Genoa or on the Venetian coast and the Istrian peninsula.

By the beginning of August German attention had thus been very effectively focussed on Italy, as 'A' Force had intended. But the preparations for a landing on the scale of *Dragoon* could not be concealed, and indeed on 29 July FHW reported that 'the necessary prerequisites as to manpower and shipping space as well as the required concentration of aircraft for a large-scale landing operation in the western Mediterranean can be said to be now fulfilled. The imminent launching of such an operation is indicated by the sailing of 4 AA Cruisers to Gibraltar. Since we have no definite information as to their destination, a landing must be expected either near Genoa or in southern France'.[75]

FHW was thus still hedging its bets, but during the first week in August it gradually made up its mind that the landings really were going to come in the Genoa sector. On 4 August it reported that all information that it had received about troop movements (including the transfer of the notional British XIV Corps from north Africa to Italy) confirmed the messages it was receiving from agents about the Allied decision to postpone the landings in the south of France. 'Although a leap across to south France from the Naples area is at any time possible, yet in summing up we have to state that in weighing up the enemy's possible moves in the western Mediterranean on the basis of the information at our disposal *a landing in the area of Genoa* appears more likely to us than a south of France operation'.[76] And on 7 August, noting the invasion build-up which aerial reconnaissance had revealed in such ports as Oran, Ajaccio and Naples, FHW pronounced 'these to be, in our judgements, a further indication of the plan to land in Genoa, since the employment of Clark's [Fifth Army] in the Italian area seems more likely than in the south of France'.[77]

The actual landings took place on the coast between Hyères and Nice early on the morning of 15 August. Until the last moment Genoa was maintained as the cover objective. The convoys carrying the assault divisions from Naples were routed through the Straits of Bonifacio and up the west coast of Corsica on a course due north towards Genoa, from which they diverged to the west only after dark on the evening of 14 August. The convoys from Algeria crept along the north African shore to a point due south of Sardinia before turning north to rendezvous with the rest of the expedition off Corsica. Shortly before dawn on the 15th small parties simulated, by sonic deception, large seaborne forces advancing on objectives well to the east and to the west of the assault areas. Dummy paratroops were dropped inland from Toulon. Then after a brief and violent bombardment from sea and air, the assaults went in in the early morning of 15 August.[78]

So overwhelming were the naval and air forces which covered the *Dragoon* operation, and so overstretched were the forces available to the Germans to deal with them, that surprise in fact played a far less important role in securing the process of the operation than it had in the case of *Overlord*. General von Blaskowitz himself had never had any doubt that the attack would come in on his front,* and the pattern of air attacks had convinced him that the threatened sector lay somewhere to the east of the Rhône. Even if OKW had shared his fears, it had no resources left to send him.[79] Yet *Ferdinand* was quite the most successful of 'A' Forces strategic operations. As in the case of *Fortitude South*, the Germans were persuaded to swallow the 'cover story' almost entire. They did so, as they had in the case of *Husky* a year earlier, very largely because Hitler himself had a predisposition to expect landings in the cover area. This was reinforced by the reports of agents who had built up a reliable reputation, which were borne out by the movement of such forces as the enemy was able to observe. Even when the Germans suspected momentarily that they were the victims of a deception, the overwhelming weight of the evidence presented to them finally convinced them to the contrary. And even after the landings in the Riveria had established a firm lodgement, it was some days before the Germans decided that a second blow against Genoa was not still imminent.

□

Much of the responsibility for implementing the *Ferdinand* deception – indeed virtually all that part of it connected with the Adriatic – had fallen to the Tactical HQ of 'A' Force with General Alexander's Headquarters at Caserta, in southern Italy. The story of its activities strictly speaking belongs to the history of the Italian campaign, but it deserves to be briefly recapitulated here.

We have already mentioned Operation *Chettyford*, which was mounted in January 1944 as cover for the Anzio operation: a notional pincer attack from the sea against Pisa and Rimini by the US Seventh Army and Polish forces from the Middle East under the overall command

---

* Nor had German naval intelligence; whose appreciations during the first fortnight in August had all indicated south of France as the most probable objective.

of General Patton. In support of this the divisions of the US Fifth Army factually intended for the Anzio landings were notionally designated as part of the assault force for Pisa, and received copious briefings about their target area; while on the Adriatic coast Eighth Army simulated preparations for an attack in Corps strength to coincide with the notional operations against Rimini. These preparations involving plentiful displays of dummy tanks and guns, sonic deception and radio traffic, together with the usual frantic activity in the ports of Barletta, Brindisi and Bari. As we have seen, the surprise achieved at Anzio owed very little to any of these measures; but a secondary objective of the activity on the Eighth Army front was to pin down the German forces in the Adriatic sector until the Anzio beach-head was secure; and this it very successfully did. Throughout the early stages of the Anzio operation two of the most formidable units under Kesselring's command, 1st Parachute Division and 26th Panzer Division, were retained opposite the Eighth Army in the Eastern sector of the front. Not till the Anzio defences had been strongly established were these forces transferred to that sector.

Chettyford was to establish a model for the greater part of tactical deceptions in Italy for the rest of the year.[80] These consisted for the most part of amphibious feints either against the western coast of Italy, in the region of Civita Vecchia, Leghorn or Genoa, or against the east coast: Pescara, Rimini or the head of the Adriatic. Sometimes, as in *Chettyford* itself, they threatened both simultaneously. In the immediate aftermath of the Anzio landings the overriding concern of Lieut Col Hood and his team was to keep German attention focussed on their Adriatic flank, and to this end they improvised an amphibious threat against Pescara by a force assembling at Termoli. For this the quiet harbour of Termoli was transformed. All civilians in the neighbourhood were evacuated, the docking facilities were extended and a plentiful supply of dummy craft were displayed together with the usual radio deception. This activity came to the notice of FHW, which on 12 February suggested that it pointed 'to the possible intention of a tactical outflanking landing operation, perhaps in the Pescara area'.[81] The intelligence evaluation staff at OKW, with statistics of Allied shipping at their disposal, were not so easily taken in. Their information, they stated, on 11 February, was that the shipping in the harbours of Sicily and south Italy was sufficient only for the existing needs of the Allied armies, and gave no indication of major forthcoming landing operations.[82] Nevertheless the Seekriegsleitung War Diary for March reported the German Second Panzer Army to be assuming that 'outflanking movements to the north of Pescara are in prospect'; and certainly substantial German forces remained on the Adriatic front throughout the month of February, while the fighting at Anzio was at its most bitter.[83]

The most important task however which fell to Lieut Col Hood, and that which was perhaps, after *Ferdinand* and *Husky*, the greatest triumph of deception in the Mediterranean, was the operation which 'A' Force mounted to cover *Diadem*, the major attack launched by General Alexander on the night of 11 May to crack open the defensive line based on Cassino which the Germans had held throughout the winter and to open the way for an Allied pursuit which did not flag until it reached the Gothic line three months later.

Alexander's plan involved the secret accumulation of an overwhelming superiority of force on the western part of his front, between Cassino and the mouth of the Garigliano river. Six Army Corps, totalling fifteen divisions, were deployed between the watershed of the Appenines and the Tyrrhenian sea; II US Corps, the French Expeditionary Corps, X and XIII British Corps, the Polish Corps and I Canadian Corps. The Adriatic front was held only by V British Corps, consisting of two Indian divisions and a single armoured brigade. The task of the deception authorities was to prevent Kesselring from effecting a comparable strengthening of his own right wing and above all to dissuade him from massing his powerful mobile force in its rear to reinforce it and deal with any breakthrough that occurred.[84]

To cover this operation 'A' Force devised its plan *Nunton*, which was approved and put into operation on 10 April, a full month before the attack began. It was accepted that the movement of Allied forces from east to west (or, to be geographically accurate, from north to south) on so massive a scale could not possibly be concealed from the enemy. At best he could be misinformed about it by contradictory reports which would throw his intelligence staff into confusion, and, more especially, deceive them as to the date by which the redeployment would be complete. But in addition the enemy was to be deceived about the scope of the Allied operation. General Alexander was concerned not simply about the toughness of the resistance which the Germans might put up in their forward defensive positions but about the armoured and other forces they held in reserve; and these were to be dealt with by the threat of an amphibious operation, on a scale comparable to the Anzio attack, against the coast of Civita Vecchia, north of Rome.[85]

For this deception 'A' Force was allotted a real Corps HQ and four actual divisions, together with real forces from the British and US navies. The divisions concerned were in fact being held in reserve to exploit the breakthrough, when it came, at Cassino; but they were stationed in the area between Naples and Salerno, where they were given ample and well-publicised training, including plenty of exercise in combined operations. The ether was filled with their radio traffic, and the Bay of Naples filled up, as it had before Anzio, with an impressive array of naval craft. A French division in Corsica, carrying out amphibious exercises in preparation for the attack on Elba, was also notionally part of this force.

The object of this deception was similar to that being simultaneously mounted in the United Kingdom under the umbrella of *Fortitude:* to compel the enemy to delay committing his reserves to battle, by posing an alternative threat, until it was too late for them to tip the balance. The difference was that whereas the forces used for this purpose in the United Kingdom were very largely notional, those in Italy were for the most part real. But the Germans were equally taken in by the deception. Already in the second half of March, agents' reports of Allied plans to land at Civita Vecchia were being passed up to OKW and noted without adverse comment.[86] By the end of April the existence of a 'Naples Group' of 4–6 divisions had been registered both by Kesselring's intelligence staff and by FHW.[87] It seems to have been taken for granted that these were intended for an amphibious thrust; the only question was where. Kesselring considered landings at Gaeta or at Nettuno, to extend the Anzio bridgehead, to be at least as likely as one north of Rome, but at OKW opinion favoured Civita Vecchia.[88] Kesselring spread out his reserves to cover all bets. 29th Panzer Division watched Civita Vecchia, 90th Panzer Grenadier Division watched Nettuno, and 15th Panzer Grenadier Division watched Gaeta; with 26th Panzer Division stationed south-east of Rome to be able to help whichever of them needed it.[89] In addition Jodl at OKW took the threat so seriously that he left the Hermann Göering Division in its positions north of Rome instead of transferring it to France as had originally been intended.[90]

The deception continued until 25 May, two weeks after *Diadem* had been launched. Only when the Canadians were identified in battle, about 17 May, did Kesselring begin to suspect that no fresh landings would in fact occur. Then he committed his reserves piecemeal, much as von Rundstedt was to do a few weeks later in Normandy; and like the reserves in Normandy, they were swallowed up in the general rout.

A German situation map captured in the course of the battle gave 'A' Force considerable gratification. Its location of Allied units was wildly wrong. Allied strength on the left wing was under-estimated by seven divisions, that on the Adriatic wing over-estimated by an entire Corps. The 'Naples Group' was faithfully depicted carrying out its amphibious training in the Bay of Naples, and no less than eight divisions, half of them non-existent, were despairingly described as 'unlocated'. In his congratulatory message after the battle was over General Alexander told Lieut Col Hood that 'your contribution towards the success of this operation has been enormous'.[91] He did not exaggerate.

The next task of 'A' Force in Italy was to cover the attack on the German defences between Pisa and Rimini, the Gothic line, which Alexander began to plan at the end of June. The deception plan devised for this was *Ottrington*, about which something has already been said in connection with the deception for *Anvil/Dragoon*. Since Alexander originally intended to breach the Gothic line in its centre, north of

Florence, *Ottrington* consisted of amphibious feints at the German flanks; Genoa and Rimini. The first has already been described. The second involved preparations in the region of Pescara of a now familiar kind. The attention of the Germans was drawn to the northern and western shores of the Adriatic, a region about which they were already highly sensitive. But in August plans for attack were changed. General Sir Oliver Leese, who was now commanding the Eighth Army, argued successfully against the plan for a concentrated attack through the highest passes of the Apennines and persuaded Alexander instead to transfer the Eighth Army to the Adriatic sector, where it would attack along the coast towards Rimini and the Po valley.

Since the deception in that area was now well under way, this presented 'A' Force with a major problem. They solved it brilliantly. The deception measures continued, but steadily grew more clumsy. Camouflage was inadequate, dummy craft laid out anyhow, and bogus radio traffic was betrayed by mistakes easily recognisable to an expert. It was made as clear as possible to the Germans that the deception *was* deception. The real troop movements in the area were kept as secret as possible, while the units which remained in the Florence sector were given conspicuous training in mountain fighting.

In so far as the Germans did not immediately reinforce the Adriatic front when the attack began on 25 August, the deception was not unsuccessful. But the original indications of an attack in that area had already led Kesselring to reinforce it by 1st Parachute Division, among others,[92] and within four days these were joined by 26th Panzer Division. The attack, after its initial success, was gradually brought to a halt, and Allied operations in Italy bogged down for another winter.

'A' Force did not enjoy putting across this double bluff. 'They found it very difficult' as the War Diary records, 'to make a deception appear false without in the course of it disclosing that that was exactly what they were intending.' There was of course the further problem of maintaining its credibility for future operations, but about this 'A' Force had been told not to worry. For one thing it was generally assumed, in August 1944, that the war would last no more than a very few weeks. For another, 'A' Force as a whole had considered *Zeppelin* to be its swan song; once that deception had achieved its object, all else was an anticlimax. For *Zeppelin*, Clarke had ordered, 'the machine will be run to a standstill ... In the past when nearing the climax of any plan we have been at pains to conserve our machinery for another day, this time that policy will no longer hold ... Once we have entered the month of June all considerations regarding the safety of our channels (outside Italy) are to be subordinated to the demands of the plans on which we are now working and every risk accepted which can further the success of these plans'.[93] The party, it was believed, was very nearly over.

In October 1944 indeed, 'A' Force began to close down. On the first day of that month Brigadier Clarke was informed that no further overall deception would be practised in the war against Germany, if only because the German intelligence services were no longer capable of acquiring or interpreting the information that the Allies might wish to feed them. Their capability for air reconnaissance was non-existent, their agents were everywhere running for cover, and in the twilight of the Third Reich their organisation at home was tottering to collapse. Main HQ of 'A' Force, which in July had moved from Algiers to Caserta, was dissolved. Tactical HQ however remained active.* Command had passed in May from Lieut Col Hood to Lieut Col R A Bromley Davenport but when Main HQ closed down Lieut Col Crichton assumed command at Tactical HQ. The arrangement was shortlived. In December Field Marshal Alexander was promoted to become Supreme Allied Commander in the Mediterranean, and took Crichton with him, as a full Colonel, to reactivate Main HQ at Caserta; and tactical deception was once again to play a significant part in Alexander's final victories in the spring of 1945. As for Rear HQ in Cairo, where it had all begun, it dwindled to a useful outstation in the Middle East; its function now to serve the deception authorities in Delhi in the war against Japan.[94]

REFERENCES

1. CAB 154/3, 'A' Force War Diary, Vol III, pp 173–180.
2. CAB 154/100, Historical Record of Deception in the War against Germany and Italy (Sir Ronald Wingate's Narrative), Vol I, pp 39–41; CAB 154/4, 'A' Force War Diary, Vol IV, pp 98–99.
3. CAB 154/4, pp 2–4.
4. Full details in CAB 154/2, 'A' Force War Diary, Vol II, pp 35–44.
5. CAB 154/4, p 88.
6. Cover and Deception, General Administration Files 1943–52, The *Wantage* Order of Battle (Record Group 319, National Archives of the United States).
7. Imperial War Museum, AL 761, Seekriegsleitung (SKL) War Diary, 2 March 1944.
8. CAB 81/78, LCS(44) 4 of 20 April.
9. CAB 154/4, p 6.
10. ibid, pp 6–13.
11. CAB 146/47, Enemy Documents Section (EDS) Appreciation 16, Chapter 1, p 66.
12. ibid, p 23.
13. ibid, p 24.
14. ibid, p 64.
15. ibid, p 46.
16. ibid, p 52.
17. Imperial War Museum, AL 1828/2.

---

* A second Tactical HQ had been created to serve General Patch and the US Seventh Army in France, and had now come under the control of Ops B at SHAEF. Since this was a purely American organisation and its activities were primarily tactical, its adventures have not been recorded here.

18. C A B 146/47, pp 64–65.
19. ibid, p 67.
20. Helmuth Greiner and Percy F Schramm, *Kriegstagebuch des Oberkommandos der Wehrmacht* (Frankfurt am Main 1965), Vol IV, p 81.
21. C A B 146/47 p 11.
22. ibid, pp 18–21.
23. ibid, pp 29–30.
24. Imperial War Museum, MI 14/499, Kurze Feind Beurteilung West (KFW) 1151 of 21 January 1944.
25. Imperial War Museum, A L 1828/2.
26. ibid
27. ibid
28. C A B 146/55, E D S Appreciation 17, Chapter 1, p 24.
29. Imperial War Museum, A L 1828/2.
30. C A B 154/4, Entry for 3 April 1944.
31. ibid, p 58.
32. C A B 146/49, E D S Appreciation 16, Chapter 3, p 18; F H Hinsley and C A G Simkins, *British Intelligence in the Second World War*, Vol 4, [1989], Chapter 12.
33. ibid, p 20. See also Greiner and Schramm, op cit, Vol IV, p 624.
34. Greiner and Schramm, op cit, Vol IV, p 621.
35. C A B 146/51 E D S Appreciation 16, Chapter 5, p 11.
36. C A B 146/55, pp 1, 29.
37. Imperial War Museum, A L 1828/2, Appreciation of Allied Landing Operations against the Balkans, 5 May 1944.
38. C A B 146/57, E D S Appreciation 17, Chapter 3, p 14.
39. ibid.
40. Greiner and Schramm, op cit, Vol IV, p 478.
41. C A B 154/4, p 64.
42. C A B 154/101, Historical Record of Deception in the War against Germany and Italy (Sir Ronald Wingate's Narrative), Vol II, p 285.
43. C A B 154/4, pp 71–75.
44. C A B 146/49, pp 1, 10.
45. ibid, p 11 et seq.
46. Greiner and Schramm, op cit, Vol IV, pp 287-288.
47. Imperial War Museum, A L 1828/2.
48. C A B 146/51 p 11.
49. All these reports in Imperial War Museum, A L 1828/2.
50. ibid.
51. C A B 146/62, E D S Appreciation 18, Chapter 1, p 9.
52. Imperial War Museum, M I14/499, Lagebeurteilung West (LBW) of 19 June 1944.
53. C A B 154/4, pp 80–84.
54. ibid.
55. Imperial War Museum, A L 1828/2.
56. ibid.
57. ibid; Imperial War Museum, MI14/499, K FW 1279 of 28 May 1944.
58. Imperial War Museum, MI 14/499, KFW 1283 of 1 June 1944.
59. Imperial War Museum MI 14/481/1, K FW 1325 of 13 July 1944.
60. ibid, K FW 1341 of 29 July 1944.
61. Greiner and Schramm, op cit, Vol IV, p 670.
62. C A B 154/4, p 96.
63. ibid, pp 103, 110; C A B 81/78, L C S(44) 17 of 4 July.
64. C A B 105/60, C O S(W) 147 of 7 July 1944.
65. W O 219/2250.
66. ibid, Serial 8A.
67. ibid, Serial 10A.

68. CAB 154/4, p 117.
69. Greiner and Schramm, op cit, Vol IV, p 537.
70. Imperial War Museum, MI 14/499, KFW 1320 of 8 July 1944.
71. Imperial War Museum, MI 14/481/1, KFW 1329 of 17 July 1944.
72. ibid, KFW 1333 and 1335 of 21 and 23 July 1944.
73. Greiner and Schramm, op cit, Vol IV, p 510 for SKL reports for 24 July 1944.
74. ibid, p 540.
75. Imperial War Museum, MI 14/481/1, KFW 1341 of 29 July 1944.
76. ibid, KFW 1347 of 4 August 1944.
77. ibid, KFW 1350 of 7 August 1944.
78. S W Roskill, *The War at Sea*, Vol III Part 2 (1961), pp 93–100.
79. CAB 146/66, EDS Appreciation 18, Chapter 5, pp 10–11.
80. For these see CAB 154/4, passim.
81. Imperial War Museum, MI 14/499, KFW 1173 of 12 February 1944.
82. Imperial War Museum, AL 1828/2, Comments on V-Mann report of 8 Febuary 1944.
83. Imperial War Museum, AL 761, p 42.
84. C J C Molony, *The Mediterranean and Middle East* Vol VI pt I (1984), p 55.
85. CAB 154/4, p 50 et seq.
86. For example, reports of 21 and 22 March 1944 in Imperial War Museum, AL 1828/2.
87. CAB 146/57, p 8.
88. ibid, p 30.
89. Molony, op cit, p 68.
90. Greiner and Schramm, op cit, Vol IV, p 480.
91. CAB 154/4, p 53.
92. CAB 146/64, EDS Appreciation 18, Chapter 3, p 37.
93. CAB 154/4, p 94.
94. ibid, p 132.

CHAPTER 8

Crossbow: The Flying Bombs, June–December 1944

T HE FIRST 'flying bombs' (the name by which the German
VI pilotless aircraft were initially known to the British public)
fell on British soil on the night of 12–13 June 1944. They came
as no surprise to the British authorities. Something of the kind had
been expected ever since intelligence reports of activities at the German
research station at Peenemünde had led the Prime Minister, in April
1943, to set up a special committee under Mr Duncan Sandys to evaluate
intelligence of German preparations for rocket attacks and make proposals for counter-measures.[1] By August of that year it seemed possible
that the Germans were working both on a rocket projectile and on
a pilotless aircraft, and a major controversy developed over which presented the greater threat.[2] Air reconnaissance flights were meanwhile
mounted over northern France, and these revealed, around Cherbourg
and in the Pas de Calais, a number of curiously-shaped sites, known
as 'ski-sites' from their configuration, which were correctly identified
as launching pads for pilotless aircraft and subjected, in December 1943,
to heavy and effective attack from the air.[3] This led the Germans to
devise less conspicuous sites which were not identified by Allied intelligence until April 1944. With preparations for *Overlord* nearing their peak,
only a limited number of aircraft could be spared to deal with them,
even when it became clear that they were being prepared for action.
But by June 1944 the authorities in the United Kingdom had no doubt
that an attack was imminent, and had made considerable preparations
to deal with it.[4]

The Twenty Committee had been brought into the picture as early
as July 1943, when it was asked to report any indications of rocket
attacks that might reach it through the double agents or any other
source. The first hint received through these channels came two months
later, in September, when *Tricycle* was warned by the Abwehr against
continuing to live in London, since this was likely to become a target
for rockets sited on the French coast. This emboldened the Twenty
Committee to put out some feelers, and *Garbo* was chosen to do so.
In October he wrote to Madrid reporting that his wife had been alarmed
by reports in the British Press of 'an enormous rocket gun which is
installed on the French coast to bombard London as a reprisal'. What,
he asked, was the truth of the matter, and what ought he to do about

it? Should he evacuate his family from the capital? 'I, naturally, would go and live with them and would come into London regularly to attend to matters connected with the service'.

'It has also occurred to me (*Garbo* continued) that I might take on the work of making daily observations (if the rocket really exists) and let you have by radio an exact report on objectives hit so that you will be able to correct any possible errors of fire. The news makes me think that if it were true and we were able to make use of this weapon to liquidate all these English dogs we would produce a rude and terrible blow to our enemy, for it is certainly time that we brought them down from their clouds of power'.

The initial response was reassuring. 'With regard to the rocket gun' *Garbo*'s control told him on 18 November; 'there is no cause to alarm yourself'. But a month later, on 16 December, the tune changed, and *Garbo* was advised to leave London. Further advice followed, until in May 1944, just as the flood of misinformation he was purveying about the second front was reaching its peak, *Garbo* was advised to expect a special questionnaire and instructed to give his answers a prefix which would ensure their immediate transmission to the Abwehr station at Arras. MI5 was puzzled by this until their colleagues of MI6 pointed out, at a meeting on 19 May, that it was from Arras that the flying bomb offensive, now termed *Crossbow*, was likely to be directed.

The initial salvo of 12–13 June was a premature effort, imposed on the V-Weapon units against their better judgement by the impatience of their High Command. The serious attack began on the night of 15–16 June, when 217 missiles were fired,* of which 45 landed in the area of central London. On the evening of 16 June *Garbo* received an apologetic message from his control in Madrid, maintaining that he had himself only heard of the beginning of the attack through the news agencies, and continuing

'It is of the utmost importance to inform us about the effect of the bombardments. We are not interested in partial details but wish you to communicate results as follows. Take as your basis a plan of London by the publishers Pharos which I suppose you have in your possession and indicate how many targets (sic) or missiles have fallen in determined squares on the plan, defining those by 'ordinates' and 'co-ordinates' and the approximate hour. Example: during the bombardment from 3–4 six shells fell in the East End in the square K10. No further details are necessary. The foregoing is only for your guidance, knowing that it will be almost impossible to obtain these details ... Your primary objective is not to endanger or take risks with the rest of the service, which continues to be of primordial importance'.

Other double agents, notably *Brutus* and *Tate* received similar orders. These came as no surprise, since Bletchley Park had already decrypted the instructions that Abwehr HQ in Berlin had sent to Madrid on

---

* Figures of launchings throughout are taken from the War Diary of Flak Regt 155(W). Those of landings are from Air Ministry summaries.[5]

the morning of June 16th, before these were transmitted to *Garbo* almost word for word.

Garbo's immediate response was synthetic indignation. 'It has upset me very much', he radioed back on the evening 16 June, 'to have to learn the news of this arm having been used from our very enemies ... I would be grateful if you would communicate to Berlin to ascertain whether it is intended to continue these operations every night against London as if so I will arrange all my affairs in order to remove the service from this city'. Two days later however he had recovered his equanimity. 'I am proud', he informed his control on 18 June, 'that you have been able to prove this fantastic reprisal weapon, the creation of German genius ... when the scale on which it is used is increased I am certain that you will be able to terrify this very pusillanimous people who will never admit that they are beaten'. He reported rumours that the bombs were falling in a wide arc to the north and west of London and promised to find out more.

Even the Abwehr, however, was likely to grow suspicious if its agents delayed for long in providing information about events that were presumably occurring under their very eyes. On 18 June a meeting of the officials directly concerned decided that for the time being they should treat the flying bomb attacks as they had previous air raids, and not try to use them for deceptive purposes. Reports about damage were to be substantially accurate, but minimised, while the effect on public morale would be represented as creating an increased demand for retaliatory raids on German towns. But more specific demands for information received by *Tate* made it clear that this would not do for long, and on 22 June the Twenty Committee agreed to suggest to the Air Ministry that the agents should give accurate reports of isolated explosions, some of them with times and dates, and should occasionally report groups of incidents.

That evening *Garbo* did in fact report, though without times and dates, half a dozen incidents that had occurred in the West End and could hardly be kept quiet; including the destruction of the Guards Chapel in Birdcage Walk with heavy loss of life during morning service on Sunday 18 June. But, he added, the general opinion was that the weapon was now being brought under control, and 'the nervousness of the public created at the beginning has now disappeared'. This was a point which he elaborated in a long letter of the same date; a letter so hilariously typical of his style that we include it in an appendix to this volume. The key passage ran as follows:

'Now that a few days have passed during which [the new weapon] has been used I ask myself 'What is the use of this new arm? has it a military aim? No'. Its effect is nil. Is it then intended for propaganda? Possibly yes! ... I do not challenge that in this respect it had at the beginning flattering success ... [but] the best propaganda are deeds, and these only take place in the field of battle ... This weapon is not only ineffective from a military point of view but also from the point of view of propaganda ... If one goes about the streets of London one sees the scars of the period of destruction which occurred during the years 1940–41. The effects of what is taking place now are no more than light editions (*sic*) which do not add to the whole a further ten thousandth part of the destruction of the city ... If we study the amount of explosives then used and the number of casualties suffered through our action and we compare this with the present expensive construction of the new arm we can then decide on a basis of effort-value which of these has been the most effective. The following important detail which I learnt ... is that only 17% of the bombs fall in 'Greater London' ... [so] until a way of improving can be found its effectiveness is nil, and therefore all the efforts which have been spent on it have been wasted, and they should be employed in the manufacture of war weapons which may have more disastrous effects on our enemy'.

Having planted this barb, *Garbo* delayed sending any detailed reports until he was able to get hold of the correct edition of the map on which he had been instructed to plot the fall of bombs. This he could not do until 16 June. On 28 June he began to transmit information in the form required, but warned that if he were to concentrate on doing this his collection of purely military information would suffer. He realised, he said further on 30 June, that it was important to discover the precise times of the explosions, but 'it is dangerous to ask questions in damaged areas since the public who lose their house is rather hostile.' He promised, however, to obtain the information himself. When his control in Madrid told him that he should regard information about troop movements as his first priority 'and you should add information about the objectives hit only to the extent that circumstances permit', *Garbo* replied bravely, on 1 July, 'I think it more important that the fire should be more concentrated and it is essential that you receive more exact information'. And he began to transmit both the times and co-ordinates of a number of bomb-falls. By then the British authorities felt that he could safely do so, and we must now consider how this had come about.

The Air Ministry was the department chiefly responsible for coping with these new weapons, and its specialists had been considering how best to deal with flying bombs that could not be shot down either by aircraft or by AA fire. Although *Garbo* had reported quite correctly when he asserted that the population of London was taking this new ordeal very much in its stride, his figure of 17 per cent hits in the Greater London area was a considerable under-estimate. By the end of June over 2,415 weapons had been launched, and although the scatter was very wide over the Home Counties, some 660 had fallen in the London area – a very uncomfortable 27½ per cent of the total. The Air Ministry assumed that the aiming point was the centre of London – Air Intelligence located it at Charing Cross – but after ten days it became clear that most of the weapons were in fact falling two or three miles short of this target. Charts compiled by the Ministry of Home Security located the 'mean point of impact' (MPI) in the region of North Dulwich station. Disagreeable as this was for the population of that region, it might have been very much worse. Many of the bombs were exploding harmlessly in the broad expanses of open ground which abound in that part of London; whereas a slight correction of aim would bring the MPI into the centre of the city where every bomb would be likely to cause dislocation, as well as damage to lives and property.

The concern of the Air Ministry and the Home Defence Executive was therefore to dissuade the Germans from correcting their aim, and if possible to persuade them to shorten it further. A means by which this might be done was worked out between Dr R V Jones, of Air Intelligence, Flight Lieut Charles Cholmondley of the Air Ministry and Mr John Drew of the Home Defence Executive. As Dr Jones was later to explain it, 'we could give correct points of impact for bombs that tended to have a longer range than usual, but couple these with the times of bombs which had in fact fallen short. Thus, if the Germans attempted any correlation, they might be led to think that even the bombs which they had reason to believe might have fallen short were instead tending to fall in north-west London. Therefore if they made any correction at all, it would be to reduce the average range'.[6]

The Twenty Committee when it met on 29 June welcomed this proposal, which accorded very well with the rumours already reported by *Garbo*, of the bombs falling predominantly in an arc to the north and west of London. Meanwhile Sir Findlater Stewart had been given overall responsibility for deception about the flying bombs; being instructed by the Chiefs of Staff, on the initiative of the Chief of Air Staff, 'to consider the impression which should, if possible, be conveyed to the Germans as to the physical and psychological effect of their attacks with flying bombs on this country', including propaganda and control of information as well as the transmission of misinformation.[7] On 6 July he submitted a preliminary report. The implications of the proposed deception, he said, had been discussed with the Government departments principally concerned. The Ministry of Production had no objection: better this, it considered, than persuading the enemy to scatter his shot more widely over the Greater London area, which would make the interference with war production yet more serious. But the Ministry of Home Security disliked the proposal to shift the MPI yet further to the south-east, since it would result in no less serious destruction of life and property. Unless shortening the range could be guaranteed to result in taking the weight off the main target, the Ministry considered, it was doubtful whether any advantage would be gained by shifting the incidence from one area to another.

Nevertheless on balance Stewart decided to recommend:

'that by special means we should try to create the impression that the bombs were appearing to overshoot the target (which was assumed to be central London) in the hope that the range would be moved further to the east and south ... Reports through special sources should so far as possible not mention areas of damage at particular incidents'.

So far as the effects on morale were concerned, Stewart saw little problem:

'Reports on morale and the disturbance to the war effort and the life of the community should be based on facts, with a tendency to minimise the effects. We presume that the real object of the enemy is not to cause military damage but primarily to bolster the sagging morale of his people, and secondly to impair the morale of the people of this country. The facts are an adequate answer to these objectives. [sic] ...'[8]

The Chiefs of Staff considered this paper on 7 July and were not at first convinced.[9] They invited Stewart to explain more fully what he had in mind. This he did in a long document which they did not consider until 18 July; by which time the situation had developed sufficiently for him to give a more complete account:[10]

'Practically all [the] agents now run by us have received urgent requests to report on the fall of bombs giving both time and place of as many incidents as possible. Two of the agents [*Brutus* and *Garbo*] on whom the main burden of supporting the plan *Fortitude* has fallen, have been instructed to provide themselves with specific maps and to report quickly on incidents by reference to co-ordinates. Another high agent, who has recently arrived here* has also been instructed to give a high priority to bomb reports, and his masters in briefing him were emphatic that time and place must be accurately given. Other agents, including a number of secret letter writers, were also expected to report on the results of attack, and we know from Most Secret Sources that the highest priority within the German Intelligence Service is given to the forwarding of these reports to the forces responsible for the operation of the weapon. It is clear from this insistent demand for information that those of the agents who are well placed to get it (practically the whole of

---

* This was *Zigzag* who had been arrested by the Germans in the Channel Islands in 1940 and parachuted as an agent into Britain in December 1942 with a sabotage mission. On arrival he had promptly reported to the police. B1A ran him as a double agent so effectively that it was decided in March 1943 to smuggle him back into Germany via Lisbon to acquire yet more information about the workings of the Abwehr. He disappeared from sight for fifteen months and was next heard of at Oslo in May 1944, instructing Abwehr agents in sabotage techniques. The following month he was once again parachuted into Britain, landing on the night of 27/28 June. His instructions included obtaining information about anti-submarine warfare equipment, the radar devices used by Allied night-fighters and the location and missions of US air force units; and 'to find out the effect of the P-plane, places where they are landing, the resultant damage to property and morale, and, in particular, the exact time of impact'. He began, under instruction, to transmit the required information on 1 July and ceased doing so on the 27th pending further decisions about policy. Thereafter he was employed on naval deception until October 1944.

them) must comply or be hopelessly compromised. Equally clearly we cannot risk losing the agents, since not only would this destroy a considerable part of the deception machine now at our command, but it would also compromise past achievements of great and continuing importance; two of these are plan *Fortitude* and a notional Order of Battle of the Allied Armies which we have succeeded in planting'.

Since they had to pass over *some* information, Stewart went on, the only way to turn this to advantage was to imply an error in bomb range. 'The agents concerned will be manoeuvred into positions in which they can best report on incidents in N.W. London ... they should report on actual incidents in N.W. London but give as the times of those incidents the actual times of incidents in S.E. London. If this is done skilfully it is hoped that the enemy will identify the bomb which fell in S.E. London with the incident in N.W. London and plot it there'.

Stewart then considered the other sources from which the enemy might derive information about the fall of his bombs. There were uncontrolled sources such as diplomatic reports from neutral embassies and the inspired guess-work of freelance agents in neutral capitals. Much of this could be monitored through Sigint. The information which they had so far passed across was vague and inaccurate and certainly not of a nature which would influence the enemy's aim. More serious were the radio direction-finding devices built in to a proportion of the weapons; but it was believed that these were carried only in 5 per cent of the weapons, and averaging a large number of results would reduce their importance. Counter-measures to distort their signals would make it even harder for the enemy to assess their significance. In any case, even after three weeks and more than two thousand launchings, the enemy was still not correcting his aim. 'It would seem to follow from this that, if the enemy has in fact radio results indicating his error, he is not relying on them as much as on the accuracy and consistency of the results established in trials of the weapon. If this is so ... our task is to work on the enemy's faith in his weapon as against his radio results'.

The Chiefs of Staff considered this proposal again on 18 July.[11] Clearly a matter of such importance for the civilian population had to be decided at the highest political level, and they agreed that the Prime Minister should now be brought into the picture. But meanwhile they accepted that the double agents should implement the proposed policy – something which, Stewart admitted, they had already begun to do.[12] The extent to which they were able to do so, however, had been deliberately limited by the decision of MI5 temporarily to close down their principal channel, *Garbo*.

This decision was largely determined by the requirements of *Fortitude South*. At the beginning of July both the Third US and the First Canadian Armies, both notionally part of FUSAG, had to be transferred to France where they would appear in their true light as part of 21st Army

Group. It was desirable to conceal this for as long as possible, but an intact *Garbo* network could hardly have failed to spot what was going on. The German appetite for information about the flying bombs added to the problem. But the Abwehr itself suggested a solution when on 30 June it urged *Garbo* not to place his military information in hazard by over-concentration on the flying bombs. *Garbo*, as we have seen, ignored this advice and gallantly set out in search of information in person. He transmitted one message on 3 July, reporting seven incidents, with map co-ordinates and times. On 5 July however the second-in-command of his network reported him missing. Two days later there came yet worse news. *Garbo* had been arrested.

The agitation of the messages from Madrid that followed showed how seriously the Germans regarded this blow to their intelligence network. But MI5 quickly put them out of their misery. On 10 July *Garbo's* deputy sent the welcome news that his master had been released, and on 14 July *Garbo* himself despatched a letter by the courier explaining what had happened. He had been investigating reports of bomb damage in Bethnal Green when he had been stopped and questioned by the police. Unwisely, he had tried to dispose of the notes he had made about his observations and been caught doing so. He was taken into custody and released only on the intervention of his employers in the Ministry of Information; who were able also to extract from the Home Office an official letter apologising for the officiousness of the police. *Garbo* enclosed both this letter and the original warrant for his arrest. On 23 July his Control joyfully acknowledged receipt of all these documents, congratulated him on his liberation, and emphasised that 'the security of yourself and of the services requires a prolongation of the period of complete inactivity on your part, without any contact with your collaborators. Cease all investigations of the new weapon'.

MI5 had thus achieved their object. But even they did not anticipate what followed. On 29 July there came another signal from Madrid. 'With great happiness and satisfaction' this ran, 'I am able to advise you today that the Führer has conceded the Iron Cross to you for your extraordinary merits'. 'I cannot', *Garbo* replied, 'at this moment, when emotion overwhelms me, express in words my gratitude'. Evidently he had given satisfaction all round.*

The near disaster to the *Garbo* network had even further-reaching results. It led the Germans, on 12 July, to prohibit *Brutus* also from communicating any information about flying bombs. With *Garbo* and *Brutus* thus effectively silenced, the Abwehr could thus provide for the time being only a thin trickle of information about the fall of bombs

---

* In fact Madrid had acted too precipitately. Difficulties arose about the award of the Iron Cross to a non-German national who was not employed with the fighting forces, and these were not sorted out until the end of the war. The British authorities listened in to the exchange of messages between Berlin and Madrid on this topic with particular enjoyment.

in London.* This was just as well; for the ingenious deception plan whose introduction was thereby hampered had meanwhile run into very heavy weather indeed.

Further discussions with the Ministries of Production and of Home Security had not silenced the doubts in these departments. Both feared that a shift of the point of impact to new areas would make the situation worse, since the civil defence services in regions which had hitherto been spared would take time to adjust themselves to the new demands made on them, and the morale of the population of these areas might be more vulnerable than in those which had learned 'to live with the bombs'. Stewart explained in reply that the shift in aim was likely to be so gradual that none of this was likely to occur, but he reported these objections in a further paper which the Chiefs of Staff discussed on 25 July.[13] At that meeting they agreed to support Stewart's recommendations, and General Ismay informed the Prime Minister accordingly; suggesting, in view of the confidentiality of the matter under discussion, that he should consult only the Minister of Home Security (Mr Herbert Morrison) and the Minister of Production (Mr Oliver Lyttelton).[14] This Mr Churchill did on 28 July, and the conclusion was negative. The Ministers concerned were not prepared to accept responsibility for deliberately directing the attack against any part of London. Instead they suggested 'that the information conveyed to the enemy as regards the point of impact and timing of arrival of flying bombs [should be] such as would create confusion in his mind and present him with an inaccurate picture'.[15]

It was understandable that the Ministers concerned should have been reluctant to accept the terrible responsibility that Stewart was pressing on them. But the alternative proposal they had put forward was not really practical, for reasons that Stewart explained in a memorandum to the Chief of Staff on 31 July:[16]

'i. We are forced to give some information in order to maintain our deception machine in being.

ii. Information cannot be given haphazardly since the enemy will draw an inference about his aim from whatever is said and we must therefore indicate some mean point of impact which would not be to our detriment.

iii. If we tell the enemy or let him infer the truth we present him with valuable information which he can use to improve his aim, and as indicated below the results of a shift to the north might be very serious.

iv. Both the Ministry of Home Security and the Ministry of Production fear that new and serious problems may face them if the enemy shifts his mean point of impact to the North. Thus any shift which involves new areas in

---

* The principal double agents left were *Treasure*, *Tate* and *Zigzag*. Unfortunately their traffic files have not been preserved and no trace of *Tate*'s messages appears in the files. About 16 messages from *Treasure* appear in traffic for June–August 1944, almost all reporting true incidents (although without times) in the West End.

heavier attacks, particularly the densely populated boroughs on the north side of the Thames, will pose afresh, possibly in a more acute form, most of the problems of organisation and public reaction which have had to be faced and dealt with in the areas at present mainly affected . . .'.

The Cabinet's directive in fact was likely to result either in the discrediting of the agents or in the enemy working out the truth of the matter for himself and reacting accordingly. Instead Findlater Stewart suggested a different directive of more modest scope:

'a. No attempt to be made to shift the weight of attack in any direction, and material to be passed over should be selected so as to deny useful information to the enemy *and to prevent him moving the mean point of impact of his attack, particularly to the north.* (emphasis added)
b. Where times are given the incidents should be selected in such a way as to prevent the enemy from linking the incident with any given bomb'.

The deception authorities had thus settled for a more cautious policy. Rather than persuade the enemy that he had got his aim wrong, they should try to reassure him that it was just about right.

The Chiefs of Staff agreed to support the new policy, and Mr Duncan Sandys and Lord Cherwell agreed to resubmit it to the Prime Minister. Meanwhile the Chiefs of Staff took the responsibility on 1 August of authorising Stewart, pending a decision, to put the new policy into effect.[17] But the paper submitted by Sandys went very much further than Stewart's draft directive had proposed. In it he renewed the arguments in favour of persuading the enemy that he was *overshooting* the target. He presented statistics to indicate that if the Germans corrected their aim so that the MPI lay at Charing Cross, monthly casualties might increase by 4,000; if they shortened their range, on the other hand, casualties might fall by as much as 12,000.[18]

This demand that the Cabinet should reverse its carefully considered decision caused some surprise in the Cabinet secretariat. Mr Morrison made it clear that he for one would not change his mind. But the Prime Minister agreed that the matter should be raised again, which was done at a meeting of Ministers on 9 August.[19] The arguments were once more presented *pro* and *con*. Doubt was cast in particular on the casualty forecasts by the Ministry of Home Security. Although the area in south-east London to which the bombs might be diverted was less heavily built up, it was pointed out that 'the type of property was largely of light construction, and despite the fact that the houses were more openly spaced, the total damage from any particular incident might in the result be found to be higher'. These arguments were strong enough to prevent any firm decision being reached at this meeting but the existing policy, that of persuading the enemy that his aim was more or less correct, was endorsed for the time being.

The following week however, on 15 August, a further conference was held, in the absence of the Prime Minister in Italy, under the chairmanship of Mr Attlee. No minute survives, but as a result of the decisions then taken Sir Findlater Stewart was informed that[20]

'it was agreed that your object should be to ensure that there is no deterioration in the position and that the enemy does not shift the pattern of his bombs towards the north-west. With this in view you should continue to convey to the enemy information that will confirm his belief that he has no need to lengthen his range. *You are also at liberty, within limits, to take such steps as you may judge safe to intensify this belief*'. (emphasis added)

The meaning of this cautious directive was spelled out a little further in a cable from Mr Attlee to the Prime Minister: 'The Cabinet reconsidered Sandys' proposals on home security... There was agreement that the direction should be to work for the maintenance of the present position with a bias towards a shift of emphasis as suggested'.[21] At a meeting of the Twenty Committee on 17 August Drew was yet more explicit. A directive, he said, had been obtained, 'namely to prevent the enemy from moving his aim towards the north-west and, to a slight extent, to attempt to induce him to move it towards the south-east'.

Findlater Stewart's hard-won victory came too late to be put into effect. On 18 August, the day after Drew reported his success to the Twenty Committee, the Germans began to close down the launching sites in northern France in face of the threatening advance of the Allied armies.[22] Those remaining fired off their ammunition very much at random. On 14 August the Home Defence Executive was alarmed by an apparent concentration on *West* London, but within a few days it concluded that 'the enemy is changing his target daily'.[23] On the night of 30–31 August the last salvo was fired – 47 bombs of which 9 reached central London. On 1 September the sites were overrun. The first stage of the V-bomb offensive had come to an end.

How effective was this attempt to deceive the enemy? Fortunately the War Diary of Flak Regiment 155(W), the unit responsible for the despatch of the flying bombs has survived, which enables us to trace German reactions with some precision.[24] This document makes it clear that the Regiment was satisfied with what it was achieving, or thought that it was achieving, and at no point thought it necessary to adjust its aim. By a stroke of good fortune one of the weapons fired in the first salvo of 16 June was fitted with a radio DF indicator [FuG23] and landed in the immediate vicinity of Tower Bridge, 'that is in the centre of the target area' commented the diary, 'right in the heart of the city'.[25] Three days later, on 19 June the Commanding Officer, Colonel Wolff, spoke of the 'complete confidence of officers and men in this weapon, the effectiveness of which has been proved for us by FuG23 bearings, by published news and by the British countermeasures'.[26] The next day a summary was given of the reports received from a 'very reliable agent' on 17 and 18 June.[27] These pronounced

'Operations a great surprise to the British public and also to military and political authorities, at least as regards timing . . .'

'Shock effect very great at first [the summary continued]. Even panic in individual places hit. Authorities, however, are making skilful efforts to boost morale and are succeeding to a certain extent. Morale more composed once initial shock overcome, but still grave. Serious loss of work in many London factories. Anglo-American military authorities admit serious indirect effect on invasion. This in their opinion of considerably greater importance than shock effect on public. Any disturbance is a danger. The new weapon is therefore being taken very seriously by the military. Damage often not so marked, as no concentrated attacks. Very many dead. Drastic censorship, even internally. Line The Wash–Bristol almost hermetically sealed off. Restricted use of telephone. Greater restrictions on travel. Often 100 per cent sealing off of towns affected. London railway stations crowded. Fantastic stories and figures quoted for dead and injured. Places hit in London: Whitehall, College Street nr Parliament (Big Ben) completely destroyed, heavy devastation with very high numbers of dead between Limehouse and West India Docks. Also devastation in East India Docks. Extensive destruction at Bromley gas works by River Lea. Gigantic blaze here. Serious damage to houses at Greenwich, Clapham, Earls Court. Large goods depot and hall burnt out. Direct hit on East Croydon Station. Eye-witnesses report many dead'.

This, of course, was exactly what the Germans were hoping to hear, and that is no doubt why the agent in question told them what he did. But it was not one of the agents controlled by MI5. Almost certainly it was a freelance agent in Madrid codenamed *Ostro* who based his reports on gossip, imagination and anything he could get from the newspapers. In fact College Street had not been hit, let alone completely destroyed. Big Ben was intact. No bombs landed on the docks until 20 June, and neither Bromley gas works nor East Croydon station had yet suffered damage. But the impression of a hail of bombs descending on the centre of London was established, and only those agents' reports which tended to confirm this were forwarded to the flying bomb sites. These included true reports from the double agents about damage in the West End, but also imaginative accounts given by *Ostro* about panic and loss of morale. 'Acute anxiety among the people has not been relieved', ran one such report: 'More evacuation is expected. The Plutocratic families in particular are leaving London.[28] A further report on 3 August was even more reassuring.[29]

'Agents' reports say that in the past weeks mainly working-class districts, especially near the docks, have been hit. Much of the London dock activity has been transferred to ports in the Bristol Channel. It is calculated that production in London will suffer a fall of 15 per cent to 20 per cent. Large-scale evacuation has caused the authorities serious trouble, and looting is the order of the day. Traffic, especially on routes to the south of England, is severely restricted. The London Underground is very overcrowded. The population is leading a hellish existence'.

It is notable, but perhaps not surprising, that *Garbo*'s report to the contrary of 22 June was *not* passed on, and the deception authorities were well served by its suppression. The last impression they ought to have given was that the bombardment was ineffective. As it was, the unanimously favourable agents' reports passed on to the batteries led the Germans not only to ignore the evidence of the FuG23 indicators, all of which showed a shortfall, but also to take in their stride a careful analysis of the performance of the weapons dated 29 June which reported quite categorically 'The mean point of impact lies, on the average, *short and to the left of the target*'. (emphasis added)[30]

But if the Germans knew, within a fortnight of the start of the bombardment that their bombs were falling short, why did they not correct their aim? One clue to their failure to take action lies in a comment in the War Diary[31] on the statement made to the House of Commons by the Home Secretary, Mr Herbert Morrison, on Friday 18 June, when he explained the prohibition on publication of details of the damage inflicted by the flying bombs as being 'in order to give the enemy no chance to make firing corrections'.[32] 'The British Home Secretary's statement', commented the diary, 'shows that they are still not very clear on the other side of the Channel as to the nature of our operations. We must keep the enemy in the dark like this for as long as possible'. But what *was* 'the nature of the operations' – that is, the object intended by the flying-bomb offensive? On this we get an indication from later pages in the diary which describe a quarrel that took place later in the year after the regiment had been withdrawn to Germany, as to what its future task should be. The regiment's new divisional commander, Oberst Walter (5th Flakdivision (W)) wanted to use it in what would today be called a 'counterforce' role, against precise military targets in Belgium such as communications and docks. Colonel Wolff on behalf of the regiment, protested:

'because of its large spread the V1 could not be used against military targets but only as a terror weapon. The most diverse sources testify to the terror effect on London and south England. Furthermore, considerable military forces were tied down by the need for defence. No details are available of the effect on Antwerp and Liège; the aim here was not to achieve a terror affect, but a military one, by disorganising supplies and holding up unloading: ... The Regiment therefore regards the operation against Antwerp and Liège as only a temporary affair, the results of which are not nearly as practicable as the bombardment of London. Every missile that falls on England is a blow which further undermines the already faltering morale of the British people and forces the British war leaders to build up a massive defence, thus calling upon forces which would otherwise be in action on the Continent'.

It is true that by December 1944 the Germans had vastly over-estimated the damage which the flying bombs had inflicted on central London as a result of a reconnaissance flight of 16 September, the first successfully carried out over the city since January 1941,[33] and which therefore enabled Wolff and his colleagues to claim credit for all the damage inflicted since that date. But the object of the bombardment was obviously considered by those who conducted it as being to inflict general and widespread damage to the civilian sector, to strike at morale and compel the diversion of resources to defence; the classic *rationale* of strategic bombing. For this it was not of vital importance where, to within five or six miles, the MPI lay. They paid little attention to the precise information about the fall of their bombs which the Abwehr was collecting for them. So long as enough were reaching central London to cause serious disturbance, and widespread damage was being inflicted elsewhere, Colonel Wolff and his men were satisfied.

The object of dissuading the Germans from correcting their aim was thus achieved, but it was not a difficult task, and its success, ironically, owed at least as much to the imaginative reports of *Ostro* from Madrid as to the efforts of the Twenty Committee and the Home Defence Executive. The real achievement of the Twenty Committee was to maintain the credibility of its agents. Their reports of damage in central London were as uncritically received as those of *Ostro*. But it was the German talent for self-deception (not unlike that of RAF Bomber Command at an earlier stage of the war) that led them to believe that they had achieved the concentration of fire on the metropolis indicated on their intelligence map, which is reprinted as Fig IA. The real scatter is shown in Fig IB. It was this degree of inaccuracy, rather than the precise location of the mean point of impact that, taken together with the increasingly successful interceptions by RAF aircraft and AA Command, prevented the flying bombs from causing any really serious damage.

The farewell barrage fired from the flying bomb sites before they were overrun were not the last of these weapons to land in England. The Germans rapidly adapted them for launching from aircraft, and a further 54 were to land at various points in the Home Counties before the war came to an end. But the threat presented by this rather haphazard bombardment was negligible compared to that from the second category of 'reprisal weapons' (Vergeltungswaffen) which the Germans brought into action at the beginning of September; the ballistic rocket missiles already known, in Britain as well as Germany, as V2s.

These were the weapons whose development had been detected even before that of the V1s, and their implications for the defence of London were very much graver. There was no means of intercepting them, and Ministry of Home Security estimates of casualties in the worst possible case were so serious – over 100,000 killed and as many seriously injured a month – that in August 1943 plans had been revived to move the seat of government out of London.[34] These had been rejected by the Cabinet, but in summer 1944 the accumulation of evidence, from Sigint, from apparatus smuggled out from Poland and Sweden, from POW interrogation, and from documents captured in France, that the use of these weapons might be imminent, reawakened official concern.[35] Evacuation of school children, hospitals and certain Government employees was put in hand, and by the end of August nearly a million and a half people had left London.[36] By then further intelligence had indicated that the attack was not likely to be made on nearly so great a scale as had been feared, and more extreme measures were suspended.[37] The rapid advance of the Allied armies on the Continent encouraged premature hopes that the attacks might be abandoned altogether, in spite of warnings from the Air Intelligence Staff that these could be improvised from sites in Holland much more easily than was generally assumed.[38] But it was confidently expected, at this euphoric moment, that these sites would shortly be overrun as well; and on 6 September the Vice Chiefs of Staff concluded that 'there should thus shortly be no further danger to this country from either of these causes [V1s or V2s] except for the possibility of the airborne launching of flying bombs'.[39] Two days later, on the evening of 8 September the first V2s landed. Over a thousand more were to follow.

The fall of the first 25 V2s, between 8–25 September, covered a wide area, from East Anglia to Sussex, but thereafter the fighting in Holland compelled the V2 batteries to fall back to positions in Friesland from which they could reach no further than East Anglia. Although the stabilisation of the front enabled them to return to West Holland on 3 October, it was not until the last week of that month that their fire began to concentrate on London.[40]

Until it became clear what targeting policy, if any, was being pursued by the V2 batteries, little could be done in the way of deception. In September no more information was put over than was strictly necessary to maintain the credibility of the agents, while in October concern was being focussed on the areas on the mainland – Antwerp, Liège – which were coming under attack from both V1s and V2s. By November, however, the situation was becoming clearer – and grimmer. From 26 October onward the fire of the V2s was clearly being focussed on London. Between 26 October and 4 November 26 rockets fell in the London area, mainly in East London and the docks, as against 19 elsewhere. But what was of equal interest was that a message passed by *Treasure* on 25 October reporting, fairly truthfully, damage done in areas as far separated as Camberwell, Mitcham, Sidcup and Edmonton, had been quoted almost verbatim in a communiqué of the German High Command. This led the Twenty Committee to consider on 9 November whether it should not once again try to manipulate the reports of its double agents so as to induce the Germans to shorten their range. Although there were those who groaned inwardly at the prospect of reopening the battle in the War Cabinet, Stewart agreed to discuss the matter with the specialists at the Air Ministry.

The Air Intelligence Staff were not encouraging. They calculated that the V2s were already being fired at their extreme range of some

200 miles. They located the aiming point at Wapping, but most of the rockets had fallen somewhat short in a 'tail-back' that resulted in the heaviest concentration landing in the quadrant north of the Thames and east of the Lea Valley, in the region of Barking, Ilford, East and West Ham and Wanstead. Less than 10 per cent had fallen west of London Bridge. But the area affected was populous and included the docks, which had been particularly badly hit during the last few days of October. The enemy's inability to extend his range was very fortunate, but there seemed everything to be said for persuading him to shorten it still further. After considerable discussion, however, the Twenty Committee agreed, on 16th November, that the agents should simply continue to send over the bare information necessary to maintain their credibility.

This at any rate was the decision minuted. But subsequent events make it clear that some members of the Committee took matters into their own hands. Out of the hundred V2s that fell on England between 26 October, when the intensive bombardment of London began, and 17 November, 30 had fallen north and east of a line running from the Lea Valley at Enfield south-east to the Thames at Erith, just short of the major built-up areas of East London. Of the next hundred which fell between 18 November and 8 December, the number falling short of this line had risen to 45. In the final hundred of the year the number had again risen, to 67. When the Twenty Committee met on 18 January 1945 the Chairman reported that sigint showed the Germans to be paying great attention to the agents' reports; and on 25 January the Committee cautiously concluded that, since the experts could give no technical explanation for the shift in the mean point of impact, it was possible that it had been due to the deception put out by 'Special Means'. The monthly report that MI5 sent to the Prime Minister in January informed him of this possibility; the subsequent report in February asserted it 'with some certainty'.

The records of the Twenty Committee make it quite clear that two agents in particular, *Tate* and a new recruit, *Rover*, a Polish seaman whom the Germans had tried to infiltrate into Britain as a refugee, were principally concerned with putting over a deception based on the principles worked out the previous July for dealing with the V1s; that is, reporting true incidents with false times to persuade the Germans that they were overshooting. Unfortunately the record of the traffic of these agents has not been preserved; few traces are available in ISOS files; and no German records have yet been found to furnish any conclusive evidence that this change of aim was in fact due to the misinformation provided. But that they were so misinformed is made clear by comparing the map at Fig 11A, on which the Germans plotted what they believed to be the fall of their V1s and V2s on London at the end of December 1944, with that at Fig 11B, which shows the true position at that time.

It is not irrelevant that a subsequent analysis undertaken for the

Ministry of Home Security indicated that if the MPI of the V2s had not altered when it did, 1,300 more people would probably have been killed, 10,000 more injured and 23,000 houses damaged – to say nothing of the disruption to the economy and administration of the country which would have resulted from the concentration of destruction which the Germans believed they were achieving between Westminster and the docks. Unless new evidence emerges to the contrary, we can state that the report conveyed to the Prime Minister in February 1945, that 'it is now possible to conclude with some certainty that the shift to the north-east of London of the mean point of impact of V2s is due to reports from Special Agents' may well have been correct.

Note: The following table has been compiled from the statistics in the Home Office Bomb Census, HO 198/178 and HO 198/107. Area A is that north and east of the Enfield-Erith line – the major built-up area of Central London. Area B is within the triangle formed by that line as a base with its apex at Camberwell. Area C includes all incidents outside the first two areas.

V2s in hundreds	Dates	Area A	Area B	Area C
1–100	Sept 9–Oct 26	71	11	18
101–200	Oct 26–Nov 17	30	45	25
201–300	Nov 17–Dec 3	45	42	13
301–400	Dec 3–Dec 30	67	23	10
401–500	Dec 30–Jan 12	55	26	19
501–600	Jan 12–Jan 26	51	35	14
601–700	Jan 26–Feb 10	45	38	17
701–800	Feb 10–Feb 20	47	29	24
801–900	Feb 20–March 6	44	36	20
901–1000	March 6–March 17	39	40	21
1001–1070	March 17–March 27	36	19	15

REFERENCES

1. CAB 101/130, Unpublished Narrative: Crossbow, by J Dawson, para 50.
2. ibid, para 61.
3. ibid, para 74.
4. ibid, para 84 et seq. See also Basil Collier, *The Defence of the United Kingdom* (1957) ch. XXIV.
5. Imperial War Museum, MI 14/1038(V), War Diary of Flak Regt 155(W); Copy also in MOD Air Historical Branch (AHB) file II/80/54/27; CAB 120/751, PM Registered file 413/4 Annex.
6. R V Jones, *Most Secret War* (1978), p 421.
7. CAB 121/213, SIC file B/Defence/2, Vol 3, COS(44) 218th Meeting (o), 1 July.
8. CAB 113/35, HDE/147/0S of 6 July 1944.
9. CAB 121/213, COS(44) 226th Meeting (o), 7 July.
10. CAB 113/40, HDE/147/5/SR.
11. CAB 121/213, COS(44) 239th Meeting (o), 18 July.
12. ibid, COS(44) 630(O) of 16 July.
13. ibid, COS(44) 652(O) of 24 July.
14. ibid, COS(44) 247th Meeting (o), 25 July; PREM 3/111A.
15. CAB 121/214, SIC file B/Defence/2, Vol 4, WM(44) of 28 July (not circulated).

16. ibid, C O S(44) 680(o) of 31 July.
17. ibid, C O S(44) 254th Meeting (o), 1 August.
18. PREM 3/111A.
19. Minutes not circulated – see PREM 3/111A.
20. ibid and CAB 121/214, Note signed by W S Murrie.
21. PREM 3/111A.
22. Imperial War Museum, MI 14/1038(V), Flak Regt 155(W) War Diary, p 207; Copy also in MOD AHB file II/80/54/27.
23. CAB 113/35, Findlater Stewart to Duncan Sandys, 24–28 August 1944.
24. Imperial War Museum, MI 14/1038(V)
25. ibid, p 126.
26. ibid, p 132.
27. ibid, p 136.
28. ibid, p 147.
29. ibid, p 193.
30. ibid, p 151. The exact wording is 'Der Treffmittelpunkt liegt im Mittel links – Kurz'.
31. ibid, p 127.
32. *The Times*, 17 June 1944.
33. Jones, op cit, p 422.
34. CAB 121/213, C O S(43) 349(O) of 28 June; CAB 121/214, WM(44) 98 of 28 July; CAB 98/39, Rocket Consequences Committee (RA(44) series).
35. CAB 101/130, para 112; JIC(44) 336(o) of 31 July.
36. CAB 101/130, para 116; CAB 121/214, WM(44) 98 of 28 July.
37. CAB 101/130, para 117; CAB 121/214, C O S(44) 299th Meeting (o), of 6 September, C O S(44) 811(O) of 6 September, WM(44) 118 of 7 September.
38. CAB 101/130, para 119.
39. CAB 121/214, C O S(44) 811(O) of 6 September.
40. HO 198/178, Bomb Census; Long-range Rockets 8 September 1944 to 4 January 1945. All subsequent information in the text is based on this source.

CHAPTER 9

Normandy and Beyond:
North-West Europe, June 1944–April 1945

WE MUST now return to take up the threads of our story where we left it at the end of Chapter 6, on the eve of the 'D Day' landings in Normandy on 6 June 1944. It will be recalled that at 0300 hours on 6 June *Garbo* went on the air to warn his control in Madrid that invasion was imminent – a warning carefully timed to arrive too late for the Germans to do anything about it – and failed to obtain any response. He got through finally at 0608 hours. The same evening he radioed again, bitterly complaining of his employer's inefficiency. 'This makes me question your seriousness and sense of responsibility', he told them sternly; 'I therefore demand a clarification immediately as to what has occurred'. Next morning, after a notionally sleepless night, he was in contact again. 'I am very disgusted as in this struggle for life and death I cannot accept excuses or negligence', he berated his unfortunate employers; 'I cannot masticate (sic) the idea of endangering the service without any benefit. Were it not for my ideals and faith I would abandon this work as having proved myself a failure. I write these messages to send this very night though my tiredness and exhaustion due to the excessive work which I have had has completely broken me'.

His German controlling officer replied at once, apologetic but reassuring. 'I wish to stress in the clearest terms that your work over the last few weeks has made it possible for our command to be completely forewarned and prepared, and the message ... would have influenced [them] but little had it arrived three or four hours earlier'. This, as we have seen, was not entirely true. Tactical surprise had been almost complete. But that the German High Command was prepared for precisely the form of attack that *Garbo* and his colleagues had warned them to expect is shown by the situation report put out by Fremde Heere West (FHW) on the evening of 6 June:[1]

'The enemy landing on the Normandy coast represents a large-scale undertaking; but the forces already engaged represent a comparatively small part of the total available. Of the approximately sixty divisions at present in the south of England, it is likely that at the most ten to twelve divisions are at present taking part, including airborne troops ... Within the framework of his group of forces Montgomery still has over twenty divisions available to reinforce his operations, which allow us to expect further air and sea landing attempts in the area of the Cotentin peninsula, to force the capture of his objective

... [But] the entire group of forces which make up the American First Army Group, comprising about 25 divisions north and south of the Thames, has not yet been employed.* The same applies to the ten to twelve active divisions held ready in the Midlands and in Scotland. The conclusion therefore is that the enemy command plans a further large-scale undertaking in the Channel area which may well be directed against a coastal sector in the central Channel area'.

Meanwhile *Brutus* had radioed from his notional observation post with FUSAG HQ 'Received this morning news of the beginning of the invasion. Extremely surprised because our FUSAG remains unmoved. It is clear that the landing was made only by units of the 21 Army Group ... FUSAG, as I reported, was ready for an attack which is capable of being released at any moment, but it is evident that it will be an independent action'. *Garbo* himself recovered from his notional *crise de nerfs* and soldiered gallantly on, transmitting prolific reports from his notional agents of notional troop movements and troop identifications in East Anglia which were logged and accepted without question at FHW.[2] The agents also gave hearsay reports of landing-craft moored in the Thames Estuary, the Crouch, the Deben, the Orwell and elsewhere which, since these were prohibited areas, they could not check; but if the German Air Force had cared to do so, it would have seen an impressive display of dummies to bear out these rumours.

In addition to all this, *Garbo* was fortunate enough in his notional capacity as a temporary employee of the Ministry of Information to receive on D-day notional official guidelines for propaganda about the invasion, which he radioed through on 7 June.[3] These instructed MOI officials to describe the invasion as 'a further important step' in the attack on Fortress Europe; but they were warned that it was extremely important to keep the enemy in the dark about future Allied intentions. Great care was to be taken to avoid speculation about further operations or areas of possible attack, and emphasis was to be laid on the significance of the present attack and its outcome for the course of the war. Next day, however, *Garbo* reported that instead 'certain allusions of a more general kind' had been laid down for the future.

To make this misinformation more credible, snippets of true and verifiable information were provided. On 8 June (D + 2) *Garbo* reported that 3rd British Division had landed with the first wave on the Normandy beaches; which was true, as the Germans had discovered already. More important, he reported that the Guards Armoured Division, regarded by the enemy as a particularly elite unit, was due to embark for Normandy the following day. In fact the Division was not due to cross for a week, but it was rightly assumed that the report would catch the eye of the German High Command. It did. On 9 June

---

* In fact the troops available for *Overlord* totalled some 20 British and Canadian divisions and 24 US (including 1 French).

Bletchley circulated a message from von Rundstedt's HQ in Paris to the Abwehr station in Madrid, confirming the identification of 3rd Division and stating that von Rundstedt had found information about the Guards Armoured Division 'particularly significant'.

During the week immediately following D-day, German intelligence appreciations continued to stress the strength of the Allied forces remaining in south-east England. Nevertheless the Germans committed the bulk of their armoured reserves to the Normandy bridgehead remarkably quickly. Responsibility for the defence of north-west France was shared uneasily between von Rundstedt, as Commander-in-Chief West, and Rommel, commanding Army Group B whose two constituent armies Seventh and Fifteenth, defended the coast from Brittany to Belgium with the River Orne marking the boundary between them. Since the middle of May Rommel had also been given operational control of the three panzer divisions, 2nd, 21st and 116th, from General Geyr von Schweppenburg's Armoured Group West. A further four panzer divisions were held in reserve by OKW, not to be committed without direct orders from Hitler; 1st SS Panzer, stationed in Belgium north of Brussels; 12th SS Panzer at Dreux, south-east of Caen; Panzer Lehr, north-west of Orleans; and 17th Panzer Grenadier, south of the Loire near Poitiers whence it could move either north to help Army Group B or south to help Colonel General von Blaskowitz's Army Group G in repulsing an attack on the Mediterranean shore.

Of these forces, Rommel committed 21st Panzer Division at once and 2nd Panzer Division within 24 hours. Von Rundstedt requested release of 12th SS Panzer, 17th SS Panzer Grenadier and Panzer Lehr Divisions from OKW Reserve, which, after some twelve hours' delay, was granted. 12th SS Panzer came into action on 7 June. Panzer Lehr, heavily bombed on its hundred-mile journey from the interior, appeared two days later.[4] SHAEF had hoped that the threat to the Pas de Calais would tie down at least 2nd Panzer Division, located as it was in the region of Amiens between the two threatened areas. Its appearance in Normandy, where on 13 June it inflicted a heavy reverse on 7th Armoured Division, took Montgomery by surprise.[5] The same day 17th SS Panzer Grenadier Division came into action on the American front. Further, on 9 June OKW ordered up not only 2nd SS Panzer Division which had hitherto been assigned to Army Group G but a regiment of 116th Panzer Division.[6] That left, of Rommel's own armoured reserve, only part of 116th Panzer Division and of OKW armoured reserve, only 1st SS Panzer Division in Belgium. The latter was released by OKW on 8 June and began to move the following day. Admittedly these formations were not made available, as Rommel had wanted, in time to smash the invasion on the beaches; but once the scale of the Normandy landings became apparent, virtually the entire strategic reserve, far from being held back to meet the threat to the Pas de Calais, was thrown into the Normandy battle as fast as possible to gain a decision there before the second landing could be made.

But it was not too late to stop at least the move of 1st SS Panzer Division, or any units of Fifteenth Army, from Belgium. On 8 and 9 June, therefore, the deception staffs mounted a major effort through all available channels to indicate that an attack on the Pas de Calais and Belgium was imminent. Bogus radio traffic and communications with resistance networks in the area were intensified, and shortly after midnight on 8–9 June *Garbo* radioed an emphatic warning:

'After personal consultation on 8 June in London with my agents, *Donny*, *Dick* and *Derrick* whose reports I sent today I am of the opinion, in view of the strong troop concentrations in SE and E England, that these operations are a *diversionary manoeuvre designed to draw off enemy reserves in order to make an attack at another place*. In view of the continued air attacks on the concentration area mentioned, which is a strategically favourable position for this, it may very probably take place in the Pas de Calais area, particularly since in such an attack the proximity of air bases will facilitate the operation by providing continued strong air support'.

This message was passed to OKW where it arrived at 2220 hours on the evening of 9 June. The Chief of Intelligence, Colonel Krummacher, underlined the passage marked above, and minuted it 'confirms the view already held by us that a further attack is expected in another place (Belgium?)'. Jodl himself underlined the words 'in S and SE England'. The message was marked as having been shown to the Führer.

By a great stroke of good fortune, another message to the same effect had reached OKW a few hours earlier; this one from an uncontrolled agent *Josephine*. *Josephine* was in fact a German Abwehr officer in Stockholm, Karl Heinz Kraemer, whose information came largely through Swedish military circles and intelligent study of the Press. He had stated in this report that according to 'authoritative military circles' in London 'a second main attack across the Channel directed against the Pas de Calais is to be expected'. To which source of misinformation this rumour should be attributed it is now impossible to say. But whereas either the *Josephine* or the *Garbo* messages on their own might not have been enough to secure action, together they were decisive, as both Jodl and Keitel after the war were to agree. Keitel telephoned direct to von Rundstedt, who at 0730 next morning issued the message:

'As a consequence of certain information, C-in-C West has declared a "state of alarm II" for the 15th Army in Belgium and North France. (For Netherlands command too, if Army Group 3 thinks fit). The move of 1st SS Panzer Division will therefore be halted.'

1st SS Panzer Division therefore remained as a reserve in the rear of Fifteenth Army, and was not to be moved to Normandy for another week.

Too much should not be made of this. Even had the Division moved,

Allied Air Forces and the forces of the Resistance would have harassed its 250 mile journey across Belgium and northern France, whether it travelled by road or rail, and the eventual intervention of such units as arrived intact would hardly have been in itself decisive. Still, the sceptics who had doubted whether the Germans would move a single division on the strength of an agent's report alone had been confounded, and the deception authorities could justifiably congratulate themselves on the direct impact they had made on the course of the battle.

Garbo's German employers were as delighted with his performance as were the British. On 9 June Bletchley decrypted a message from Berlin to the Abwehr Stelle in Madrid: 'In the name of Fremde Heere West I express appreciation of previous work in England. The object of further reconnaissance must be to ascertain in good time when embarkation begins and the destination of the group of forces in south-east England'. And two days later they repeated in more emphatic terms, 'The reports received in the last week from the *Arabel* undertaking (ie *Garbo's* network) have been confirmed almost without exception and are to be described as especially valuable. The main line of investigation in future is to be the enemy group of forces in south-eastern and eastern England. It would also be especially valuable to learn in good time when the formations which are at present assembled in western Scottish ports put to sea, and what their destination is'.

What had in fact happened was that German identifications of Allied units fighting in Normandy had confirmed all *Garbo's* information about 21st Army Group. All the more credible, therefore, was his information about FUSAG, whose imminent attack across the Channel continued to pin down the nineteen infantry and two armoured divisions of the Fifteenth Army – units whose intervention in the Normandy battle really might have tipped the scales.[7] As FHW put it in its report on 9 June, 'The fact that not one of the formations still standing by in the south east and east of England has been identified in the present operation strengthens the supposition that the strong Anglo-American forces which are still available are being held back for further plans'. An attack on Belgium, FHW decided two days later, was improbable, since so much of the Allied close-support air strength had been committed to Normandy; but this made it likely that FUSAG would operate in close co-operation with 21st Army Group, probably between the Seine and the Somme, in a direct thrust on Paris.[8]

It was of course the task of the deception staffs to keep this supposition alive for as long as possible, and they found no difficulty in doing so. For the remainder of the month *Garbo* and *Brutus* continued to feed in information about the growing concentrations in south east England, backed up by alarming accounts of the rate at which fresh American forces were flooding into the country. *Garbo* reported on 16 June that one of his agents had just returned from Liverpool, which he had found surrounded by enormous transit camps. He had been told that 'the rate of arrival in north-west ports of US troops has been so fast that it became impossible to cope with transport on the spot, and so camps were made available for temporary encampment of new arrivals until posted to their areas. Enormous convoys on roads, massive war material, great activity in the docks, especially hundreds of small assault craft'.[9] A further refinement was added in case the Germans were wondering about the capacity of the Channel ports to handle these vast numbers. Because of the danger from V-weapons, they were told on 22 June, many of these units were being held in the west country and would be embarked at ports in the Bristol Channel. Of all the forces available in Britain for the invasion, *Garbo* assured them, only 38 per cent had been committed to Normandy by 21 June.[10]

All this misinformation was faithfully logged and transmitted by FHW, which now built up a firm picture of Allied intentions. 'It is assumed', it reported on 28 June, 'that an attack by the Army Group Patton would be timed to coincide with the moment when Mont-gomery's armies have gained ground in the direction of the River Risle sector ... As regards the targets set for the operation of the American Army Group, some further captured documents (maps issued to the English Army Group) indicate that for Montgomery's troops there is no plan for operations on the north bank of the Seine. Thus it appears more probable that the Army Group Patton will make a co-ordinated thrust directed against the middle Channel Coast area'.[11]

Enough of the FHW situation reports were decrypted to give the deception authorities a very good idea of the success of their plans. But another equally prolific source was the traffic between the Japanese embassy in Berlin and Tokyo, which carried regular and detailed reports by the Japanese Naval and Military Attachés on the progress of the war. The German military and naval staffs gave their Allies full and frequent briefings. One of the most extensive was given by Jodl himself on 3 July, which the Japanese Naval Attaché reported as follows:

'The main enemy force used in the landings was Montgomery's Army Group. This Group now has in England no more than 4 to 5 infantry divisions and 2 armoured divisions. On the other hand it is obvious that Patton's Army Group (18 infantry divisions, 6 armoured divisions, 5 airborne divisions) is being made ready in London and in southern England for the next landing. It is also evident, from the operational sectors of the two enemy army groups and the state of preparations, and from the fact that it would be difficult for the port of Cherbourg alone to supply two army groups, that the landing area will be the Channel region facing the German Fifteenth Army. We con-clude that the enemy will plan operations with both army groups on both sides of the Seine, heading towards Paris. Reports of preparations for large enemy landings on the Mediterranean coast of southern France appear to be largely deliberate propaganda reports by the enemy. We are prepared for landings in the vicinity of Bordeaux and on the coast of Belgium and the Netherlands, although there is little probability of such landings; it is believed at present there is almost no probability of landings in Denmark and Norway.

The defences on the front of the German Fifteenth Army are extremely strong, and moreover our troops are disposed with an equal number of coastal defence divisions and of rear groups (9 or 10 divisions) directly behind them. Nearly all of the enemy's seasoned troops with experience in the African and Italian fighting have been exposed in the present landings; there are not more than two divisions acknowledged to be seasoned troops in Patton's Army Group which is to carry out the next landing. Moreover, since this Army Group intends to land in the face of strong German defences, we have every confidence in defeating them'.

The nature of the Allied deception measures in the Mediterranean to which Jodl referred have been described in the previous chapter. *Fortitude North* was anyway being wound down; on 11 June *Garbo's* agent on the Clyde reported that the shipping concentrations there had gone, probably moving south to join the Channel forces, although there was still much troop movement in and around Glasgow.[12] That story in fact was blown when one of Kraemer's contacts returned to Sweden at the end of the first week in July and reported that there were no particular troop concentrations in the north of England and Scotland, and the Swedes themselves were reported to dismiss all probability of an attack on Scandinavia. ('Good and clear', minuted Jodl's staff on this report, 'and corresponds to our information').[13] As for the threat to Bordeaux, it is interesting that the notional Operation *Ironside II* should have registered at all; though no direct link can be traced between the rumours transmitted by the double agents and the preparations made to defend that port.

Four weeks after the Normandy landings the German High Command was thus still completely convinced of the existence of FUSAG, and had some 22 divisions waiting to repel its attack. But by now *Fortitude South* had moved into a further stage. At the beginning of July some of the real formations used to flesh out FUSAG were due to be committed to the Normandy battlefront, where they would be rapidly identified by enemy intelligence. More important, General Patton himself was about to take command of the US Third Army in that theatre, as part of General Omar Bradley's 12th Army Group. The appearance of Patton in a subordinate command in a theatre hitherto commanded by his great rival Montgomery took some explaining, but it was not beyond the ingenuity of the deception authorities. The story devised was that 21st Army Group had made such unexpectedly slow progress that it had to be heavily reinforced by formations from FUSAG. In order to avoid putting so many American forces under Montgomery's command a new US 12th Army Group had been set up under General Bradley to take charge of them (which was also true). With two Army Groups in operation, it was necessary for Eisenhower himself to assume operational command. Patton furious at seeing his best units milked off before he had been committed to battle at all, exploded in a typical display of insubordination; which so enraged General Eisenhower that he demoted him on the spot. Patton, was however given the chance to retrieve his reputation in a subordinate field command. The story was transmitted, with plenty of colourful detail, by *Garbo* on 20 July as coming from his friend in the US Service of Supply. It was not easy to find a successor to Patton whose prestige would lend equal credibility to FUSAG, and it is some indication of the importance which the Allied High Command attached to the deception that General Marshall at once released one of the most outstanding senior officers remaining in the United States, Lieut General L J McNair, Commander-in-Chief Land Forces USA; it being announced that he was to take up 'an important command in the field'.[14]

The appointment had a tragic sequel. General McNair was flown to the United Kingdom, whence he visited the American forces fighting in Normandy. On 24 July he was killed, together with many other American troops, in a disastrously misdirected air bombardment by the US Army Air Force. His death could not be kept secret, but it was carefully leaked by *Brutus* on 26 July, before any public announcement had been made. When a successor was found in the person of General De Witt, Director of the Army and Navy Joint Staff College in Washington, it was announced that he was being posted 'to fill the assignment previously held by General McNair'. The Germans took the bait. A FHW situation report of 9 August commented that 'The probable transfer to the command of First US Army Group of a particularly well thought of and administratively competent General like General De Witt proves the special importance that is attached to this Army Group, which should consist of about 32 large formations ...'.

The 1st US Army Group of which first McNair and then De Witt took command had now been notionally very largely reorganised. The Third US Army, a real formation, had now been committed to battle, as had the First Canadian Army. In their place were established two notional formations; the Fourteenth US Army whose transit through Liverpool had been notionally observed by *Garbo's* notional agent, and the Fourth British Army built up for *Fortitude North* and now notionally brought south. The Fourth British Army did contain a few real formations but the US Fourteenth Army, consisting of two airborne and six infantry divisions, was entirely imaginary. Rather more realism was provided for a few weeks by Lieut General WH Simpson's real Ninth US Army, notionally allocated to FUSAG as a follow-up force, factually waiting its turn to go to Normandy.

Brutus, ideally placed to monitor all this at FUSAG HQ, missed the early stages of the reorganisation through being notionally on leave and so could report it only retrospectively; but he returned on 18 July and at once brought his Abwehr controlling officer up to date. On

27 July FHW's situation report logged the structure of FUSAG exactly as described by *Brutus*: Fourth English, Ninth US and Fourteenth US Armies. By the end of August all the notional units were correctly located on the situation maps at OKW.[15]

On 18 July, in a situation report read at Bletchley, von Rundstedt's HQ stated that 'there are no grounds for changing our appreciation of the intentions of the Army Group assembled in south-east England ... If and when the advance of the Anglo-Americans in Normandy and the compulsory draining off of our force to that area takes place, First US Army Group can be launched against Fifteenth Army'. From this the HQ drew the conclusion that it was necessary to contain Montgomery in Normandy for as long as possible. But a week later von Rundstedt's staff was more doubtful about the role of FUSAG:

'52 major formations are still assembled in Great Britain and about 42 of these can be transferred to the Continent ... [ran a situation report of 24 July]. While forces continue to be given up to the Normandy front, a widely removed landing operation becomes less probable. On the other hand Fifteenth Army's sector from north of the Somme along to the Seine continues to be particularly endangered. The more ground Montgomery gains southward from the bridgehead, and the quicker he does this, the less probable it will be that the forces still in England will carry out a seaborne landing at a new point. It is, rather, possible that in this case the English and Americans will push their remaining reserves into the bridgehead and will possibly carry out a major landing with their airborne troops south of the present bridgehead and then exploit this operationally'.

By the end of the month von Rundstedt was increasingly convinced that this was the case. 'The possibility which has already been emerging for some time that the enemy are in fact contenting themselves with the landing in Normandy and are sending the forces still assembled in Great Britain into this area as well', ran the War Diary of von Rundstedt's HQ for 27 July, 'is becoming increasingly probable'. It was an opinion shared by FHW, whose situation report on 31 July stated that 'a second major landing on the Channel coast no longer seems to be so probable in view of the development of the situation in Normandy'. As a result OKW, on 27 July, authorised the Fifteenth Army to release two divisions (84th and 33rd) to the Seventh Army followed by a third (89th) on 31 July and a fourth (85th) on 1 August. All the Panzer Divisions previously allotted to Fifteenth Army – 2nd, 1st SS and 116th – had already been committed to the Normandy battle. But it was too late. Montgomery had successfully achieved his object of drawing the German forces into battle around Caen. On 28 July General Bradley opened his attack in the west of the bridgehead, and on 3 August the US Third Army under General Patton – the *real* General Patton – began its decisive breakthrough. The Battle of Normandy had been won.

□

Three weeks later, in one of his inimitably long and chatty letters, *Garbo* told his Abwehr control what, according to his American inform-ant, had really happened. The American High Command, he wrote, had always been jealous of Montgomery, and had tried to restrict the scope of the Normandy campaign so that the real *coup de grâce* would be delivered by the Pas de Calais operation, a spectacular end to the war brought about by an American victory.

'The fact is that competition exists between the English and the Americans as to which is to win the glory of the final battle, but Montgomery, who has the fame of being an astute intriguer, once having initiated the Normandy operation was determined to maintain control and exploit the fame which he achieved at Alamein. He realised that he could only do this by allowing the Americans to have the newspaper headlines for the advances they were to make whilst he was exploiting his fame as a tactical general. So he did all that was possible that the weight of the German armies should fall against the British and the Canadians so that the Americans were able to advance more easily to the west and south, manoeuvring in order that this operation should develop into a large-scale one and should come to be considered as the principal one, in order that he should be allowed to reinforce his front from the original FUSAG, thus delaying the second operation which they were to have carried out'.

Garbo's informant further reported that the original FUSAG ope-ration had been planned for D + 40 (13 July) but had been delayed so that the (notional) US Fourteenth Army could be incorporated into the force structure. Montgomery apparently was now trying to persuade SHAEF to cancel the FUSAG operation altogether, so that he could use the Fourteenth Army himself. The Fourteenth Army, *Garbo* reported, was an unsavoury body. Originally raised to fight in the Pacific, its ranks contained 'many convicts who were released from prisons in the United States to be enrolled in a Foreign Legion of the French or Spanish type. It can almost be said that there are brigades composed of gangsters and bloodthirsty men, specially selected to fight against the Japanese, men who are not supposed to take prisoners but to admin-ister a cruel justice at their own hands …'. But Montgomery, as it turned out, had already been successful in acquiring possession of this collector's item. The order for its notional transfer was signed on 18 August, and the movement of its formations to France was reported by *Garbo* and *Brutus*. It began to appear in FHW situation reports between 31 August and 12 September.

By the end of August the German Fifteenth Army had been reduced to seven largely immobile divisions, and a new role had to be found for FUSAG. The US Ninth Army was now actually arriving in France, and at the beginning of September was committed to the capture of

Brest; so it was reported that this, with the notional US Fourteenth Army, now constituted SHAEF strategic reserve. There was thus left in FUSAG only the notional British Fourth Army, which was now joined, as *Garbo* reported on 31 August, by a notional First Allied Airborne Army. 'With this rearrangement', he pointed out, 'a great part of FUSAG will become a sort of modern version of Combined Operations. For instance, they will carry out large-scale airborne operations anywhere in France, Belgium, Holland or Germany to attack the enemy lines of communication. They will also be used to occupy any areas or countries which the Germans give up unexpectedly'.

FHW had in fact already recorded the existence of this airborne army in its situation report of 28 August. On 2 September it issued an intelligence summary which repeated the *Garbo* message of 31 August almost word for word, and speculated whether Eisenhower would use his new *masse de manoeuvre* to support Montgomery's thrust with 21st Army Group to the north, or that of US 12th Army Group, spearheaded by General Patton's Third US Army, to the east. 'Montgomery' FHW reported, paraphrasing what *Garbo* had told it, 'is said to have demanded only a *deceptive* attack towards the East by the Third American Army so as to enable him to envelop the German flank from the south (sic) with the *mass* of American formations, while Patton wanted to press forward directly towards Germany and demanded for this purpose all available reinforcements of the whole of the supply arrangements for himself. It is not clear in which direction the *decisive* effort will finally be made . . .'.[16]

It was not clear to the Allies either. No one could foresee that General Eisenhower would in fact make no decision but let the matter go by default. On 12 September, indeed, 21st Army Group submitted a cover plan to SHAEF on the assumption that the decisive thrust would be made in the north. '21st Army Group and the First US Army of 12th Army Group', this ran, 'having advanced so far as the Dutch and German frontiers, have now outrun their supplies . . . General Eisenhower has, therefore decided to hold the Second British Army and First US Army . . . and to concentrate his administrative resources in order to enable the reinforced army under command of General Patton to drive through the Metz-Nancy gap towards Saarbrücken. It is estimated that Second British Army and First US Army are likely to remain inactive until the first week of October'. If it had been Eisenhower's plan to put his weight behind the 21st Army Group this picture, transmitted by the now completely trusted *Garbo*, would no doubt have done much to help it. But he had already decided on the more cautious strategy of closing up to Germany's frontier along the full length of the Rhine.[17]

As for FUSAG itself, hardly had it been transferred into 'a sort of modern version of Combined Operations' than the opportunity arose for its use; to provide cover for the real airborne operations being planned by 21st Army Group to seize the crossings over the mouth of the Rhine, which were to culminate in the disastrous attack on Arnhem.

Field Marshal Montgomery submitted his plans for these operations, collectively termed *Market Garden*, to SHAEF on 10 September. Lieut General F A M Browning's 1st Airborne Corps, consisting of 82nd US, 101st US and 1st British Airborne Divisions, were to be dropped to secure the crossings over the Rhine at Grave, Nijmegen and Arnhem in face of the advancing British Second Army. The cover story, put across largely by *Brutus*, was that four notional airborne divisions of FUSAG, operating with the notional Fourth British Army, were being prepared for a long-range attack; possibly against north Germany itself in the region of Bremen or Kiel. This he reported on 10 September. But in order to keep the German reserves pinned down even after *Market Garden* had begun he warned them on 14 September that a second such force was being prepared, whose destination he could not discover.

Fate now took a hand in the person of the uncontrolled agent Kraemer, or *Josephine*. Kraemer's information came, as we have seen, from a wide range of sources, not least German intelligence reports themselves; but his knowledge of Allied air activities, acquired largely through his contacts on the Swedish General Staff, was particularly good. It is also possible that he had learned something about *Market Garden* from genuinely uncontrolled and indiscreet rumours conveyed through diplomatic channels in Stockholm. On 1 September he reported the movement of FUSAG units, adding 'it is quite clear that either a large-scale decoy manoeuvre is being planned, to cover the employment of FUSAG in Belgium, Holland and the Heligoland Bight, or that an operation against Denmark is actually intended'. This possibly originated with *Brutus's* own reports and fitted in very well with the intentions of the deception authorities. But on 15 September, two days before *Market Garden* was launched, Kraemer reported a rumour in London that FUSAG was not to be employed at such long range, but would be used in close association with 21st Army Group. 'The Second English Army will be advanced on a broad front as far as the Meuse and if possible as far as the Waal by 24 September. After that the employment of powerful airborne forces in eastern and northern Holland and the German frontier region is planned. Immediately on completion of the air landing action, which is intended to eliminate German river positions in the rear, it is intended to use FUSAG in Eastern Holland and the Heligoland Bight'.

This was in part alarmingly accurate. Fortunately the message reached Berlin only on 17 September, after the landings had already begun; and although there were strong German formations in the Arnhem area, of whose presence the British planners had not taken adequate account, their presence was quite fortuitous and the attack still secured total surprise. Indeed so far as the deception authorities were concerned – though not the unhappy forces on the ground – the whole enterprise turned out very well. If *Josephine*'s credibility was confirmed, so was that of *Brutus*, and the cover story remained intact. On 17 September FHW warned 'in connection with the air landings which have taken place, particular attention is deserved for an agent's report which has only just come in and which predicted these air landings correctly. In this report we are told that immediately after the air landing a landing operation by Fourth English Army (some fifteen divisions) would take place against Holland and the German Bight'. And a week later, on 23 September, a further FHW situation report summarised 'various reports by prudent agents' referring to a strong force in England preparing for further airborne operations:

'The reports above make convincing impression, [it ran], and have been partially confirmed by the course of operations and by troop identifications in recent days … On the basis of the above reports, therefore, new landings, coupled with strong airborne landings, must be expected in the area of the German Bight'.

The cover for the Arnhem operation was effectively the last act of Operation *Bodyguard*. The deception authorities had fulfilled the task given them by the Combined Chiefs of Staff after the Tehran conference ten months earlier. It was due in no small degree to their work that the allied Armies were now established in strength in western Europe and the German armies in the west had suffered a shattering defeat, that France, Belgium and much of Holland had been liberated, and that Hitler was preparing a last, despairing fight to defend the frontiers of the Reich. On 1 October therefore the Combined Chiefs ordered the cancellation of *Bodyguard*. It was assumed that the German forces were now stretched so tight that they no longer had the resources to meet new threats, whether real or imaginary; an assumption to be disproved by the Ardennes offensive ten weeks later.[18] Tactical deception, however, continued, controlled by deception staffs at Army Group Headquarters, and these were implemented where necessary by the 'Special Means' co-ordinated through Ops B at SHAEF with the London Controlling Section and the Twenty Committee. In addition, some use could be made of German 'stay behind' agents most of whom rapidly gave themselves up and could thus be used as channels of misinformation.

But deception during these closing months of the war seems to have been an unsatisfactory and largely unsuccessful affair. For one thing, few of the commanders of the huge new forces committed to battle fully understood what their deception staffs could be expected to do and what they could not; in particular, how long a successful deception operation took, and how carefully the ground had to be prepared. For another, the deception specialists themselves were now largely inexperienced. Most important of all, Allied strategy itself was so opportunistic, so lacking in long-term plans for developing enemy points of weakness and then exploiting them, that no serious cover plans could be made. The deception staffs were, paradoxically, in much the same helpless position as they had found themselves in 1941, when the British were too weak to have any offensive strategy about which they could mislead the enemy. Now the Allies were so strong that they effectively dispensed with strategy altogether and simply attacked all along the line, much as they had in the closing months of 1918.[19]

The various deception plans which fill the files of SHAEF for October 1944–March 1945 are thus largely historical curiosities. There was Operation *Avenger*, designed to cover a possible thrust into north Germany by 21st Army Group by giving the impression that the real objective was south Germany, and that the main attack would be launched across the Upper Rhine by United States Third Army and 6th Army Group. Plans for this were approved by General Eisenhower on 12 October, but on 8 November SHAEF Headquarters had to inform 6th Army Group 'it is not possible to give firm dates for the launching of future operations nor even to state with certainty that these operations will ever take place as planned'. A modification, *Avenger II*, was substituted in November which added a notional threat to the ports of north Germany; but 'although this plan received official approval' stated the file summary, 'further changes in the dates of real operations resulted in the instruction being almost stillborn, and very little implementation took place'.[20]

Much the same fate overtook *Dervish*, a project for luring German forces away from the front line by feigning a major airborne landing deep in central Germany; and *Callboy*, an attempt to pass off the crossing of the Rhine in the Weser sector in February 1945 as a feint to cover a real thrust against Kassel; and *Taper*, a month later, which involved a notional airborne landing in the Cologne-Düsseldorf area; and *Knifedge*, in December 1944, projecting an attack by the First French Army in the Mulhouse-Vesoul sector, which involved spreading prolific rumours in Switzerland; and *Jessica*, operations on the extreme right flank of the Allied forces on the Italian frontier, to pin down German troops while General Alexander's forces advanced in their rear. Much paper was generated by all these schemes for very little result.[21]

In the United Kingdom however, the deception authorities were stuck with the results of their earlier successes. They tried to disband FUSAG, thinning down its notional formations to cadres and holding units, but nothing could shake the belief of FHW that strong reserves were still being held back in Britain. On 27 October it reported as follows:

'The English Army at present consists of about 57 large formations ... to which are added 12 AA Divisions in Britain. The strength of the Air Force in 1940, which at that time belonged to the Army (sic) was about a quarter of a million men. That gives the result that today, with an army about four times as strong (about 1 million men) the present strength of the British Army is only 6 divisions less than the strength of the Army at that time. If one reckons that from the personnel strength of the present day air force 20–25 divisions could be formed, the potential total strength of Britain would be 89–94 divisions, far greater than the peak strength of their army, in the last war, of 75 divisions. Through the extension of the English arms industry to Canada and the USA as well as the heavy use of female workers, the use of manpower for industry can be almost disregarded'.[22]

From these amazing statistics the Germans reached the conclusion that there were some 14 active divisions of the British Army still in the United Kingdom. The London Controlling Section had therefore no difficulty in meeting the request of SHAEF that some notional forces should be kept on hand to pose a threat of amphibious operations in the context of its own tactical deception plans. So 'Fourth Army', now consisting of a small Army Corps and an airborne task force, was notionally moved up to Yorkshire, and *Brutus* passed across tantalising accounts of their preparations. These seem to have been highly effective. On 3 December the Japanese Naval Attaché reported to Tokyo that the German Naval Operations Department 'think it quite likely that the enemy will make a landing in the Heligoland Bight', and were also concerned about the Skagerrak. On 21 January the German Intelligence Service in Madrid had been ordered by Berlin to obtain information about the 'extensive preparations' on foot for anticipated further landings.[54] So *Garbo* was again alerted. On 19 February he was told, 'You will understand that the question of a new landing operation being undertaken from England is of the utmost importance. There are several important symptoms that this may occur although your agents have not yet discovered details. As preparations and troop concentrations in ports often do not begin until a very few days before embarkation, the situation may change from one day to another.' *Garbo* was told to report anything suspicious: 'until further notice we shall be listening here every day' said his control; adding, a little surprisingly, 'except on Sundays'.

Garbo did his best to reassure his anxious employers. On 5 March the FHW report stated that 'a hitherto trustworthy agent confirms once more on 2 March that on the English east coast and likewise in the whole of England there are no signs of any larger preparations for invasions to be noted'. Even so, on 16 and 22 March GC and CS decrypted warnings from OKW that Allied preparations for airborne and seaborne landings on the German North Sea coast were now complete. On 14 March, indeed, Hitler reorganised the local command structure so as to cope with them. As late as 9 April the Japanese Naval Attaché reported that a briefing given by the German Air Force five days earlier had categorically warned of an imminent Allied landing in the Heligoland Bight. Once an idea is established in the minds of military staffs, it is remarkably difficult to root it out. Until the very end of the war – indeed, until long after it – the Germans remained convinced of the reality of these phantom units against which they had prepared so resolutely to give battle.

REFERENCES

1. Imperial War Museum, MI 14–499, Lagebeurteilung West (LBW) 1288 of 6 June 1944.
2. Imperial War Museum, AL 1828–1, for example message from V-mann *Alaric* of 9 June 1944.
3. Imperial War Museum, AL 1828–1.
4. LF Ellis, *Victory in the West*, Vol I (1962), pp 200, 236, 237.
5. ibid, pp 261–262.
6. Helmuth Greiner and Percy F Schramm, *Kriegstagebuch des Oberkommandos der Wehrmacht* (Frankfurt am Main 1965), Vol IV, pp 313–315.
7. See map in Ellis op cit, p 130.
8. Imperial War Museum, MI 14–499, Kurze Feind Beurteilung West (KFW) 1293 of 11 June 1944.
9. Imperial War Museum, AL 1828–1.
10. ibid.
11. Imperial War Museum, MI 14–499, KFW 1310 of 28 June 1944.
12. Imperial War Museum, AL 1828–1, Message of 13 June 1944.
13. ibid, Message of 12 July 1944.
14. Documents relating to McNair's appointment are in WO 219–2226.
15. Information in Imperial War Museum, MI 14–481–1.
16. ibid, LBW 1376 of 2 September 1944.
17. See directive of 13 September 1944 in Alfred D Chandler Jr (ed), *The Papers of Dwight David Eisenhower* (Johns Hopkins Press, Baltimore 1970), Vol IV, 2136.
18. WO 219–2246.
19. ibid.
20. WO 219–2249, 2251.
21. WO 219–2242, 2253–2256.
22. Imperial War Museum, MI 14/481/2, KFW 1431 of 27 October 1944.

PART IV

The Far East 1942–1945

CHAPTER 10

The Far East 1942–1945

DECEPTION OPERATIONS in the Far East and in the Middle East were initiated by the same man: General Sir Archibald Wavell. It will be recalled that Wavell had been transferred from the Middle East to become Commander-in-Chief in India in July 1941. There he remained, apart from a brief interlude between January and March 1942 as Supreme Allied Commander American-British-Dutch-Australian (ABDA) Command, until the summer of 1943. In both capacities, as Supreme Commander and as C-in-C, in India, Wavell was faced with the same problem as had confronted him in the Middle East; how to deter attack by an adversary who, if not this time numerically superior, enjoyed all the advantages of the initiative and was vastly better trained and equipped than the forces under his own command. The weakness of his position made deception an essential element in his strategy from the very beginning.

On assuming command of ABDA in January 1942, Wavell asked that Major R P Fleming should be attached to his staff, to serve the same function as had Dudley Clarke in the Middle East. Major Fleming, better known as Peter Fleming the traveller, explorer, author and journalist, had already collaborated with Dudley Clarke in carrying out brief tactical deception activities during the last phases of the Norway campaign. Although Wavell asked for him in January, the difficulties of wartime travel made it impossible for Fleming to reach India until March; but a delay in Cairo enabled him to brief himself very thoroughly in the organisation and techniques of 'A' Force. By the time he arrived in Delhi Singapore had fallen, the ABDA Command had dissolved and British Forces were in headlong retreat from Burma. Wavell at once set him to improvise a piece of 'instant' deception: Operation *Error*.[1]

Compared with the elaborate and professional operations which deception authorities were now mounting in other theatres, *Error* was no more than a piece of light-hearted amateur improvisation, but it was the best that could be done under the circumstances. It did not even have the merit of originality, being virtually a re-run of the famous ploy that Wavell had described in his life of Allenby[2]; when Colonel Richard Meinertzhagen, scouting in front of the British lines in Palestine in September 1917, had drawn Turkish fire and fled, dropping as he galloped away a saddle bag containing a complete set of marked maps and orders which successfully misled the Turks as to the location of Allenby's forthcoming attack. This time the misinformation indicated a formidable defensive build-up of British forces in India, more than sufficient to block any further Japanese advance. The documents were contained in a brief-case which, together with other items of the Commander-in-Chief's personal effects, was left in a staff-car ditched on the further side of the Ava bridge over the Irrawaddy river, a few hours before the bridge was blown by 17th Division's rearguard on 30 April. Wavell's biographer commented a shade hopefully that 'after the British withdrawal into India, the Japanese made no effort to extend their advance, [and] it is possible that their decision was not unaffected by Wavell's and Peter Fleming's old ruse in the Jordan valley'.[3] No evidence, however, has come to light to suggest that the Japanese ever found the documents, let alone acted on them.

Once the front was stabilised in Assam, Wavell returned to his old command post in Delhi, and Fleming set about establishing his new organisation. This consisted of a small inter-Service staff within the Military Intelligence Directorate, known as GSI (d), which enabled Fleming to enjoy the unrestricted access to the Commander-in-Chief that had characterised Dudley Clarke's early days in Cairo. There was little call for more during 1942, when contact with the Japanese was minimal. But in May 1943, Wavell was recalled and in September the creation of South-East Asia Command under Vice Admiral Lord Louis Mountbatten made a more elaborate apparatus necessary. When the following March Mountbatten set up the Supreme Allied Command, South East Asia (SACSEA), the deception staff was redesignated as 'D' Division. It was as 'D' Division that it remained generally known; but when Mountbatten moved his HQ to Kandy in Ceylon, a nucleus of 'D' Division, the Policy and Plans Section, moved with him, leaving the main force behind in Delhi. This was reconstituted in December 1944 with the title Force 456. A further Tactical HQ was set up in Calcutta, with an Advanced HQ at Barrackpore, later moving to Rangoon, to keep in touch with the fighting forces in Burma and supervise tactical deception. Eventually 'D' Division was to total, on paper, 30 officers, 32 other ranks, and 9 secretarial staff.[4]

Like 'A' Force, 'D' Division thus found itself divided into three parts. A rear HQ at Delhi kept the records, supervised the main channels of misinformation and kept in touch with 'A' Force and the London Controlling Section. Main HQ was located with the Supreme Commander, while a Tactical HQ operated with the main land force Command. Initially officers of Tactical HQ were allocated to all major field formations to advise their commanders on deception activities, but in October 1944 a special unit was created, 'D' Force, consisting of eight companies equipped with sonic and pyrotechnic apparatus to provide deception in the field.

By now all the expertise of four years' fighting in the Western Desert and Europe had become available to equip these units with material, much of it air-portable, to simulate a battle on almost any scale, lasting if necessary for hours. A similar naval group, No 1 Naval Scout Unit, was formed with all the devices needed to simulate a seaborne attack. The manner in which these units were employed belongs to the operational histories of the Burma campaign, but one major deception, Operation *Cloak*, was sufficiently important to deserve a brief description later in these pages. As for radio and visual deception outside a strictly operational role, there is little to be said. Although a certain amount of bogus radio traffic was mounted in India in support of the Order of Battle deception that occupied the bulk of 'D' Division's time, the enthusiasm of the participants was tempered by an entirely justifiable scepticism as to the capacity of the enemy radio intercept services to read the traffic, or to make much sense of it if they did.[5] Absence of Japanese air reconnaissance activities made visual deception pointless except in immediate contact with his forces, and even then the thickly-covered terrain of Burma gave little opportunity for the camouflage experts. As a result, the only serious tool for strategic deception, at least until 1944, was to be the channels provided by the Intelligence and the Security Services: 'Special Means'.

The most dramatic and perhaps the most effective of these channels was provided by Britain's Chinese allies, the intelligence services of Chiang Kai-shek's government in Chungking. The links between these services and those of the Japanese occupation forces in China were, and remain, obscure, but they were certainly close as Fleming learned when he paid his first official visit to Chungking in June 1942. It would be possible, he then decided, to use them to present the Japanese with a series of red herrings so considerable as to deserve the title of *Purple Whales*; and so this channel came to be called.

Fleming's first proposal was for a document to be conveyed to the Japanese which would bear the real signatures of Mr Churchill and President Roosevelt, outlining the agreed strategy of the Grand Alliance for the forthcoming year. This grandiose suggestion had to be cleared with the Chiefs of Staff through the London Controlling Section, where it was considered a little excessive. So instead Fleming presented his Chinese colleagues with the *procès-verbal* of a notional discussion that had taken place at a meeting of Allied Commanders in Delhi on 31 May 1942. This indicated among other things that a second front was due to be opened in Europe some time during the coming summer; that all idea of an offensive in the Western Desert had been abandoned since substantial forces had been transferred from Egypt to India; that the United States was strengthening its defences in the south-west Pacific (where further Japanese attacks were expected) and preparing an offensive in the central Pacific; that heavy air raids were being planned against Formosa and the Japanese mainland; and that India was very heavily garrisoned indeed.[6]

This information appears to have vanished into the maw of the Japanese intelligence system without producing any noticeable effect, but further documents were to follow in support of successive deception plans: purloined operational orders, a sketch-book with portraits of senior officers, official telegrams, and the occasional personal letter between senior officers of the kind that proved so successful in *Mincemeat*. Their notional source was a weak-willed and impecunious British staff officer in Calcutta who sold them to a Chinese pilot on the Chungking air ferry, who then sold them to a Japanese agent with a radio-link to Macao. The channel was later reinforced by the addition of a notional Chinese official in Chungking who had access to the traffic between Chiang Kai-shek and his military representative at Mountbatten's head-quarters.[7]

In addition to this Chinese channel, Fleming had access to those developed in the European theatre. These included the contacts established by 'A' Force via Ankara and a particularly valuable source in Stockholm controlled by MI6 who commanded high credibility both with the Abwehr and with Japanese intelligence. But Fleming developed his own stable of agents and double agents as well. The first group of these, the *Hiccoughs*, were purely notional and their function was simply to distract Japanese counter-intelligence authorities in Burma. It was a group notionally left behind the Japanese lines and communicated with from India in a low-grade cypher over All India Radio. Further particulars about them were conveyed to the Japanese through the *Purple Whales* channel via Chungking. In August 1943 a container with supplies, documents and a new cypher was dropped to them which was successfully directed into Japanese hands, and it is clear that hunting them down occupied a certain amount of Japanese time and attention. The experience, Fleming reported later, 'shows how – just as infantry in a quiet sector can and should dominate No Mans Land by offensive patrolling – a deception staff, even when they have no policy to go on, can and should seek out and impose their will on the Japanese intelligence'.[8] When the British took the offensive in Burma in 1944 such a policy did develop, which was to attract Japanese forces towards the south-west coast of Burma so as to prevent them from reinforcing the Arakan and central Burma fronts. The *Hiccoughs* channel was used to spread alarm about this region, and the Japanese did indeed reinforce their garrison there; but there is no direct evidence of any causal connection.

The apparent success of *Hiccoughs* led to the establishment of a further notional party in Siam (*Angel One*), which was to be much used during the final months of the war, and a similar group in North Sumatra (*Coughdrop*) which was projected to Japanese intelligence by a carefully devised two-way radio traffic from Calcutta indicating that theatre as a target for forthcoming amphibious attack. There is, unfortunately, no sign that this traffic was ever intercepted by the Japanese.[9].

Hiccoughs was no more than a holding action. In 1943 however the Japanese played a number of cards into the hands of the British when they began to land their own agents on India's shores by submarine. These were either members of or associated with the Indian National Army organised under Japanese and German auspices; a body closely watched and partly infiltrated by the Intelligence Bureau of the Indian Government. The motivation of these agents was low, their training minimal, and they were easily captured and, once captured, turned round. Their value was limited, for their Japanese controls were as incompetent as they were themselves. 'Incoming (radio) traffic abounded with mistakes which had a stultifying effect, and which included the wrong cypher, the wrong call sign and the wrong frequency'.[10] At its very best, communication, maintained by clandestine sets over huge distances, was uncertain. Such double agents were thus of greater value to the security than to the deception authorities, providing as they did prolific information about the structure and progress of the various subversive movements with which the Japanese were in touch. But they were able to communicate a substantial quantity of misinformation as well – especially cumulative material dealing with the British and Indian Order of Battle.

The most effective of these channels was *Pawnbroker*, a party which was landed by submarine in December 1943 with the mission of establishing Indian National Army centres in Benares, Bombay and the North-West Frontier Provinces, with a head office in Calcutta; mainly with the object of relaying information back to the INA Headquarters in Rangoon. This party was caught almost at once, and its Calcutta set was put on the air in March 1944. Contact was not made with Rangoon until the end of August, but thereafter almost until the last days of the war, a stream of political and military misinformation was conveyed. The sources of the latter were notionally disaffected Indian serving officers in touch with such nationalist organisations as the All India Youth League. Other similar parties were *Travel*, a small group which landed on the Orissa coast in December 1944; *Trotter*, a team which landed in Madras about the same time; and *Hat Trick*, eight agents landed on the Malabar coast and captured with rather too much publicity for them to be effectively used, though two sub-groups, *Audrey* and *Doubtful*, were added to the list.[11]

Then there were the air-dropped agents. In April 1943 the Japanese tried to infiltrate a number of groups into Assam by parachute. All were caught and two were turned round. Known collectively as *Bats*, one of these, *Owl*, was brought back to Calcutta whence he relayed fairly low-grade military information which gradually progressed to higher levels as his standing with his Japanese employers appeared to be confirmed. The other, *Marmalade*, remained in Imphal but proved of little value. Comparable to these was *Frass* – a group of Karen agents dropped by the British near Rangoon in November 1942, who were themselves captured and turned round – or at least, their transmitter was used – by the Japanese. So clumsily was this done that 'D' Division continued to communicate with them so as to relay misinformation for two and a half years. A similar party of Malays was captured by the Japanese near Khota Bharu in October 1944. Known as *Oatmeal*, this group was used by both sides to mislead the other; but since the Japanese had now acquired a great deal more experience in this complex game, honours rested very much more even.[12]

Finally there were two double agents from the stable of MI5 in London, one real, one notional. *Father* was a real Belgian pilot attached to the RAF who in July 1943 found himself being pressed by his German control with such specific questions that it was thought best to transfer him to the Far East. There he began to send very full information back to his control in Madrid, but, as this had to go by surface mail, by the time it arrived it was very out of date. Not to be thwarted, the Abwehr sent him a radio set, via Istanbul and Bombay, and he began transmitting high-grade misinformation in August 1944. Within a few months however real personal difficulties made it necessary to send him home; but not before he had found a notional successor, an Indian attached to Strategic Air HQ in Calcutta, to whom he handed over his set.[13]

His companion from the United Kingdom was one of *Garbo's* numerous notional offspring, a member of the Womens Royal Naval Service codenamed *Gleam*. Her very improbability made her credible. Before enlisting, she had been connected with the Welsh Nationalist group (splendidly if confusingly entitled the Welsh Nationalist Aryan World Movement) from which *Garbo* had recruited so much talent. She was in fact the mistress of its most improbable member, an Indian poet known as 'Rags'. Perhaps it was this emotional involvement that led her on enlistment to request posting to the Far East. The British gave her a course in Hindustani, the Abwehr instructed her in the use of secret ink. Reaching Kandy in August 1944, she was posted to the office of the Deputy Chief of Staff, Information and Civil Affairs, and began a secret correspondence with *Garbo* under the cover of chatty letters to a girl friend in London. Her information was excellent, notionally derived from her close friendship with amiable senior officers; but since it took all of six weeks to get from India to London, whence it had to be transmitted via Madrid to Berlin and thence to the Japanese, it was of little operational value by the time it arrived. But at least it added lustre to the *Garbo* network.

But India had a figure comparable with *Garbo* himself; comparable, if not in inventiveness, then certainly in intelligence, personality, and the dominance he established over his control. He was given the codename *Silver* by the British and owed his loyalty to one master only; the cause of Communism, and hence of the Soviet Union. Highly gifted, personable, well-educated, he would no doubt have been an unequivocal supporter of the Indian National Army if that force had not been sponsored by the Axis powers, and an equally unequivocal opponent of the British in India if the British had not been allied with the Soviet Union. This complication of his loyalties made him suspect to all his employers in turn – German, Russian, British, Japanese – but he was meticulous in fulfilling the duties entrusted to him by 'D' Division. He first appeared on the scene early in 1942, when he helped the leader of the Indian National Army, Subhas Chandra Bose, to escape from India to Kabul. Thereafter his adventures would require the pen of Rudyard Kipling to do them justice. The Abwehr was active in Kabul, and he presented himself to them – not without reason – as a kind of Lawrence of Arabia, a master of disguise, held in numinous respect by the hill tribes of the North-West Frontier and deeply knowledgeable about the various revolutionary movements in India itself. The Germans gave him a questionnaire to take back to India, which he promptly delivered to the Soviet legation in Kabul. The Russians after some delay put him in touch with the British. He returned to India in October 1942 and was enlisted as a double agent by the Intelligence Bureau of the Government of India Home Department, whose interest in his activities was certainly not less than that of 'D' Division. Since the German interest in him was initially political rather than military, he presented himself to them on his return to Kabul in January 1943 as coming from a notional body, The All India Revolutionary Committee, which through its branches throughout India controlled all revolutionary activities and provided a magnificent espionage network comparable to that of *Garbo* in the United Kingdom.[14]

The report which *Silver* took back to Kabul was in two parts. The first consisted of an analysis of the political situation in India. The second was a military survey, a carefully concocted mixture of fact and fiction, in which strategic speculation was combined with a detailed Order of Battle of all three Services. Somewhat to the chagrin of his British case-officers, the Germans showed far more interest in the first part of his report than the second, and appeared to be in no hurry to reveal the existence of *Silver* to the Japanese. They regarded him primarily as an associate of Bose, a valuable tool of subversion and sabotage; the military affairs of south-east Asia enjoyed a low priority in their estimation. Not until 1944 did they start to pass over his information to the Japanese. But when he returned to India in March 1943 the Germans equipped *Silver* with a radio set with which he began to communicate with Kabul in July and with Berlin in September.

The British in India now enjoyed a direct line to Berlin. But it was of limited value unless their signals were passed to Tokyo, which for many months they were not. Meanwhile the Russians, perhaps suspicious of an agent who had now passed so completely out of their control, made a half-hearted effort to 'blow' *Silver* to the Germans. He succeeded in retaining the confidence of his German employers but by 1944, for obvious reasons, they were losing interest in the theatre, and in May they at last put him directly in touch with the Japanese.

But his communications with them remained circuitous. The rest of 1944 was spent in setting up a direct radio-link between his transmitter in India and the Japanese in Burma, but it was not until the last week in April 1945 that he at last made contact with Rangoon. It was by then getting rather late. Almost immediately the Japanese had to transfer their station from Rangoon to Bangkok, with which contact was so weak that it could not be put to practical use. Nevertheless in spite of all these problems *Silver* had for some 19 months provided Berlin with a mass of misinformation over his radio link, and had in the course of his visits to Kabul handed over to the German legation a total of six reports whose contents averaged twelve foolscap pages. He well deserved not only the Iron Cross bestowed on him by the Germans, but also the very large funds they placed at his disposal; a very fair proportion of which found their way into British hands.[15]

From very unpromising beginnings, therefore, Fleming had by 1944 built up an orchestra of deception almost as impressive as that created by Dudley Clarke in Cairo and BₐA at home. Like Clarke, he suffered from the disadvantage that he could not, as was possible in the United Kingdom, control all the channels of information available to the enemy, so he could not create in the enemy's mind a clear and false picture of Allied intentions. At best he could conceal those intentions behind a cloud of well-authenticated false information. He suffered however, from a further drawback which affected neither his colleagues in Cairo not, after 1942, those in London; that is, a total absence of any settled Allied strategic intentions in the Far East at all – at least, until the final year of the war. But the intervening years from 1942 until 1944 were put to the same use of they were in Cairo and in London; in building up, patiently and with scrupulous accuracy, a false Order of Battle, carefully geared to that being constructed in London by Bevan and in Cairo by Clarke. As early as November 1943 captured enemy documents showed that the Japanese estimated Allied strength in India and south-east Asia at nearly 52 divisions. 72 per cent of these formations were the creations of 'D' Division, the rest little more than cadres. By the end of the war the apprehensive Japanese garrison of Malaya and Thailand stood ready to repel an onslaught by six Army Corps and one Airborne Corps, each consisting of three divisions backed up by ample trained reinforcements; an exaggeration of Allied strength by nearly one hundred per cent.*[16]

There was a further, and massive complication. Deception in south-east Asia had to be integrated not only with that in the Middle East and European theatres. It was even more important that it should be carefully co-ordinated with the Americans, whose interest and commit-

---

* At their strongest SEAC land forces comprised twelve formed divisions, none of them either armoured or airborne.[17]

ment in the Far East was so very much greater than that of the British. The London Controlling Section had, as we have seen, established intimate links with Joint Security Control in Washington, but Fleming had little contact with his American colleagues in the south-west Pacific, and none whatever with those further east. It was a deficiency of which the importance became evident in the spring of 1943, when the Allies, having stabilised their fronts at the limits of the Japanese offensive, began to contemplate a coherent counter-offensive strategy; which in its turn called for a coherent cover plan.

Once again it was Wavell who took the initiative. In February 1943 he communicated to London a deception plan covering his own theatre. At the time he was planning the seaborne attack on Burma, *Anakim*, which had been authorised at the Casablanca conference for the coming autumn, and his object therefore was to prevent the Japanese from reinforcing Burma and interfering with British amphibious operations. The cover was a notional attack, mounted from India and Australia, on the south-west corner of the Japanese occupied region with a view to gaining control of the Sunda Straits, neutralising the Straits of Malacca and recapturing Singapore, the immediate objectives being southern Sumatra and western Java.

'Later (continued the outline plan) we should put it out that, as a diversion to cover these operations, to placate China and meet the pressures of public opinion (developed by our manipulation of the Press) we are undertaking a feint land offensive into northern Burma to be followed by seaborne expeditions ostensibly against southern Burma. In other words, sell our *real* plan as a *cover* plan, and our *cover* plan as the *real* plan. To back up the belief that our cover plan is the real plan we should initiate actual preliminary operations such as occasional PRU (photographic reconnaissance) of north and south Sumatra, Java, Andamans, north Malaya, Timor, gradually closing in to concentrate on the Sunda Straits area, followed by bombing raids, commando raids and the initiation of political warfare operations including leaflet dropping, radio broadcasts and attempts at landing arms, etc. Suitably-timed liaison visits should also be exchanged on a high level between India and SW Pacific and inter-command conferences staged, both open and secret publicity being given to them. More or less secret leakages should be arranged, regarding the appointment of commanders for these expeditions, especially at the Australian end'.[18]

The document was wildly optimistic about the resources that could be made available, political as well as military. Publicity in the Press was to be manipulated, political personalities should make injudicious statements, senior commanders should commit calculated indiscretions, there should be complaints of inaction from the Chinese government, upbraidings from the United States, pressure from Australia and 'apologetic statements from British sources stressing the physical difficulties of the campaign'. The failure of the Arakan campaign in the spring of 1943 was to produce all too much of this without any help from the deception authorities. With hindsight one can condemn this ambitious proposal for global thought-control as unrealistic and absurd, the product of inexperience and despair. But it was at least recognised that the implementation of any such cover plan would need not only careful planning and execution but meticulous and world-wide co-ordination; and Wavell proposed 'that this co-ordination must be done from Washington both as regards the manipulation of the world Press and public opinion and of the use of secret channels to influence the enemy High Command'.[19]

The Chiefs of Staff in London, advised by the London Controlling Section, sent back a guardedly encouraging reply. They agreed with the general proposals, except those for political manipulation. 'There are strong reasons', they stated, 'against using Press and personalities in this country for these purposes. We are examining this aspect further. There will probably be considerable clamour, both here and in America, in connection with aid to China through Burma without any press manipulation'. They agreed that there should be a preliminary conference to co-ordinate plans with Washington, but warned that 'no action should be taken to implement any deception plan in connection with *Anakim* until the CCS have confirmed that the operation is to be mounted'.[20]

Within a few months *Anakim* was to be cancelled for lack of resources, but the conference went ahead none the less. It was held in Washington in May, simultaneously with the 'Trident' conference of the Combined Chiefs of Staff, and it was attended by Fleming and by Sir Ronald Wingate of the London Controlling Section. At this conference the British brought forward proposals based on their now quite considerable experience, involving the complete integration of deception for the war against Japan under the auspices of the US Joint Chiefs of Staff. Under the JCS, they proposed that there should be a Combined Deception Planning Staff located in Washington comparable to the London Controlling Section whose task it should be to draw up a strategic outline plan. This would be communicated to the relevant theatre commanders, who would make their own cover plans in the light of it, submitting these to the Combined Deception Planning Staff for the elimination of contradictions and overlap. Also responsible to the Combined Deception Planning Staff would be a Combined Implementation Staff, responsible for all action to mislead the enemy by 'special means'. This would build up channels to the Japanese intelligence and work closely with 'A' Force and the London Controlling Section. The head of this (who should, the British considered, be an American) would enjoy much the same position as did Dudley Clarke; responsible for servicing the theatre commanders, but working to the Combined Deception Planning Staff much as Clarke did to the London Controlling Section.[21]

It was a plan which drew on British experience while giving the

Americans final control, and as such might have been expected to recommend itself in Washington. But substantial changes would be needed if it were to fit into the US command structure. The Americans would accept neither the idea of Combined Deception and Implementation Staffs, acting independently of their own Joint Staff Planners, nor the subordination of their theatre commanders to the overall control of a staff in Washington. In the document which was eventually drafted by the US Joint Chiefs of Staff for the approval of the Combined Chiefs of Staff, it was laid down, first, that responsibility for the formulation of overall deception plans for the war against Japan rested with the US Joint Chiefs of Staff, while responsibility for planning deception measures within the various theatres rested with the theatre commanders subject only to review and approval by the appropriate Chiefs of Staff. Deception plans for combined US–British operations would be submitted to the CCS for approval. Co-ordination in planning deception measures would be the responsibility of the US Joint Chiefs. Co-ordination for execution, and continuity of deception measures would rest with US Joint Security Control. Channels of responsibility thus continued to run along purely national command structures, and successful co-ordination depended on good communications between the London Controlling Section and their opposite numbers in Joint Security Control. The approved proposals merely authorised direct communications between theatres for the implementation of authorised plans, and urged the maintenance of close liaison between all concerned.[22]

During their stay in Washington Fleming and Wingate came to appreciate the impossibility of imposing a British-style integration on either General MacArthur, who deeply resented any interference from Washington, or the US Navy, who were equally reluctant to accept that the British should have any say in what they regarded as their own private theatre of war in the Pacific. They therefore accepted the revised proposals as the best they could get.

The British were more successful in obtaining agreement to a general Deception Plan for the War against Japan. Inevitably couched in very broad terms, this really made only two specific points. The first was that the greatest possible effort should be made to persuade the Japanese to retain a considerable proportion of their forces at home by threatening air attack on their home islands from aircraft carriers and from the Chinese mainland. The second was that, in view of the number of operations still being considered by the planning staffs, it would be better to deceive the enemy as to the timing and sequence of actual operations rather than by any specific cover plans. Detailed proposals however were made for feints, exaggerations of strength and deceptive naval and air bombardments in all Pacific theatres; while Wavell's proposals for a feint against north Sumatra were included, together with another plan for drawing the Japanese away from Burma by a threatened attack against the Netherlands East Indies from the south-west Pacific theatre. Finally, the Japanese were to be persuaded that the volume of traffic being ferried by air from India to China was insignificant, at least until September 1943, so as to dissuade them from attempting to interfere with it; but after that its volume should be magnified as much as possible; to add credibility to the threat presented to their Japanese mainland by US aircraft operating from bases in China.[23]

It took many months for these recommendations to receive final approval by the Combined Chiefs of Staff,[24] but the decision to leave both planning and implementation in the hands of the respective national authorities at least enabled Fleming to get down to work as soon as he returned to India. While he and his colleagues had been conferring in Washington, the Combined Chiefs of Staff had been recasting their strategy for south-east Asia. The ambitious proposals for amphibious attack, for which no resources were available, were abandoned. Instead it was agreed that the British should concentrate their resources on a series of offensives in the north of Burma so as to improve the air link with China and ultimately to open the Burma Road from Rangoon to Chungking over which, it was hoped, plentiful supplies could then be sent to Chiang Kai-shek. In June 1943 Wavell was replaced as Commander-in-Chief in India by General Auchinleck, but plans were already on foot for the creation of a new South-East Asia Command to take charge of all operations in the theatre. Fleming's own organisation was, as we have seen, overhauled and enlarged, and he drew up his cover plan for the new Allied strategy; Operation *Ramshorn*.

Allied operations were now in fact to consist of overland thrusts into northern Burma (powerfully assisted, it was hoped, by the large-scale Chindit operations proposed by Major General Orde Wingate), together with limited amphibious assaults against the port of Akyab and the island of Ramree. Fleming outlined his cover plan in a letter to the London Controlling Section of 12 July.[25] It would, he pointed out, be virtually impossible to conceal the preparations for the attack on Akyab and Ramree, so the enemy must be misled as to its scope and purpose. The major advantage which the deception authorities enjoyed in the Far East, as in the European theatre, lay in the enemy overestimation of the forces available to the Allies. Japanese intelligence was estimating its adversary's strength at 10 British, 22 Indian and 3 US Divisions.* It would thus be possible to depict the Akyab assault as a cover, designed to distract Japanese attention from the Allies' real, and more far-reaching intentions. These were, notionally, to bring to battle and destroy as much of the Japanese Air Force as possible in

---

* In fact the forces available for operations in India in autumn 1943 totalled 4 British and African divisions and 9 Indian Divisions, with half a dozen independent brigades. The figure of three American–Chinese divisions was correct.[26]

order to divert it from opposing either the operations of General MacArthur in the south-west Pacific or those of General Chennault's air forces based on the mainland of China. The operations being prepared against Akyab were thus a mere demonstration, a feint to bring about a battle in the air. The feint would be supported by an overland advance on the Arakan front. In upper and central Burma Allied military activity would likewise consist of no more than feints and harrassing operations which would be given plenty of publicity in order to pin down the maximum number of Japanese forces. Real attacks, however, would be mounted against the Andaman islands as soon as the feint against Akyab had run its course; while later in the campaigning season, in February 1944, a further assault would be mounted from Ceylon against the island of Sumatra, in preparation for further advances against Singapore. The Japanese would thus, it was hoped, leave the minimum forces to oppose Allied activities in Burma, and make preparations to meet the wide-ranging amphibious operations which the Combined Chiefs of Staff at the 'Trident' Conference had decided should *not* take place.

Unfortunately, unknown to Fleming, the decisions taken at the 'Trident' conference were still surrounded by so much uncertainty that they provided a very unsure basis for any kind of planning. Political disagreements with the Americans and the Chinese, logistical difficulties and the doubtful availability of forces from the European theatre made it uncertain from the beginning whether the agreed operations would take place at all, and if so on what scale; while the Prime Minister, for one, refused to accept that amphibious operations against the Andamans, Sumatra or anywhere else were an entirely lost cause. In commenting on Fleming's proposals for the Chiefs of Staff, Bevan suggested that in view of the fluid state of Allied plans it would *not* be wise to draw attention to the Andaman islands or Sumatra. Instead it might be better to give the impression that Allied forces based on India were incapable of mounting any operations, owing to lack of naval and amphibious forces, the low morale and poor state of training of land forces, the unreliability of Indian units as a result of subversive propaganda and the overstraining of rail communications in India; all of which, as Bevan wryly commented, had 'a sub-stratum of truth'. The Chiefs of Staff therefore decided, on 6 August, that until operational plans were more firmly decided it would be unwise to draw up any cover plans at all.[27]

The cover story proposed by Bevan was in fact uncomfortably near the truth, and the landings at Akyab had to be cancelled for lack of the necessary amphibious support. But the operations in northern Burma, in spite of all difficulties, went ahead during the dry season of 1943–1944. Bevan therefore accepted an amended cover plan that Fleming sent to London in December, which stated that owing to operational difficulties Mountbatten had called off the overland operations in Burma and was concentrating on the assault on Akyab. A further story, that SEAC was co-operating with South-West Pacific Command in an assault on the island of Timor (comfortably remote from any conceivable British operations) was shelved pending consultations with General MacArthur. No evidence has emerged to suggest that these ever took place.[28]

The results of the Anglo-American Conference on Deception, and the directives that flowed from it, thus seemed negligible. Strategic uncertainty had paralysed the British, while the American decision to make deception a theatre responsibility was a recipe for inaction. In February the British Joint Staff Mission in Washington pointed out to the Chiefs of Staff in London that no action appeared to have been taken on the decisions reached about deception by the Combined Chiefs of Staff, and asked whether they should raise the matter again. The British Chiefs of Staff advised waiting until strategic intentions in the Pacific had been clarified. But before the month was out the Americans themselves had taken the initiative, and produced the outlines of a new common plan.[29]

This plan had been made possible by agreement on Allied Grand Strategy for the Pacific theatre which had been reached between the American, British and Chinese leaders at the 'Sextant' conference in Cairo in November–December 1943. This provided for a joint advance by US forces across the islands of the central Pacific and by the forces under MacArthur's command through the archipelago of the south-west Pacific, while the greatest possible Allied air strength was built up on the mainland of China. Operations in South-East Asia Command were to concentrate on facilitating this latter objective by gaining ground in upper Burma. Amphibious operations in south-east Asia could not be discounted – not only was Mr Churchill still pressing for them but Generalissimo Chiang Kai-shek considered them a *sine qua non* for Chinese participation in the Burma campaign – but they would not take place until after the 1944 monsoon season, by which time the necessary forces should be available from the European theatre.[30]

The American deception proposals were initiated by their Joint Staff Planners in a document dated 17 February 1944.[31] They were based on the assumption that the Japanese had now lost the strategic initiative in the Pacific, though they retained it in China, Manchuria and possibly Burma (a shrewd exception, as the Japanese attack on Imphal the following month was to show). 'The deployment of their forces is generally defensive but the launching of a limited offensive by the Japanese to disrupt Allied plans is a possibility'. The object of deception measures, in addition to those approved the previous autumn, should therefore be 'to entice the Japanese fleet into areas where we can bring it to battle under conditions favourable to ourselves. This object is of prime importance, since the destruction of the Japanese fleet would give us freedom of movement throughout the Pacific'. They therefore recommended that theatre commanders should be ordered to prepare deception measures in order to:

a)   Bring the Japanese fleet to battle under favourable conditions;
b)   contain the maximum Japanese air and ground forces in their homeland;
c)   draw Japanese strength into the Kuriles (almost the only area where the Americans did *not* propose to attack);
d)   draw the Japanese into the south-west Pacific at the times when operations were pending in the central Pacific and in Burma;
e)   lead the Japanese to believe that amphibious operations would be launched in the Indian Ocean before the onset of the 1944 monsoon; and
f)   persuade the Japanese to concentrate forces in Malaya and Sumatra in September 1944.

It took more than three months for this deception plan – roughly the equivalent of *Bodyguard* in the European theatre – to receive the final approval of the Combined Chiefs of Staff; a fair indication that deception in the Pacific theatre was not regarded in Washington as a matter of very great urgency.[32] Even when it was approved it was almost impossible to implement. The London Controlling Section understandably looked to their US colleagues in Joint Security Control to take the initiative; but the initiative had been explicitly removed from them and placed with the various theatre commanders, most of whom gave strategic deception a very low order of priority indeed.

Even within SEAC very little could be done during 1944. The British had considerable reservations about the last of the proposals listed above – persuading the Japanese to concentrate forces in Sumatra and Malaya.[33] In spite of the decision taken at the 'Sextant' conference to abandon any major amphibious operations in the Indian Ocean until after the 1944 monsoon, plans continued to drift around Delhi and London, and any deception contrived by Fleming and his team might at any moment find itself being seriously considered as a plan for actual operations. *Buccaneer*, the plan for an amphibious attack on the Andaman islands, was taken seriously until the end of 1943, when it received its *coup de grâce* shortly after the 'Sextant' conference. After the conference Mountbatten concentrated on planning for the overland operations in upper Burma (*Capital*), but the British remained stubbornly reluctant to abandon the amphibious alternative. Throughout the winter of 1943–1944 SEAC planners were discussing a possible attack on Sumatra (*Culverin*); and when in the spring of 1944 this was abandoned another amphibious proposal took its place: *Dracula*, a seaborne assault on Rangoon. Even though the resources for this could not be made available until early in 1945, it was accepted by the Combined Chiefs of Staff at the 'Octagon' conference in August 1944 as a supplement to *Capital*, and a modified version of it, with resources from within the theatre itself, was launched in April 1945 to assist General Slim's victorious

Fourteenth Army when, in the overland assault that developed from their repulse of the Japanese attack on Imphal during the summer of 1944, they drove the enemy out of upper Burma and recaptured Rangoon on 3 May 1945. 'D' Division continued to feed Japanese intelligence with rumours of Allied landings on the Burmese coasts, but it cannot be said that in the triumphant defence of Imphal and Kohima and the equally triumphant offensive that followed it, strategic deception played a major part.

But tactical deception did. Only general reference can be made to the activities of 'D' Force, whose creation in October 1944 has already been mentioned and of whose facilities General Slim and his subordinates made frequent and imaginative use. But in the climactic battle for the reconquest of Burma, that for the capture of Meiktila and Mandalay which the Fourteenth Army fought throughout February 1945 and which broke the power of the Japanese Army in Burma as decisively as the Battle of El Alamein broke the power of the Axis forces in the Western Desert, deception played – as it had at Alamein – an essential part.

The story of these deception measures has been told, both in the Official History and in General Slim's own full and vivid description of the battle.[34] Here it is necessary only to remind the reader that General Slim intended to bring the main enemy forces in central Burma to battle and destroy them in the plains of the Irrawaddy around Mandalay as the climax to the pursuit of the retreating Japanese Army which began once the Fourteenth Army began to advance out of the Chin Hills in January 1945. Slim had at his disposal two Corps, IV and XXXIII, comprising five divisions, two tank brigades and three independent brigades, to deal with Japanese forces not only superior in strength but enjoying greatly superior communications. Of their total available forces, Slim calculated that the Japanese would be able to deploy at least half on his front; while the strength he could himself bring to battle was limited by the fact that his railhead was 400 miles distant, that only a limited stretch of the roads connecting it to his front had all-weather surfaces, and that even his airlift, on which he was heavily dependent, could deliver only to airfields two hundred miles or more behind his front. What even he could not foresee was that a substantial proportion of that airlift was to be removed without warning, on the eve of battle, to reinforce the China front.[35]

In face of these odds, Slim could only hope to succeed by the use of stratagem. He had hoped to bring the Japanese to battle on the western shore of the Irrawaddy, trapping them in the bend of the river at Mandalay; but his opponents were too skilful to be caught in such a trap. Slim's difficulties were thus compounded by the need to make an opposed crossing over one of the widest waterways in the world. His plan therefore was to make the Japanese believe that his real objective was Mandalay, on the right flank of the Japanese front, and that he was advancing on it with both his Corps; IV Corps moving down the river, which they had reached and crossed upstream at Kyauk-myaung and Thabeikkyin between 9–14 January while XXXIII Corps kept pace on their right down the western bank of the river, which they crossed at Myinmu on February 12th. These two advances thus appeared to be squeezing Mandalay in a nutcracker grip, and the Japanese concentrated to deal with it.

What was actually happening was very different. The crossings at Kyaukmyaung and Thabeikkyin were indeed carried out by formations of IV Corps, in particular 19th Division. These formations were then however transferred to the command of XXXIII Corps. A bogus IV Corps HQ took over radio communications from the real HQ (among other things relaying orders from XXXIII Corps to 19th Division) while the rest of IV Corps, comprising 7th and 17th Divisions, a mixed brigade and a brigade of Sherman tanks, moved westward over virtually non-existent roads to the Gangaw valley far beyond XXXIII Corps' right flank, and advanced southward in deepest secrecy via Pauk to the Irrawaddy downstream at Pagan and Nyaungu. Their objective was Meiktila, 70 miles south of Mandalay, which Slim had rightly diagnosed as an objective of even greater strategic importance than Mandalay. It was there that the Japanese had established their main complex of bases. It was like the wrist of an extended hand. 'Crush that wrist,' as Slim put it, 'no blood would flow through the fingers, the whole hand would be paralysed and the Japanese armies on the arc from the Salween to the Irrawaddy would begin to wither'.[36]

The surreptitious movement of IV Corps (if such an adjective can be used to describe so huge an enterprise) together with all the radio and visual deception involved, went by the name of Operation *Cloak*. And there were deceptions within the deception. Because it was the function of XXXIII Corps to draw in the bulk of the Japanese forces to oppose their landings upstream at Myinmu, they had been allotted the bulk of such river-crossing equipment as could be made available. For its crossings at Pagan and Nyaunga, IV Corps (7th Division) had to depend largely on surprise, which was achieved by a number of feint landings at other points, in which the sonic deceptive apparatus of 'D' Force was put to full use. The crossings took place on 13 February, a day later than the attack by XXXIII Corps upstream. It was almost unopposed, the Japanese seeing in it only a minor diversion from the main attack, and aiming not at Meiktila but at the oilfields of Yenan-gyaung further downstream. On 21 February the rest of IV Corps passed through 7th Division's bridgehead and moved on to Meiktila. The Japanese reacted swiftly and fought courageously, but Meiktila fell on 4 March, Mandalay two weeks later. The whole operation was almost a text-book example of how deception made possible tactical surprise which in its turn produced complete and economical victory.

The clearing of Burma was completed some six weeks later when, as we have seen, Rangoon fell at the beginning of May to a combination of overland and amphibious attack. The strategic objective of the Burma campaign had been achieved, and communications to China, both by air-ferry and overland, had been freed from all interference by the enemy. But the Combined Chiefs of Staff meeting at the 'Argonaut' conference at Malta at the end of January 1945 had now given Mountbatten the further task of liberating Malaya and opening the Straits of Malacca; and plans for this were already in hand.[37]

The recapture of Singapore was of course the object on which the British had set their hearts, but the resources for this would not be available until the war in Europe was over. As an intermediate step SACSEA was planning what was to prove the last in the long series of abortive amphibious operations for the reconquest of south-east Asia: Operation *Zipper*, a landing on the coast of Malaya near Kuala Lumpur at Port Swettenham and Port Dickson. This, it was hoped, would take place in August. With a clear operational objective at last approved, 'D' Division was able to draw up a full deception plan: Operation *Sceptical*, which was submitted to London and approved on 30 April 1945.[38] The overall 'story' was that the Allies now had such huge forces at their disposal, sixty infantry and five armoured divisions in SEAC alone (in fact there were twenty infantry and no armoured divisions in the theatre) that major assaults were being planned directly against Singapore and Siam. An Army three divisions strong, reinforced with an Airborne Corps of four divisions, was based on Burma and poised to launch an overland and airborne attack on Bangkok. Further forces based on India and Ceylon were preparing seaborne operations against Sumatra and Java to establish air and naval bases in order to cover a direct assault on Singapore through the Sunda Straits. The Chinese armies in north Burma (which had now in fact been diverted to the fighting inside China) would advance into Indo-China from the north, while other forces from the south-west Pacific would assault the coasts of Indo-China from the sea. To this a further deception was later added (*Slippery*) to cover the preparations for *Zipper* itself. The landing-craft so conspicuously evident in Indian harbours were said to be intended for an assault on the Kra Isthmus.[39]

It was typical of the frustrating nature of the Far Eastern campaign in general, and of the deception activities in particular, that the war ended before the effectiveness of this cover story could be tested. It was put over through all the channels that 'D' Division had now developed and certainly reached Japanese intelligence. But it cannot be said to have done more than obscure Allied intentions. The Japanese took sensible precautions for the defence of northern Malaya and the Kra Isthmus, as indeed of Sumatra, Java and Siam, but the Kuala Lumpur area received attention as well, where a landing some three to six divisions strong was expected; not a bad estimate of the four divisions that XXIV Corps in fact planned to put ashore. The weakness of the forces available to defend the area was due to the weakness of the Japanese position as a whole – they had only two divisions available to defend the whole of Malaya – rather than to any misreading of British strategic intentions.[40]

Strategic deception in the south-east Asia theatre was not a success story, as Fleming was the first to admit. 'The achievements were in themselves of a minor order and largely devoid of operational significance' he wrote in his subsequent report; 'But the principles and techniques employed are of some interest, while the enemy's reactions throw a unique and curious light on the workings of the mind behind the most formidable military machine so far created by an Asiatic race'.[41] This last sentence refers to the ease with which the deception authorities persuaded Japanese intelligence 'to swallow the most outrageous and implausible fabrications' combined with the reluctance of the operational staffs to pay the slightest attention to them. What became clear at an early stage was the low esteem in which the Japanese military held its intelligence services, and the limited value it attached to any information emanating from that quarter.

The real problem which confronted the British deception staff in India, however, was that created by its own side; the continuing uncertainty as to what Allied strategic intentions really were. In default of firm actual plans the best that the deceivers could do as one of them ruefully put it, was to ensure that the enemy remained as confused as they were themselves. But in fact they could, and did, do a great deal more. As in Europe and the Middle East, their lasting achievement was to build up in the minds of enemy intelligence a totally erroneous idea of available Allied operational strength. What mattered in 1945 was not whether the Japanese were expecting to be attacked at one point rather than at another. It was that, like the Germans in Europe, they believed their opponents capable of delivering multiple attacks, and had in consequence to spread their forces so thinly to meet them that the actual assault, when it came, achieved overwhelming local superiority. It was in this vital respect that 'D' Division could at the end of the war, like their colleagues in the European theatres, congratulate themselves on a job well done.

REFERENCES

1. Duff Hart Davis, *Peter Fleming* (1974); John Connell, *Wavell Supreme Commander 1941–43* (1973).
2. Archibald Wavell, *Allenby* (1940), p 202.
3. Connell, op cit, p 213.
4. CAB 154/99, Strategic Deception in the War against Japan, pp 3–5.
5. ibid, p 43.
6. CAB 121/105, SIC file A/Policy/Deception/1, Fleming and Stanley notes to Hollis, 25 April 1942, COS (42) 131st Meeting, 27 April, Fleming telegram to ISSB (C-in-C

India to War Office 11084/1) of 7 May, Hollis note to COS 8 May, with appreciation of Operation *Purple Whales*.

7. CAB 154/99, p 43.
8. ibid, p 37.
9. ibid, pp 42–43.
10. ibid, p 9.
11. ibid, p 19.
12. ibid, p 27.
13. ibid, p 24.
14. ibid, p 44.
15. ibid, pp 44–58.
16. ibid, p 7.
17. SW Kirby, *The War against Japan*, Vol IV (1965), Appendix 18, p 477.
18. CAB 84/53, JP (43) 89 (O) (T of R) of 25 February.
19. ibid.
20. CAB 105/27, COS to C-in-C India, COS (India) 140 of 29 March 1943.
21. CCS Decimal File 1942–45 (Record Group 218, National Archives of the United States).
22. CAB 121/105, JSM 1091 of 21 July 1943.
23. CCS 385 (4–8–43), Memo for JCS, Decimal File 1942–45 (Record Group 218, National Archives of the United States).
24. CAB 121/105, CCS 284/3/D of 6 August 1943, 284/5/D of 17 September 1943.
25. CAB 81/77, LCS (43) 12 of 12 July.
26. Kirby, op cit, Vol III (1962), Appendix 10, p 466.
27. CAB 121/105, COS (43) 441(o) of 4 August, COS (43) 121st Meeting, 6 August.
28. CAB 81/77, LCS (43) 19 of 5 December.
29. CAB 121/105, JSM 1483 of 3 February 1944, COS (44) 34th Meeting (o), 4 February, CCS 284/6 of 20 February 1944.
30. Kirby, op cit, Vol III, pp 59–65.
31. COS 385 Pacific Theater (4–1–43), JCS 498/1, Section 2, Geographic File 1942–5 (Record Group 218, National Archives of the United States).
32. CAB 121/105, CCS 284/10/D of 26 May 1944.
33. ibid, Air Ministry telegram to JSM, OZ 1949 of 14 April 1944.
34. Kirby, op cit, Vol I (1957) Chapter XXIII and Appendix 20; Sir William Slim, *Defeat into Victory* (1956), pp 380–457.
35. Slim, op cit, pp 380–398.
36. ibid, p 393.
37. Kirby, op cit, Vol V (1969), p 209, Directive of 3 February 1945.
38. CAB 121/105, SEACOS 370 of 21 April 1945, COS (45) 112th Meeting, 30 April.
39. CAB 154/99, p 64.
40. Kirby, op cit, Vol V, pp 71–75.
41. CAB 154/99, p 1.

APPENDIX I

Naval Deception

The great bulk of the deception practised by the Royal Navy during the Second World War was 'strategic', in that it was concerned to project to the enemy a misleading picture of British weapons, capabilities and intentions. Since naval strength was a question of quality as well as quantity, of the characteristics of vessels as well as their numbers, much of this deception was technical in nature. For the rest it was concerned with the quantity of vessels available to the Navy, their dispositions and their movements. And naturally during the early years of the war the object was normally to project an image of British naval strength as being greater than was in fact the case.

From the earliest stages of the war naval interest in deception was due very largely to the initiative of the Director of Naval Intelligence, Rear Admiral John Godfrey, though all relevant branches of the Admiralty were quick to see its importance. We have described in the text of this volume the active part which his representative on the Twenty Committee, Lieut Cdr the Hon Ewen Montagu, played in that body; and double agents played as great as role in naval deception as in every aspect of deceptive activities. One of the tasks entrusted to *Tricycle* by his German control when he first came to Britain in December 1940 was to infiltrate the entourage of the Commander-in-Chief of the Home Fleet, Sir John Tovey, and we have seen how Montagu and others provided him with enough information for him to claim a considerable degree of success. *Tricycle* remained an important channel for naval misinformation, and when in August 1941 he departed for the United States his place was filled by the sub-agent he had notionally recruited, *Balloon*, who as a business man dealing in armaments was in a good position to obtain information about the introduction of new weapons and naval vessels, At a later stage in the war *Tricycle* was joined by a group of his countrymen, officers in the Royal Yugoslav Navy whose arrival in Britain he had engineered through his Abwehr connections and who were particularly suitable for naval specialisation. The *Garbo* network was also used where appropriate, and so was *Tate*. *Tate* indeed was provided with a notional girl friend, Mary, who allegedly worked not only in the Admiralty but also, on loan from that body, with the United States Naval Mission. Mary introduced *Tate* to officers in both Services, some of whom occasionally stayed the night in his London flat where they displayed deplorable laxity in the custody of classified documents. A number of seamen travelling to Spain and Portugal were also used as witting or unwitting channels; and two Abwehr agents, landed in Iceland and immediately apprehended, *Cobweb* and *Beetle* were used to pass misleading information, especially about shipping movements. Altogether naval deception provided a substantial proportion of the traffic of all double agents; and although at the operational level radio, sonic and visual deception assumed the highest importance, that traffic was probably the principal channel used by the Admiralty to deceive the enemy as to Britain's naval capabilities and deployment.

The earliest attempts to deceive the enemy about Britain's naval strength was visual. In 1939 three merchant ships of 7,900 tons were fitted out with the appropriate dummy guns and superstructure to simulate two R-class battleships of 33,500 tons, and the 12,000 ton aircraft carrier *Hermes*. This force was stationed at Rosyth to decoy German air attacks away from the Home Fleet in Scapa Flow. In due course it was hoped that the units could also be used as decoys for U-boat attacks, and to confuse the enemy as to the true strength of the British fleet. At that stage of the war unfortunately no channels had been developed for informing the Germans of their existence except their physical display for reconnaissance aircraft; and the German Air Force does not appear to have picked them up. The need for the harmonisation of multiple channels for deception had not yet been fully appreciated.

Somewhat later in the war, in 1942, the same ploy was attempted again with better success. An old battleship, *Centurion*, that had been disarmed under the terms of the Washington Naval Treaty of 1922, was rigged up to resemble the new battleship *Anson*, and was sent out with a crew of 16 officers and 265 men on a 20,000 mile trip round the Cape to Bombay. This time her commissioning and voyage were reported to the Abwehr by the appropriate agents under the aegis of the Twenty Committee. So convincing was her appearance that in June 1942, sailing with a convoy to the relief of Malta, she attracted heavy attacks by enemy bombers. Her active career ended ignominiously when a monsoon in the Indian Ocean swept overboard one of her dummy turrets, complete with a 14 inch gun whose appearance among other flotsam surprised uninitiated observers; but she survived as a blockship off the Normandy coast in June 1944.

By 1942 more subtle measures were being taken to exaggerate the numbers of British capital ships. The target of the deception was now the Japanese rather than the Germans, the object being to deter them from pursuing their advantage in the Indian Ocean theatre. It was no good reporting the launching of entirely notional vessels unless their existence could be permanently sustained; the agent concerned would simply lose credibility. Instead it was decided to report the launching of each real new capital ship in advance of the actual event. Enemy intelligence would always have one extra heavy unit in their Order of Battle of the Royal Navy, and the agent concerned would reap the credit when the vessel was finally identified. This information was passed to the Germans, who were known from Sigint to communicate significant items of naval intelligence to the Japanese. The increment was not great, but given the narrow margin on which the Royal Navy had to work in the middle years of the war it was significant, and above all it was credible. In 1944 however this policy was reversed. It was no longer the strategy of the Allies to deter the Japanese from using their naval strength. Rather it was to encourage them to attack and exhaust it as quickly as possible; so both the numbers and the capabilities of new vessels under construction and launching were now underrated rather than the reverse.

Two other deceptions directed against the Japanese need to be noted. In December 1942, when the demands of the Battle of the Atlantic, the northern convoys and the landings in French north Africa were imposing on the Royal Navy the greatest strain on the entire war, the East Indies Fleet under Admiral Sir James Somerville had on its strength only one aircraft carrier, *Illustrious*, and that was due to be withdrawn. No other carrier could be made available, but there was one, *Indefatigable*, in course of construction.

By a combination of radio traffic and agents' reports the story was put over that the *Indefatigable* had been commissioned and was sailing in company with two other vessels to reinforce the *Illustrious* with modern aircraft. The voyage of the *Indefatigable* was projected to the enemy entirely by radio traffic put out by the appropriate commands *en route* until she notionally reached Simonstown, where she came under Somerville's command. Throughout 1943 her existence was sustained through all channels of deception until December, when she returned to the Clyde; notionally for a refit, in practise to merge her identity with the real *Indefatigable* which was now ready for commissioning. Both German and Japanese intelligence believed there to be two British carriers in the Indian Ocean throughout this period, when in fact there were none.

Finally a deception was practised less with the intention of giving a misleading impression of British naval strength than of changing the composition of the Japanese fleet itself. In 1942 it was learned that the Japanese were attempting to counter the huge American construction of new aircraft carriers by building a new type of vessel, part battleship, part aircraft carrier, to which the British gave the name 'battle carrier'. This was a programme that the Admiralty wished to encourage, as it seemed an admirable way of wasting scarce resources. The new hybrid, the Admiralty were convinced, would be effective neither as a battle ship nor as a carrier. So the message was put out that the British were building battle carriers themselves, and that the battleship *Vanguard* which was actually being constructed in John Brown's yard was one such. Not only was this story fed into known Japanese intelligence sources in Stockholm, but an actual blue-print of the notional vessel was transmitted to the Japanese through the channels opened by Lieut Col Fleming *via* Chung-king. The effectiveness of all this cannot be assessed; but by July 1943 the Director of Naval Plans decided that Japanese construction was far enough advanced for the British notionally to abandon their project as impracticable. The story was therefore transmitted, through a seaman agent known to be in contact with the Japanese sources in Spain, that the development of new types of aircraft had created insoluble constructional problems for the battle carriers, and that *Vanguard* would be completed as a battleship after all.

Attempts were also made to affect the deployment of enemy fleets. In December 1942, for example, when U-boat successes in the Atlantic were reaching a dangerous level, an effort was made to persuade the Germans to deploy the bulk of their U-boat strength in the Mediterranean where they could be more easily dealt with. Messages were passed through the double agents indicating a great reinforcement of escort strength in the Atlantic, with a corresponding weakening in the Mediterranean. A friend of *Tricycle*'s who had been commanding a corvette in the Mediterranean was switched to duty in home waters. *Garbo*'s agents reported the arrival of three destroyers at Milford Haven whose officers were complaining at having to leave the Mediterranean for the bleak waters of the North Atlantic in the middle of winter. *Balloon*'s contacts in the Admiralty were concerned about the strain imposed on the inadequate escort strength in the Mediterranean by this shift in emphasis; while *Tate* reported high-level gossip among Mary's friends in the Admiralty and the US Naval Mission about the background for this decision, which had notionally been successfully carried through by the British Naval Staff over the strong protests of the Americans. No judgement can be made as to the success of this enterprise, but nothing was lost by making the attempt.

Since the activities of German U-boats presented the gravest and most continuous problem with which the Royal Navy had to deal, a great deal of naval deception was directed towards countering them. Demands for information about convoy routes were frequent and deeply embarrassing to the double agents. They fended them off as best they could with the excuse that this information was quite impossible to extract from seamen who knew that their own lives depended on keeping it secret. Eventually *Tate* did give one route, notionally extracted from Mary, but only after it had been discontinued. But in the autumn of 1944, when the bulk of convoys from the United States were sailing direct to French ports, hints were dropped indicating that old routes to Britain via the Western Approaches to the north of Ireland were still carrying most of the traffic.

Most of the deception practised in the U-boat war, however, related to the weapons with which it was being waged. In September 1943 an attempt was made to discourage U-boats from diving deep to evade attack by putting it about that the Royal Navy had developed a new rocket-propelled depth-charge that exploded with more force and accuracy and at greater depth than the weapons used hitherto. This deception (*Fernbank*) was supported by messages from one of *Tricycle*'s Yugoslav naval associates, *Meteor*, who notionally learned about it while on an anti-submarine warfare course. *Meteor* was also valuable in a more elaborate scheme concerning the projectors used by the Navy for firing volleys of depth-charges simultaneously over the bows of anti-submarine vessels, codenamed *Hedgehogs* or *Squids*. The object of this was to conceal the effectiveness of certain new anti-submarine devices such as the Mark XXIV mine, which were responsible for an increasing number of U-boat sinkings, by attributing these to the *Hedgehogs*, which were alleged to be detonated by a proximity device that activated all of them simultaneously. A further object of this deception was to discredit the reports of an uncontrolled agent in Madrid who was suggesting that these devices were in fact activated by some kind of radar; a suggestion that German naval intelligence found particular persuasive. The questionnaires they provided to double agents repeatedly asked about Allied devices to set off underwater explosions which not only revealed the exact location of the U-boats but automatically triggered highly accurate depth-charge attacks.

The Admiralty decided to encourage this belief. A real *Hedgehog* was modified and photographed in such a way as to make it appear one-third of its real size. This was to be passed off as the activator whose explosion triggered off the complete series of explosions. Another photograph showed a modified depth-charge fuse allegedly capable of greatly improved depth-settings. These photographs were allegedly stolen, together with other documents, from a research laboratory in Manchester by the double agent *Zigzag*, who had been parachuted back into England by the Abwehr in 1944 as described on page 172 above. His haul included a letter written to a colleague by an official at the Admiralty Research Department describing those new mechanisms as being 'a wonderful improvement on the old method of depth finding', capable of dealing with targets moving not only at the known U-boat top speed underwater of 13 knots but at much greater speeds than the Germans were likely to achieve in the foreseeable future. *Zigzag* transmitted the text of the letter by radio, but arrangements to send over the photographs by a seaman agent via Lisbon could not be completed before *Zigzag*'s indiscretions made it necessary to close down his case. ISOS decrypts showed that the Abwehr accepted his information at its face value, but there is no evidence that the German Navy was equally convinced.

They were convinced, however, by a deception put over by *Tate* in the autumn of 1944, which was perhaps the most important naval deception of the entire war. Even at this late stage in the conflict the balance could once again be titled against the Allies by a technical development in naval warfare; this time the development of the *Schnorkel* device fitted to submarines which enabled them to lie or move submerged for an indefinite period without having to surface in order to re-charge their batteries. Vessels equipped with this were virtually undetectable by radar, and could therefore lie in wait in those terminal areas off the British coasts where convoys converged and where coastal trade ran unescorted. In such waters, where draught was shallow, currents strong and the bottom studded with wrecks, not even Asdic could be relied on to identify a stationary or slow moving vessel. The only solution would be to lay minefields deep enough not to interfere with the passage of shipping, which would trap submarines diving to avoid surface attack. Plans for this were set on foot, but shortage of both mines and of minelaying craft delayed their implementation. So deception channels were brought into play.

Several attempts had already been made to convince the German Navy of the existence of bogus minefields. There was, for example, the chart provided for *Tricycle* by Lieut Cdr Montagu in 1941. The same trick was tried again in December 1942, this time using *Tate. Tate* was provided with a notional friend in the Royal Navy employed in minelaying who occasionally spent the night in *Tate's* flat. This operation fizzled out, but the officer concerned reappeared in November 1944 with news of greatly increased minelaying activities. The mines, he reported, were of a new design, and were being laid in small groups dotted about near the sea bottom. Their depth made it possible to sow them outside declared mined zones and inside mine-free channels where they might catch U-boats pursuing or lying in wait for convoys. These mines were apparently being concentrated off the Fastnet Rock on the coast of southern Ireland, though northern Irish waters were being sown as well. *Tate* continued to make these reports throughout the winter and into the spring of 1945; indeed the last was sent only four days before the end of the war. By this time mines were also being notionally laid in the Channel and off the north coast of Norway. The reports were given added credibility when *Tate* was in a position to give advance news of real U-boat sinkings when it was clear that the Germans did not know the circumstances in which the U-boat had been sunk, and when the sinking occurred in an area where the notional mines had been laid. The effectiveness of the deception was revealed when, on 1 January 1945, the Germans ordered their U-boats to avoid the area of the Fastnet Rock and haul off to the southward. Providentially, early in March a U-boat actually hit a mine off Fastnet. As a result on 13 March the Germans instructed their U-boats to avoid an area of some 3,600 square miles south east of Fastnet and ordered them, if they had to traverse it at all to do so at a lesser depth than ten fathoms. The memorandum by the Naval Intelligence Department bearing on this matter is printed as an Annex to this Appendix.

Annex

Tate laid a minefield 30 miles SE of the Fastnet Rock and the Germans in ZTPGU 34919* of 1 January notified U-boats of that report, and ordered them to avoid the area and haul off to the southward.

2. *Tate* was asked for details of the minefield, including the exact position and its size, etc., and, before he had answered, the Germans in ZTPGU 35227* of 9 January sent out corrections to their standing War Orders, including *Tate's* minefield.

3. By 8 February, *Tate's* details of the position of the minefield not yet having had a chance of reaching and being appreciated by the Germans, a further correction to the standing orders was sent out in ZTPGU 36330,* suggesting that *Tate's* minefield SE of the Fastnet Rock is probably near the coast and giving reasons for this view. The words 'if there at all' were used later in the message, but it is not clear whether these throw doubt on the existence of *Tate's* minefield, or on the exact position.

4. On 18 March in ZTPGU 37291,* the Germans sent out a notification to U-boats that there was no danger of mines in the actual operational areas (*Tate* had not laid any mines in such areas) and suggested that the fouling was at conspicuous navigational corner points across what the 'enemy' considered to be the main direction of approach of the U-boats ('if that fouling exists at all') and gave as an example the SW corner of Ireland, Scillies and N of the Shetlands. It is noteworthy that the SE corner of Ireland and the Scillies were *Tate's* favourite areas and the description that he had given of the exact location of the Fastnet Rock minefield was based on the fact that the area was a 'conspicuous navigational corner point across the main direction of approach of the U-boat' to the Irish Sea.

5. Meanwhile a U-boat had scuttled itself owing to damage by mining and the crew had gone ashore near Galley Head in S Ireland. If a U-boat had been mined in the notional Fastnet minefield the Galley Head area would be a quite likely spot for the crew to have made land. In fact the U-boat must have hit one of the deep minefields fairly near *Tate's* Fastnet Rock minefield. As a result of this the Germans sent out ZTPGU 37374* of 13 March, in which they stated that a U-boat had reported being mined in a square in this area which confirmed the agent's report concerning mining SE of the Fastnet Rock. It ordered U-boats to avoid an area of four grid squares (a very large area about 60 miles square, i.e. 3,600 square miles) and ordered U-boats if they got into that area, to proceed at a depth shallower than ten fathoms. Boats on passage to the Irish Sea were either to come close

---

* All these are references on decrypts issued by Bletchley.

inshore at a lesser depth than ten fathoms, or to keep S of the area mentioned above.

6. The advantage of these orders from our point of view are fairly considerable, in that they hamper the movements of U-boats. they must increase the worry of U-boat captains, they provide an area in which U-boats are unlikely to operate, and it is possible if U-boat captains do keep clear of the banned area they might find it necessary to fix their position on a particular shallow sandbank which is, in fact, really mined, thus bringing them into a deep minefield.

7. There is as yet no evidence whether a suspicion of a minefield in the position given by *Tate* had anything to do with the destruction of this particular U-boat, and, *prima facie*, there does not seem to be any reason why it should have.

APPENDIX 2

The *Garbo* Network

Garbo reached England on 24 April 1942 and began work for BIA under the guidance of his case-officer, who was bilingual in Spanish and English and in peacetime specialised in the collection and sale of works of art. It was to prove one of those rare partnerships between two exceptionally gifted men whose inventive genius inspired and complemented one another.

Garbo was a man of phenomenal industry. For the first year of his stay in England he communicated with his control in Madrid entirely by letter; messages in secret ink with covering letters written over them, notionally carried to Portugal by the employee of an airline running a regular service between London and Lisbon ('the Courier'), who posted them to Abwehr accommodation addresses in Lisbon and collected the replies from a safe deposit box in a Lisbon bank. In fact delivery and collection was arranged by MI6. *Garbo* wrote altogether 315 such letters, their length averaging 2,000 words, as well as the equally garrulous covering letters that concealed them. After March 1943 he was able to supplement these by radio messages, notionally transmitted by a radio 'ham' of left-wing sympathies who had built his own set and who believed that the cyphered messages he transmitted were the communications of a group of left-wing Spanish exiles with their comrades at home. A total of 1,200 messages were passed over this channel before the end of the war.

Garbo began to operate before there was a coherent deception policy for him to implement; so for lack of anything better to do, as his case-officer put it, 'we tried to report in as much confusing bulk as possible and, in the absence of another objective, to increase our network of notional agents'. The 'confusing bulk' was highly effective in that the Madrid Stelle of the Abwehr became so glutted with information that it made no further attempt to infiltrate agents into the United Kingdom. It became entirely dependent on *Garbo*, regarding him a a sensitive quarrelsome genius of priceless value who had at all costs to be humoured and satisfied. By the end *Garbo* and his British case-officer were able to treat his German case-officer as a temperamental mistress might treat an elderly and besotted lover. No assertion that *Garbo* made might be questioned; no demand go unmet.

By 1944 *Garbo* and his British case-officer had between them built up a notional network of some 27 agents. In the first place there were five immediate contacts, labelled J1 to 5. J1 was the courier who carried the letters to Lisbon. He was himself involved in a smuggling racket and believed that *Garbo* was also. J2 was a RAF officer employed at Fighter Command HQ, a casual acquaintance who unwittingly occasionally let slip important information. J3 was a most useful friend, an official in the Spanish section of the Ministry of Information, who eventually found *Garbo* part-time employment in the Ministry, where he occasionally saw interesting policy documents. J4 was another official he met at the Ministry, a man of extreme left-wing views who worked in the censorship department. J5 was a girl secretary in the 'Ministry of War' (sic) who was a little in love with *Garbo* and who could be relied upon for the occasional silly indiscretion.

Then there were the agents themselves. The first two had been notionally recruited even before *Garbo* actually arrived in England, while he was writing his hilariously inaccurate letters from Lisbon. Agent 1 was a Portuguese commercial traveller named Carvalho, based at Newport, Monmouthshire; well placed to observe traffic in the Bristol Channel and, as it turned out, to make contact with dissident Nationalist elements in south Wales. Agent 2 was a German-Swiss businessman named Gerbers domiciled in Bootle, who reported on traffic in the Mersey. Tragically, it became necessary for Gerbers to die of cancer during the autumn of 1942 before he could observe the assembly, in the Mersey estuary, of the convoys for *Torch*. But his unfortunate widow proved willing to carry on the activities of her deceased husband. She was recruited as Agent 2(1) (though usually referred to simply as 'the Widow') and became virtually *Garbo's* personal assistant.

Agent 3 was a Venezuelan based on Glasgow, who observed traffic on the Clyde. A man of enthusiasm and efficiency, he became second in command of the network and took it over after *Garbo* had been notionally 'blown' in 1944. He had three sub-agents of his own: a NCO in the RAF (3(1)); a talkative lieutenant in the notional 49th Infantry Division (3(2)); and a useful Greek sailor who operated on the east coast of Scotland (3(3)). The first two were unconscious agents, the last a Communist who believed that he was working for the Soviet Union. This network received from the Germans the codename *Benedict*.

Agent 4 was a Gibraltese, 'Fred', who originally worked as a waiter in Soho, where he put *Garbo* in touch with the radio-operator already referred to. He was then directed by the Ministry of Labour, first to employment in a subterranean munitions depot in the Chislehurst caves, about which *Garbo* and his British case-officer wove a rich fantasy for the benefit of the Abwehr; then to work in military canteens, where he picked up much useful information; and finally to one of the sealed military camps in the region of Southampton where he was able to observe the final concentrations for *Overlord*. Strict security precautions prevented him from leaving his camp to report on these in detail until he broke out, as will be recalled, on the very eve of the operation with the news which *Garbo* transmitted to his control in Madrid; just too late to be of any value.

In addition to the Radio Operator (Agent 4(1)), 'Fred' recruited a guard in the Chislehurst caves (4(2)) and, much more usefully, an American sergeant who worked in London for the US Service of Supply (4(3)). This man was a particularly valuable source. Not only was he well informed about the movements and constitution of the 1st US Army Group, but he was the son of a senior American officer on Eisenhower's staff who was ferociously anti-British and passed on to his son all the gossip about high-level disagreements that came his way. The Patton deception owed much to the information he so indiscreetly communicated.

Agent 5 was the brother of the Venezuelan, Agent 3, and was eventually despatched to Canada to observe matters there. He had a colleague, an American commercial traveller (5(1)) who filled in with information about the United States. Agent 6 was an anti-British South African whose linguistic skills gained him employment with the War Office. He was posted to north Africa, where he collected much high-level and accurate information; but since he could transmit it only by letter to *Garbo*, who then had to forward it to Lisbon, by the time it reached the Germans it was very out of date. He died, unfortunately, in an air crash in July 1943.

Finally there was a group of eight agents of whom the leader 'Stanley' (7), was an anti-British Welsh nationalist, a seaman operating in Swansea. His network, known to the Germans as *Dagobert*, was recruited largely from Welsh dissidents like himself. It contained two rather curious characters: an Indian poet known as 'Rags', who although he was recruited in Swansea lived in Brighton, where he was well placed to observe troop movements, and his mistress, Theresa Jardine, in the Women's Royal Naval Service. A little later this lady was posted to Ceylon, and passed under the control of 'D' Division in the Far East.

The reader should bear in mind that none of these people actually existed.

By the summer of 1943 the existence of these networks was well established and *Cockade* gave *Garbo* and his British case-officer valuable practise in using them. A procedure was established by the London Controlling Section which was to become the regular pattern by the time of *Overlord*. The cover story was broken down into a number of serials. Each serial contained a story to be passed to the enemy, the date by which it had to be in his possession, and the factual evidence for it. The evidence was then compared and collated with the observing capacity of the *Garbo* network and appropriate messages were devised for the agents which, after clearance with the Service authorities (at first through the Twenty Committee but increasingly direct) were then passed on to Madrid in *Garbo's* inimitably florid style. From Madrid, as Sigint revealed, these were sent direct to Berlin, where they made an excellent impression. After *Starkey* had passed its climax on 8 September 1943, his Abwehr case-officer wrote enthusiastically to *Garbo* on 18 September: 'Your activity and that of your informants gave us a perfect idea of what is taking place over there; these reports, as you can imagine, have an incalculable value and for this reason I beg of you to proceed with the greatest care so as not to endanger in these momentous times either yourself or your organisation'.

Four months later, in early January, his Abwehr case-officer warned *Garbo* once more to prepare for action. German intelligence, he informed him on 5 January 1944, had learned that preparations were far advanced for a major operation based on the United States, which might materialise at a very early date. *Garbo* was therefore to find out everything he could about Allied military intentions, the dates of forthcoming operations, and the locations and strength of all land, sea, air and amphibious forces that might be employed. This, he was told, included possible operations against Norway and Denmark, as well as those against the Channel coast.

To tackle this new assignment, *Garbo* redeployed his agents. *Fortitude North* was covered basically by the Venezuelan (3) in Glasgow, and by the Greek sailor (3(3)) on the Scottish east coast. 'Fred' from Gibraltar had, as we have seen, insinuated himself into the heart of the Allied concentration around Southampton, while the *Dagobert* network covered the rest of the south coast, with agents in Harwich, Dover, Brighton, and the west country and south Wales. *Garbo's* informants in Whitehall had only to keep their eyes and ears open, and he himself picked up a lot of useful news and one or two documents in his capacity as part-time employee in the Ministry of Information. The agents sent their messages to him in secret ink, but *Garbo* now communicated with Madrid very largely by radio, sending an average of 5 or 6 messages a day. The information in *Garbo's* reports now found its way into the daily situation reports of Fremde Heere West; in particular, the Order of Battle projected by him and by *Brutus* (now established at FUSAG HQ) was accepted without question. All was carefully co-ordinated directly with Ops B at SHAEF, and a great deal of accurate information was included about 21st Army Group. When the formations specified by *Garbo* as belonging to this Army Group were identified in Normandy, it made his further information about FUSAG all the more credible.

The manner in which *Garbo* was able to give warning (alas, too late) of the actual assault in the small hours of 6 June, thanks to Agent 4 breaking out of his camp, has been described in the text; and we have also seen how his German case-officer reassured him the following day 'that your work over the last few weeks has made it possible for our command to be completely forewarned and prepared, and the message of Four would have influenced but little had it arrived three or four hours earlier'. Undeterred by this set-back, *Garbo* summoned a meeting of all available agents, as a result of which he transmitted a long report, on the night of 8 June about the existing Allied dispositions.

'From the reports mentioned', this ran, 'it is perfectly clear that the present attack is a large-scale operation but diversionary in character for the purpose of establishing a strong bridgehead in order to draw the maximum of our reserves to the area of operations to retain them there so as to be able to strike a blow somewhere else with ensured success ... the fact that these concentrations which are in the east and south-east of the island are now inactive means that they must be held in reserve to be employed in the other large-scale operations. The constant aerial bombardment which the area of the Pas de Calais has suffered and the strategic disposition of these forces give reason to suspect an attack in that region of France which at the same time offers the shortest route for the final objective of their illusions, which is to say, Berlin ... I learned yesterday that there were 75 divisions in this country before the present assault commenced. Suppose they should use a maximum of 20–25 divisions they would be left with some 50 divisions with which to attempt a second blow'.

All this his Abwehr case-officer acknowledged gratefully on 10 June. 'With reference to your extensive information of the 8th on the concentrations still existing in the south-east of the Island, I am interested in the transmission with the maximum urgency of as much news as you can obtain of the embarkation and destination of these forces'. At the same time Bletchley Park decrypted the congratulatory messages to *Garbo's* German case-officer from Berlin. 'In the name of Fremde Heere West', ran one on 9 June, 'I express appreciation of previous work in England'. And on 11 June the message stated 'The reports received in the last week from *Garbo** have been confirmed almost without exception and are to be described as especially valuable'.

The Germans now began, as we have seen, to press *Garbo* embarrassingly closely for information about the fall of VIs on London. To deter them from this undesirable practice, BIA arranged to have *Garbo* notionally arrested, on 3 July, while he was making indiscreet enquiries about V-bomb damage in Bethnal Green. Nothing could be proved against him and he was eventually released with an official apology which was duly transmitted to Madrid. When his Abwehr case-officer congratulated *Garbo* on his release he informed him also that the Führer had been graciously pleased to bestow on him the order of the Iron Cross Class II.† But the lesson had been learned. *Garbo* was asked no further questions about V-weapons and he continued to put across prolific information about the reconstruction of FUSAG. This elicited from his Abwehr case-officer the further message, on 21 August: 'Headquarters entrust me with the mission which I fulfil with the greatest satisfaction of again expressing to you our special recognition for the results achieved by you and your organisation. They also made reference

---

* Sic in the file, but the original presumably read *Cato* = *Garbo's* German Code-name.
† See above, p 174.

in this connection to the information which you have supplied to us since the invasion of France – news which has been of the greatest value to them . . .'.

By the end of August MI5 had begun to fear that *Garbo's* cover could not be preserved for very much longer. The growing number of Abwehr defectors in neutral countries must, MI5 thought, lead the Germans to assume that the Allies would by now have been informed of the existence of this network operating so effectively in their midst; and it would look very odd if it continued to operate undisturbed. In the middle of August a Spanish informant did in fact tell MI6 about *Garbo*, and this was taken as the excuse for sending *Garbo* into notional retirement. *Garbo* informed his Abwehr case-officer on 12 September that he had been warned of this betrayal by friends in Spain, and was going to ground. The network would henceforth be operated by his Venezuelan lieutenant. *Garbo* himself would still master-mind operations from a cottage in Wales, but the British would be led to believe, by a forlorn and distraught Mrs *Garbo*, that he had returned to Spain.

It was a neat solution. *Garbo's* deputy could not be blown, since his name had never been revealed to the Germans. An even more important guarantee of his security was that he did not exist. Communications ceased to be written in *Garbo's* inimitably baroque style, but they still continued, now conducted direct by MI5. For the last six months of the war, therefore, the British security services were in direct radio communication with German intelligence. keeping it supplied with a stream of misinformation to which the latter attached the highest degree of credibility.

The Abwehr paid good money for their information. *Garbo's* notional expenses were paid, partly to an address in Lisbon where the money was notionally collected by 'the courier', in fact picked up by MI6, and partly by a transfer of funds effected through a nominee of *Garbo* in Spain who held a sterling balance in London.

Annex

Garbo's letter to his Abwehr case-officer re *Crossbow*

Strictly Personal for Carlos

Dear Friend and Comrade,

In writing this letter I do so in order to address my Chief as the head of the organisation which I represent here being absolutely sure that this letter will be received by you as a statement of opinion between two friends who share the same ideals and are fighting for the same end.

My work is not that of a propagandist and still less is it my intention to sustain false opinions, programmes or intentions of Ministries which are removed from our vital work of military information. My work and duty is to inform my chief secretly, which is yourself, as to the truth about what I see in the very camp of the enemy, even if the truth is harsh or unsatisfactory, as in the present case. Having satisfied my conscience about the truth it is for you to decide whether or not to transmit to Berlin this class of report.

As both you and I proudly belong to the German Secret Service we do not require propaganda or empty words to maintain our morale. We are too level headed to allow our spirits to be weakened by adverse incidents or to allow our hopes to be smashed. This only happens to pusillanimous people who gradually adjust their views alternatively as they are influenced by optimism or pessimism. For me, individual incidents in this hard war have been nothing more than evolutionary scenes in a gigantic development of a grandiose act. The war continues, and within it the daily events, the official communiques, the temporary battles, are only episodes of the day, of the week, or of a month, but the magnitude of the great undertaking carries on and at least for me the temporary adverse episodes have no significance whatsoever. Always remember the saying 'He who laughs last laughs best'. I do not know why it is that I have the feeling that you share this opinion with me and therefore I address this letter of a strictly personal character to you so that nobody in the Madrid office can read it or interpret the contents in the wring way. For the same reason I have kept from all my agents any knowledge as to the contents or the reason of the present letter. This is, therefore, I repeat, a matter between you and me, leaving it to your judgment as to whether you should show it to our chief in Berlin or any other personality who shares our views because we must always avoid any possibility of there being differences of opinion amongst our Ministries. In talking to you in this way I feel that I must clarify this paragraph and I wish to point out that I refer to our Ministries of Propaganda and War, the synthesis of the present letter. The theme involved is the new secret weapon.

Now that a few days have passed during which it has been used I ask myself 'What is the use of this new arm? Has it a Military aim? No! Its effect is nil. Is it then intended for propaganda? possibly, yes!' I do not challenge that in this respect it had at the beginning flattering success. In considering these two questions I must give priority to one of the greatest importance. I do not wish to deny or try to belittle the importance of an arm as strong as that of propaganda but when one comes to analyse these two questions the thing which immediately comes to my mind, as I imagine it does to yours, is the tangible and net conclusion. This is, that we must win the war with fighting weapons. The other weapon, which is that of propaganda, has its limitations and its very name would not make a complete phrase or commonsense if the subject for its oration did not exist. The best propaganda are deeds and these only take place in the field of battle. In talking in this way it is only in the fear that in order to justify one thing we have sacrificed the other. I do not know what the production is, neither have I the least idea technically of the labour involved in the production of the device to which I allude, but if it is being produced at the partial sacrifice of the production of battle weapons, the mistake which we will have suffered is serious and the consequences fatal to the outcome of our undertaking. I speak thus, because it is my duty to inform you of what is taking place, and as is natural, no one is in a better position than I am to speak the truth, so that if it is accordance with what you are wanting to know you will be able to find a solution before it is too late, and before we have to lament the past.

The new arm has passed through two completely opposed phases. The first lasted for three or four days, and was surprisingly successful, if not destructive, it was at least destructive to morale. The second phase is the present one. This is what I am commenting on and can be summed up in a simple phrase 'We are wasting our time'. To continue I will explain my use of this phrase.

When I was first told about this weapon and its existence was confirmed by you (I am referring to several months ago) I had hoped to see my ambitions realised in the destruction of this useless town which surrounds me. Though the employment of this weapon was delayed I had not the slightest doubt that its effect would one day be felt when once it had been perfected, and thus I had the key to what I had imagined was going to materialise and be put into effect. Days passed and at last it arrived and the effect which it produced, as I say above, if it was not altogether destructive, was at least a bloody weapon against the morale of these people, because the fear of the unknown is sufficient to break down the highest spirit. I must, however, deal with facts and not with arguments, and you will remember that I then sent you a message in which I made clear my illusions about the future employment of this weapon, then conceiving the first episode as being a trial. Without, therefore, paying much attention to the decomposition which this might bring about on the phlegmatic English, I awaited the second phase which I thought would be the vital one which I expected to bring about, if not the total destruction, at least a partial destruction, which would have counterbalanced the work of genius which had been put into this and would have out-weighed the energy and material expended in its fabrication. Days have passed and to-day I can sum up what has happened as follows.

This weapon is not only ineffective from a military point of view but also from the point of view of propaganda. Analysing these two points and putting my arguments crudely I have the following to say. First, the morale of the public was for a moment brought down to the point of this weapon taking first place to the battle front as a theme of conversation. The new arm is now being discussed in quite a different strain and what is happening is not only that the situation has quietened down but the device is now being ridiculed both by words and insinuations about its effects. What has happened to produce this change? It is that measures have been taken not only to counterbalance its effectiveness but to destroy its usefulness. Even now though a state of precautious alertness still exists in case one of these weapons should fall on London, the public in spite of hearing the sirens, do not go to the shelters nor do they interrupt their daily work. The traffic in the streets continues normally and the activity in the city remains unchanged. The public has absorbed the counter-propaganda which is that they give out for their own benefit what is said in German sources, such as, London is burning; London is evacuating; the railway communications have been stopped; the Metropolitan system has been suspended; Big Ben has been destroyed; etc., etc. This, as is only natural, is checkable by the ordinary citizen with ease and as they can see with their own eyes that none of it is true they calm themselves in the knowledge that this arm is created to terrorise them. The result is unproductive from our propaganda point of view, not only so far as this country is concerned, but also for the neutrals, who, as soon as they receive their reports from their representatives in London, will be faced with the truth. This may not be the case in districts outside the capital where quite a number have fallen but this is not what we were aiming to achieve, since these weapons may destroy, ten, fifty, a hundred, a thousand houses in a city where buildings are to be found in hundreds of thousands, but they do not destroy the capital of its industry or the important centre of national communication which would make the manufacture of such an arm worth while.

Second: If, in order to put this weapon into operation forces have to be taken away from military industries the consideration is still less pardonable, as this does not add in the very least to the strategic aims of the war which we are following. I have not the slightest idea of the time or the material which is taken up in the fabrication of this weapon neither can I make comparisons as to how many bombers or fighters might have been produced in their stead, nor their proportionate value. This is a matter for technicians whose intelligence and good will take care of these interests for the German nation, and know the respective importance of each of these weapons and where vital energies can best be used, not only for the continuation of the war, but also for final victory. Naturally they cannot analyse this conception because they are not in the least aware of the effects of this new weapon, therefore I am going to give you some facts.

If one goes about the streets of London one sees the scars of the period of destruction which occurred during the years 1940–41. The effects of what is taking place now are no more than light additions which do not add to the whole a further one ten thousandth part of the destruction of the city, though of course the periods covered are very unequal. If we study the amount of explosives then used and the number of casualties suffered through our action, and we compare this with the present expensive construction of the new arm we can then decide on a basis of effort value which of these has been most effective.

The following important detail which I learnt from J(2) should be taken into account, which is that only 17% of the bombs fall in 'Greater London'. 22% in other urban towns were either destroyed by the defences or fell in open country due to lack of precision. As I have never liked to embark on a problem with out at the same time finding its solution, and as I am not a technician I can only make the suggestion that the two following questions should be dealt with.

Firstly, the speed of the weapon, and secondly its precision. If we can remedy the first in such a way that the fighters and anti-aircraft of the enemy should be unable to cope with the apparatus and the second point can be dealt with, then we will have been successful in our aims. Possibly the second matter is one in which I can help you, and if through my reports you are able to improve your aim it would be most satisfactory. But before this can be of any use our scientists who created this wonder must find a way of protecting it and this can only be done if the speed can be increased.

My conclusion therefore is the following—

Until a way of improving it can be found its effectiveness is nil, and therefore all the efforts which have been spent on it have been wasted and they should be employed in the manufacture of war weapons which may have more disastrous effects on our enemy. I do not know whether you are now working on its improvement or whether there may be in production others which are better. Since I remember that when we were dealing with this we had always referred to it as the rocket weapon, which seems to me to have nothing to do with what is now being used.

I base all I have said on what I have seen as I know nothing about what may come. The present trials have shown me that the High Command does not have absolute confidence in me or my service to advise me in advance as to what is taking place. I say this not because I am annoyed at not being told in advance the date that this was to be used but because I feel some bitterness at not having been shown the recognition of my loyalty by my superiors by their having strictly kept this information from me. This is a matter which does not really affect the case as I know that I have fulfilled my part in obtaining the military information, having given it most scrupulous care and my conscience rewards me for these small annoyances which, when all is taken into consideration, merely means that I have been relieved of further responsibilities. I end this letter, my dear chief, in the same strain as I started it, giving you a strictly impartial opinion as you requested in your message. I speak to you as a comrade, as if we were equals and frank as always, I speak my mind. Another person who did not know me as you do without the proof of the conduct of the work which I have achieved might think this letter disillusioning and demoralising. On you, or on me, it can only produce a vigorous reaction and call for urgent and necessary counter-measures. This can bring perfection in our work, which after all we share by mutual ideals and sincere wishes.

I am now going to confess to you something which, being opposed to flattery, I have never before expressed, but which I now feel obliged to say, which is that I have always had a very strong feeling of respect and admiration for your advice which you have offered me in all moments of danger. It has been advice full of good sense and calmly expressed, and in it I have found a value which I can never overlook. This is perhaps why I could never cheat you with false hope, but I feel that I must be frank and open up my heart to you and unload the truth which in the long run is never malignant. I have been a severe critic of our faults, just as I have praised our victorious achievements. The latter one can fulfil with pleasure but too much of this can create a state which can be dangerous. The former are bitter to administer, but by talking freely about them we awaken our common-sense and strengthen our decision to continue to look for a solution which will lead us on a better path towards the objective we wish to reach. These things can only be dealt with between men of spirit and tenacity, and by people who follow a doctrine, by fighting men and bold combatants. This unfolding of confidence can only be made between comrades. One could not say to an English Lord what one may say to a National Socialist Comrade. The former would consider himself ridiculous if he had to accept an observation from a subordinate. We accept, within the discipline of hierarchy, the advice of subordinates. Thus, the great Germany has become what it is. Thus, it has been able to deposit such great confidence in the man who governs it, knowing that he is not a democratic despot but a man of low birth who has only followed an ideal. The Fatherland! Humanity! Justice and Comradeship!

On approaching the completion of the third year of my stay here I now, more than ever, feel pride in my work, and desire to prove myself worthy of all the evidence of friendship which you have expressed on me. I feel more than ever a sensation of hatred, more than death, for our enemy, and an ever increasing irresistible urge to destroy his entire existence. The arrogance of this rabble can only be conceived when you live among them.

Receive a cordial embrace from your comrade and servant,

JUAN.

APPENDIX 3

Directive To Controlling Officer*

You are appointed Controlling Officer of the Controlling Section for Deception.

2. The section forms part of the organisation under the Chiefs of Staff. For cover purposes it will continue to be considered as part of the Future Operational Planning Section of the Joint Planning Staff.

3. You are to—

a. Prepare deception plans on a world-wide basis with the object of causing the enemy to waste his military resources.

b. Co-ordinate deceptions plans prepared by Commands at home and abroad.

c. Ensure that 'cover' plans prepared by ISSB fit into the general frame-work of strategic deception.

d. Watch over the execution by the Service Ministries, Commands and other organisations and departments, of approved deception plans which you have prepared.

e. Control the support of deception schemes originated by Commanders in Chief, by such means as leakage and propaganda.

4. In the initiation and preparation of your plans you are to work in close co-operation with the Joint Planning Staff, through which your plans are to be submitted when necessary to the Chiefs of Staff.

5. You are also to keep in touch with the Joint Intelligence Sub-Committee, Political Warfare Executive, Special Operations Executive, SIS, and other Government organisations and departments.

6. Your work is not to be limited to strategic deception alone but is to include any matter calculated to mystify or mislead the enemy wherever military advantage may be so gained.

7. You are to be prepared to keep the Chiefs of Staff informed regarding all matters of deception both at home and abroad and are authorised to report to them direct insofar as this may be necessary.

8. Should the United States authorise the setting up of a similar organisation in Washington, you are to arrange for mutual co-ordination of British and United States plans. For this purpose the exchange of liaison officers may prove necessary.

---

* Reproduced from CAB 80/63, COS(42)180(0) of 21 June.

APPENDIX 4

Copy of a letter from Lieutenant General Sir Archibald Nye to General the Hon Sir Harold R L G Alexander dated 23 April 1943

I am taking advantage of sending you a personal letter by hand of one of Mountbatten's officers, to give you the inside history of our recent exchange of cables about Mediterranean operations and their attendant cover plans. You may have felt our decisions were somewhat arbitrary, but I can assure you in fact that the COS Committee gave the most careful consideration both to your recommendation and also to Jumbo's.

We have had recent information that the Bosche have been reinforcing and strengthening their defences in Greece and Crete and CIGS felt that our forces for the assault were insufficient. It was agreed by the Chiefs of Staff that the 5th Division should be reinforced by one Brigade Group for the assault on the beach south of CAPE ARAXOS and that a similar reinforcement should be made for the 56th Division at KALAMATA. We are earmarking the necessary forces and shipping.

Jumbo Wilson had proposed to select SICILY as cover target for 'HUSKY'; but we have already chosen it as cover for Operation 'BRIMSTONE'. The COS Committee went into the whole question exhaustively again and came to the conclusion that in view of the preparations in Algeria, the amphibious training which will be taking place on the Tunisian coast and the heavy air bombardment which will be put down to neutralise the Sicilian airfields, we should stick to our plan of making it cover for 'BRIMSTONE' – indeed we stand a very good chance of making him think we will go for SICILY – it is an obvious objective and one about which he must be nervous. On the other hand, they felt there wasn't much hope of persuading the Bosche that the extensive preparations in the Eastern Mediterranean were also directed at SICILY. For this reason they have told Wilson his cover plan should be something nearer the spot, e.g. the Dodecanese. Since our relations with Turkey are now so obviously closer the Italians must be pretty apprehensive about these islands.

I imagine you will agree with these arguments. I know you have your hands more than full at the moment and you haven't much chance of discussing future operations with Eisenhower. But if by any chance you do want to support Wilson's proposal, I hope you will let us know soon, because we can't delay much longer.

I am very sorry we weren't able to meet your wishes about the new Commander of the Guards Brigade. Your own nominee was down with a bad attack of 'flu and not likely to be really fit for another few weeks. No doubt, however, you know Forster personally; he has done extremely well in command of a brigade at home, and is, I think, the best fellow available.

You must be about as fed up as we are with the whole question of war medals and 'Purple Hearts'. We all agree with you that we don't want to offend our American friends, but there is a good deal more to it than that. If our troops who happen to be serving in one particular theatre are to get extra decorations merely because the Americans happen to be serving there too, we will be faced with a good deal of discontent among those troops fighting elsewhere perhaps just as bitterly – or more so. My own feeling is that we should thank the Americans for their kind offer but say firmly it would cause too many anomalies and we are sorry we can't accept. But it is on the agenda for the next Military Members meeting and I hope you will have a decision very soon.

APPENDIX 5

Plan 'Bodyguard'*

Overall Deception Policy for the War against Germany
Intention of this Paper

1. The intention of this paper is to formulate an overall deception policy for the war against Germany in accordance with CCS 426/1 of 6 December 1943, paragraph 9(e).

Object

2. To induce the enemy to make faulty strategic dispositions in relation to operations by the United Nations against Germany agreed upon at EUREKA.

Present Situation

3. The German General Staff will this winter be considering the strategic disposition of their forces to meet offensive operations by the United Nations in 1944. Though they will be forced to maintain the bulk of their forces on the Russian front, they already suspect that large-scale Anglo-American operations will be undertaken in Western Europe sometime in 1944. It is, however, doubtful whether they have at present sufficient information regarding the timing and scope of this threat to justify any immediate changes in their strategic dispositions.
4. At a later stage, however, preparations for 'OVERLORD' and to a lesser degree for 'ANVIL' will be on such a scale and of such a type that the enemy cannot fail to appreciate our intention to carry out a cross-channel operation and an amphibious operation in the Western Mediterranean.

Deception Problem

5. The problem to be solved is twofold –

   a. *Overall Problem*
   We must persuade the enemy to dispose his forces in areas where they can cause the least interference with operations 'OVERLORD' and 'ANVIL' and with operations on the Russian Front.

   b. *Tactical Problem*

---

* Reproduced from CAB 80/77, COS(43) 779(0)(Final) of 23 January 1944.

As soon as our preparations for 'OVERLORD' and 'ANVIL' clearly indicate to the enemy our intention to undertake a cross-channel operation and an amphibious operation in the Western Mediterranean, Theatre Commanders concerned must implement their tactical cover plans to deceive the enemy as to the strength, objective and timing of 'OVERLORD' and 'ANVIL'.

Choice of Areas in which to contain Enemy Forces

6. In view of SEXTANT decisions our overall deception policy should be to contain enemy forces in areas where they will interfere as little as possible with operations on the Russian Front and with 'OVER-LORD' and 'ANVIL'. Such areas are –

a. *Northern Italy and Southern Germany*
It should be possible by means of real operations and feints to contain a number of first quality divisions in this area.
'POINTBLANK' operations from Italy should also help to contain enemy fighter forces.

b. *South East Europe*
The JIC appreciate* that the enemy will do his utmost to hold South East Europe, though limited withdrawals from the islands and Southern Greece might be undertaken. Provided that we can persuade the enemy to believe that considerable forces and landing craft are being concentrated in the Eastern Mediterranean it should be possible to contain enemy forces in the Balkans. Our chances of success would be increased if Turkey joined the Allies, but even if she refused we might still induce the enemy to fear the results of our continued infiltration. The deception plan would be assisted to a marked degree if the Russian General Staff staged an amphibious threat to the Bulgarian-Roumanian coasts across the Black Sea.

c. *Scandinavia*
A threatened attack against Scandinavia should help to contain some first-quality divisions and limited naval and air forces. Such a deception plan would be assisted if the Germans were induced to believe that Sweden was prepared to co-operate with the Allies and if the Russians mounted a threat against enemy occupied territory in the Arctic.

Allied Preparation for 'OVERLORD' and 'ANVIL'

7. a. *'OVERLORD'*
It will be impossible wholly to conceal the gradual build up of Allied forces and other preparations in the United Kingdom during the

---

* JIC(43)385(0) of 25.9.43.

next few months. In addition the enemy will appreciate that considerable American forces in the USA are available for transfer to Europe.

In these circumstances our best chance of deceiving the enemy would be to indicate that Anglo-American strategy is dictated by caution and that we have no intention of undertaking the invasion of the Continent until we had assembled an overwhelming force and the necessary landing craft; these would not be available until the late Summer. To support this story we must try to indicate that the assault and follow-up forces at present available in the United Kingdom are less than they in fact are, and that during the next few months we could only re-enter the Continent against little or no opposition.

b. *'ANVIL'*

Preparations and the build-up for 'ANVIL' should not be so apparent in the early stages, therefore the tactical cover plan eventually put into operation by Allied Commander-in-Chief, Mediterranean Theatre, should suffice to cover this assault.

In the Mediterranean theatre the enemy has in the past been induced to overestimate Allied forces by 20 to 30 per cent. It would be an advantage if such exaggeration could be maintained especially in the Eastern Mediterranean.

Russian Front

8. The Russian offensive will presumably be continued during the next few months but it would be of assistance to our plans if we could lead the enemy to believe that the Russian main Summer offensive would not start before the end of June.

It would be plausible that this operation should thus precede 'OVERLORD' and 'ANVIL' thereby rendering the maximum assistance to these far more hazardous seaborne assaults.

Factors Against the Achievement of the Object

9. a. Preparations for 'OVERLORD' during the next few months and any announcements of the appointment of prominent commanders in the United Kingdom will indicate to the enemy that our main strategy is switching from the Mediterranean to North Western Europe.

b. Statements both in the press and on the radio and the platform may continue to emphasise the likelihood of operations in 1944 from the United Kingdom against North Western Europe.

c. 'POINTBLANK' operations from the United Kingdom will compel the enemy to keep strong GAF fighter forces in North Western Europe.

Factors for the Achievement of the Object

10. a. Germany's armed forces are dangerously stretched by current operations and provided we can induce her to retain surplus forces in Scandinavia, Italy and the Balkans, she will find it difficult simultaneously to provide adequate forces for Russia, France and the Low Countries.

    b. Germany's defensive commitments are likely to be increased since –
    i. The political and economic situation in Germany and occupied countries is deteriorating and may necessitate the maintenance of strong garrison forces in these areas.
    ii. The attitude of neutrals and satellites may move further in favour of the Allies and compel Germany to dispose reserves to meet unfavourable developments.

    c. The assembly of the Rosyth force in NE Scotland will reinforce the threat to Scandinavia.

Overall Deception Policy

11. The following Overall Deception Policy is based upon the considerations outlined above.

12. *Allied Intentions*
    We should induce the enemy to believe that the following is the Allied plan for 1944.

    a. 'POINTBLANK' operations were seriously affecting the enemy's war potential and, if continued and increased, might well bring about his total collapse. Consequently, reinforcement of the United Kingdom and the Mediterranean by long-range American bombers has been given such a high priority that ground forces build-up in the United Kingdom has been delayed.

    b. The Allies must be prepared to take advantage of any serious German weakening or withdrawal in Western Europe and preparations to this end must be put in hand forthwith.

    c. To concert in Spring an attack on Northern Norway with Russia with the immediate object of opening up a supply route to Sweden. Therafter to enlist the active co-operation of Sweden for the establishment of air bases in Southern Sweden to supplement 'POINTBLANK' with fighter bomber operations and to cover an amphibious assault on Denmark from the United Kingdom in the summer.

    d. Since no large-scale cross-channel operation would be possible till late summer, the main Allied effort in the Spring of 1944 should be against the Balkans, by means of –

i. An Anglo-American assault against the Dalmatian coast.
ii. A British assault against Greece.
iii. A Russian amphibious operation against the Bulgarian-Roumanian coast.
iv. In addition Turkey will be invited to join the Allies to provide operational facilities including aerodromes to cover operations against the Aegean Islands as a prerequisite to the invasion of Greece. Her refusal would not materially modify the Allied intentions.
v. Pressure against the satellites to induce them to abandon Germany.

e. Anglo-American operations in Italy would be continued, and in order to hasten their progress, amphibious operations against the north-west and north-east coast of Italy would be carried out. Provided these were successful, 15 Army Group would later advance eastwards through Istria in support of the operations mentioned in d. above.

Note: The operations in c. d. and e. above would enable us to employ our amphibious forces and retain the initiative until preparations for the final assault in the late summer were completed.

f. Though Russian operations would presumably be continued this winter it would not be possible for them to launch their summer offensive before the end of June.

g. In view of the formidable character of German coastal defences and the present enemy strength in France and the Low Countries, possibly as many as twelve Anglo-American Divisions afloat in the initial assault and a total force of about fifty divisions would be required for a cross-channel assault. This operation would not be launched until the late summer (i.e. after the opening of the Russian summer offensive).

13. *Allied strength and dispositions*

We should induce the enemy to believe the following information regarding Allied strength and dispositions –

a. *United Kingdom*
i. Shortage of manpower has obliged the British Army in the United Kingdom to resort to cannibalisation, while several of their formations are on a lower establishment, or still lack their administrative and supply units. The number of Anglo-American Divisions in the United Kingdom available for offensive operations is less than is, in fact, the case. Some United States Divisions arriving in the United Kingdom have not yet completed their training.

ii. Personnel of certain Anglo-American Divisions in the Mediterranean with long service overseas are being relieved by fresh divisions from the USA. British troops will, on relief, return to the United Kingdom where they will re-form and be utilised for training inexperienced formations.

iii. Invasion craft remains the principal bottleneck due to operations in the Pacific and the full number required for the initial assault cannot be made available from home production and the USA before summer.

b. *Mediterranean*

i. Anglo-American forces in the Mediterranean, especially in the Eastern Mediterranean, are greater than is, in fact, the case.

ii. French forces are taking over responsibility for the defence of North Africa, thus leaving Anglo-American forces free for offensive operations elsewhere in the Spring of 1944.

iii. Certain British Divisions and landing craft are being transferred from India to the Middle East.

iv. Fresh Divisions from the United States of America are expected to arrive in the Mediterranean.

Tactical Cover Plans

14. a. *United Kingdom*

When the enemy realises that cross-channel operations are imminent, the story indicating that no cross-channel attack will occur until late summer, will tend to lose plausibility. At this juncture the tactical cover plan prepared by Supreme Commander, Allied Expeditionary Force will come into force with a view to deceiving the enemy as to the timing, direction and weight of 'OVERLORD'.

b. *Mediterranean*

In due course the enemy will probably appreciate, especially from air reconnaissance, that an amphibious operation is being mounted in North African ports and Western Mediterranean Islands. At this stage, a tactical cover plan prepared by Allied Commander-in-Chief, Mediterranean Theatre will come into force with a view to deceiving the enemy as regards the timing, direction and weight of 'ANVIL'.

Timing

15. The selection of the D day of all cover and deception plans mentioned above is a question to be decided by Supreme Commander, Allied Expeditionary Force. In this connection, it is recommended that the dates chosen should, in each case, be later than 'OVERLORD'

or 'ANVIL' D days, with a view to delaying the despatch of enemy reinforcements for as long as possible.

The Supreme Command, Allied Expeditionary Force after consultation with Commander-in-Chief, Mediterranean Theatre and the Controlling Officer will decide the tempo of the 'OVERLORD' and 'ANVIL' tactical cover plans.

Means of Implementation

16. a. *Physical Means*

Implementation by means of movements of forces, camouflage devices, W/T deception and other activities will be carried out in accordance with detailed plans prepared by Supreme Commander, Allied Expeditionary Force and Allied Commander-in-Chief, Mediterranean Theatre.

b. *Diplomatic Means*

Genuine diplomatic approaches will be required to lead the enemy to believe that we intend persuading Sweden to join the Allies and assist us in operations in Scandinavia.

Even if Turkey refuses to join the Allies in the near future, the enemy should be led to believe that our continued infiltration may give the Allies important opportunities in connection with a Balkan campaign.

c. *Special Means*

Implementation by means of leakage and rumours in support of plans prepared by Theatre Commanders will be co-ordinated by the London Controlling Section.

d. *Political Warfare*

The Political Warfare plan while not departing from its main purpose, should conform to the above general policy.

e. *Security*

Plan 'BODYGUARD' cannot succeed unless the strictest security precautions are taken to conceal the true nature of 'OVERLORD' and 'ANVIL' preparations.

Index